Disarmament
Without Order

Recent Titles in
Contributions in Political Science
Series Editor: Bernard K. Johnpoll

Disarmament Without Order

The Politics
of
Disarmament
at the
United Nations

AVI BEKER

CONTRIBUTIONS IN POLITICAL SCIENCE,
NUMBER 118

GREENWOOD PRESS
WESTPORT, CONNECTICUT
LONDON, ENGLAND

Library of Congress Cataloging in Publication Data

Beker, Avi
  Disarmament without order.

  (Contributions in political science, ISSN 0147-1066 ;
no. 118)
  Bibliography: p.
  Includes index.
  1. Atomic weapons and disarmament. 2. Disarmament.
3. United Nations. I. Title. II. Series.
JX1974.7.B44 1985   341.7'33   84-6722
ISBN 0-313-24362-X (lib. bdg.)

Library of Congress Catalog Card Number: 84-6722
ISBN: 0-313-24362-X
ISSN: 0147-1066

First published in 1985

Greenwood Press
A division of Congressional Information Service, Inc.
88 Post Road West
Westport, Connecticut 06881

Printed in the United States of America

10 9 8 7 6 5 4 3 2 1

To Zvia

Contents

Illustrations

Abbreviations

ACDA	Arms Control and Disarmament Agency
CCD	Conference of the Committee on Disarmament
CD	Committee on Disarmament
CPD	Comprehensive Program of Disarmament
CTB	Comprehensive Test Ban
CW	Chemical Weapons Treaty
DC	Disarmament Commission
ENDC	Eighteen Nation Disarmament Conference
ERW	Enhanced Radiation Warhead
GCD	General and Complete Disarmament
HEU	Highly Enriched Uranium
IAEA	International Atomic Energy Agency
ICRC	International Committee of the Red Cross
INFCE	International Nuclear Fuel Cycle Evaluation
MAD	Mutual Assured Destruction
MBFR	Mutual and Balanced Force Reductions
MEOP	Middle Eastern Oil Producing Countries
MLF	Multilateral Nuclear Force
NATO	North Atlantic Treaty Organization
NIEO	New International Economic Order
NNWS	Non-Nuclear-Weapon States
NPT	Nuclear Non-Proliferation Treaty
NRC	Nuclear Regulatory Commission
NWS	Nuclear-Weapon States
OPEC	Organization of Petroleum Exporting Countries
PTBT	Partial Test Ban Treaty
RIO	Reshaping International Order
SALT	Strategic Arms Limitation Talks

SIPRI	Stockholm International Peace Research Institute
SSOD	Special Session on Disarmament
TNF	Theater Nuclear Forces
UNAEC	United Nations Atomic Energy Commission
UNCTAD	United Nations Conference of Trade and Development
UNDP	United Nations Development Programme
UNESCO	United Nations Educational, Scientific and Cultural Organization
WDC	World Disarmament Conference

Disarmament
Without Order

1

Introduction: What Is the Problem of Disarmament?

As soon as the United Nations opened its headquarters in New York City, the Isaiah Wall across the street from the organization became a popular gathering spot for demonstrators for a variety of international causes. The inscription on the wall is perhaps the most popular bibilical quotation concerning disarmament and international security. The message, chiseled into granite, is taken from the book of Isaiah (2:4): "They shall beat their swords into plowshares and their spears into pruning hooks, nation shall not lift up sword against nation, neither shall they learn war anymore."

These words of Isaiah, the great visionary of peace, to his fellow children of Israel in Judah in the eighth century B.C., have buoyed entire peoples and inspired many great thinkers through the conflicts of history. However, what is not revealed by the admonition on the wall are the conditions of this vision of peace. The truth is that even in the religious prophecy of Isaiah, disarmament and peace among nations are not dealt with in isolation but within a broader context of a universal change of order. One should render the phrase preceding the plowshares in line, in the same verse: "And he shall judge among the nations, and shall rebuke many people."

Though Isaiah meant only to speak about "the last days" of Judgment, he emphasized two aspects of prerequisites for total disarmament: (1) a moral (in the religious sense) transformation of man; and (2) a new order with a supranational, legitimate authority to judge, rebuke, and enforce the law among the nations of the world.

Characteristically, the omissions in the admonition on the wall highlight the deficiencies in the deliberations on disarmament in the United Nations across the street. To talk about General and Complete Disarmament (GCD) or to elaborate a Comprehensive Program of Disarmament (CPD) is to forget what disarmament is really about. Disarmament cannot be dealt with as a self-contained process, disregarding the conditions of world order. In essence, disarmament is about the organization of power in the international community.

Since disarmament proposes to deprive nations of anything to fight with, taken literally, it appears frequently as the most appealing method to guarantee peace. The novel aspiration to disarmament became a recurring theme of many individuals who were appalled by the record of human history, which could easily be described as history of war and conflicts. In modern history, the concept of disarmament has occupied a prominent place in people's thinking and has been a principal goal of public movements concerned with world peace. But one has to admit that peace and disarmament have not figured among the notable achievements of mankind. They have become the most talked of and least practiced of all social endeavors. With the emergence of the modern nation-state as an institution well organized for waging war, disarmament proposals became part and parcel of international diplomacy. It has been a fruitless effort, as can be seen in the *Encyclopaedia Britannica*, which, in its last edition, was shaken from its usual composure to conclude that disarmament endeavors in our time have been "spectacularly unsuccessful."

By the end of the nineteenth century the idea of a special international conference dedicated to disarmament had achieved particular prominence with the convening of the first Hague Conference in 1899.[1] With the first international conference, disarmament was institutionalized as a major arena of international diplomacy. The framers of the League Covenant took pains to make disarmament the cornerstone of their system of collective security and the principal object of the organization. Perceived as the key for the post–World War I international order, disarmament got the first priority and was continuously in the forefront of the League's agenda, culminating in the Disarmament Conference of 1932. World War II led to the disillusionment with disarmament and, consequently, to a very low-key and weak reference to it in the Charter of the United Nations. However, because of historical circumstances (the coming of the nuclear age) and the self-propelled dynamics of the United Nations routine and polemics coupled with the dictates of political interests, disarmament soon became the subject of more continuous deliberations than any other single item on the United Nations agenda.

The League's experience represented an effort to rely heavily upon disarmament in order to establish a reformed system of international order. The United Nations, after three decades of wrestling with the politics of disarmament, seems to have reached a dead end, where disarmament is completely divorced from the realities and conditions of world order. The record of both organizations suggests a tendency, though motivated by different factors, of overreliance on the conception suggested by the Soviet Deputy Foreign Commissar Maxim Litvinov to the League of Nations that "the way to disarm is to disarm."[2] Following this approach, international organization has demonstrated extraordinary vitality in treating every possible idea on disarmament and in exhausting almost every possible structural and functional option in the field of disarmament machinery.

"Swords into plowshares" was treated alone as if this revolutionary process were possible without elaborating on the general settlement of outstanding political differences and guaranteeing the necessary conditions for maintaining international order. The advice of Salvador De Madariaga, the top official in the League dealing with disarmament, seems to have gone unheeded: "The solution of the problem of disarmament cannot be found within the problem itself, but outside it. In fact, the problem of disarmament is not the problem of disarmament. It really is the problem of the organization of the World Community."[3]

It is this inextricable connection between disarmament and world order and its manifestations in the United Nations that is the concern of this book. Proceeding from the East–West confrontation on disarmament that dominated the deliberations at the United Nations during the cold war era, we shall follow the shift toward the North–South axis during the 1970s. In both the East–West and North–South confrontations on disarmament, the essence of the debate concerns, in effect, the nature and character of international order. However, in each confrontation there have been different types of interplays and clashes between the concepts of disarmament and world order.

At the outset, we shall deal primarily with the East–West debate and the evolution of the United Nations machinery in the field of disarmament. First, we examine (in Chapter 2) the historical and legal background for United Nations activities regarding disarmament. Contrary to what Third World rhetoric would suggest a few decades later, the United Nations Charter was never designated to promote disarmament objectives. The drafters of the Charter believed in an international order based on a collective security system under which the maintenance of national armaments, particularly in the hands of the major powers, is a prerequisite to permit the discharge of international obligations respecting the enforcement of peace and security. Obviously, the advent of the atomic bomb fundamentally altered the nature of the world in which the United Nations would function, and therefore attempts were made to accommodate the "pre-atomic" character of the Charter to the requirements of the new age. However, these attempts were doomed to fail since they embodied a new concept of world order. The East–West haggling over the "Baruch Plan" of 1946 was concerned not as much with disarmament as with the idea of revising the world order envisaged in the Charter. The pattern of differences would create an impasse leaving the United Nations with no role to play in disarmament. Later, when the superpowers started to negotiate arms control measures, they did it primarily outside the United Nations, in keeping with the existing framework of world order. In the United Nations, instead, delegates and staff members were engaged in numerous bureaucratic reforms of the disarmament machinery that had no bearing on the real world outside (Chapter 3).

The dramatic changes in the balance of power within the United Nations brought about a shift in the disarmament debate from the East–West to North–South axis. Chapter 4 will examine how the politics of the New International Economic Order (NIEO), the overriding concern of the Third World, have affected the disarmament debates. It was again a debate over international order, but unlike the debate on the Baruch Plan, the issue of world government was not raised. This time disarmament was perceived as a major vehicle for the Third World in its attempt to get rid of the "law of the great powers" through disarmament of the superpowers and through reallocation of resources and power from them to the Third World. The Third World challenged the right of the great powers (recognized by the Unitd Nations Charter) to maintain their privileged position as the custodians of international security (Chapter 5). They view the Non-Proliferation Treaty of nuclear weapons as discriminatory and pursue initiatives to undermine the non-proliferation regime (Chapter 6). Similarly, they reject efforts in the United Nations to discuss the conventional arms race or to restrain the international trade of arms (Chapter 7).

With disarmament debates becoming hostage to NIEO politics, East–West confrontations have reemerged. With the decline of arms control efforts between the superpowers, the Soviet Union enjoyed important advantages in the United Nations debates on disarmament over the United States and its allies. The NIEO–disarmament linkage helps the Soviets to exploit the forum to further isolate and divide the Western group.

Significant progress in disarmament cannot be achieved without addresssing the issues of world order. The United Nations seems to foster disarmament plans in terms of grandiose ethical statements and sweeping programs instead of proceeding toward limited bargains and workable measures that recognize international realities. Caught between these East–West and North–South axes, the United Nations cannot play an effective role in promoting achievable agreements of arms control.

NOTES

1. For historical and documentary reviews of disarmament efforts and proposals, see Trevor N. Dupuy and Gay M. Hammerman, eds., *A Documentary History of Arms Control and Disarmament* (New York: R. R. Bowker, 1973); Merze Tate, *The Disarmament Illusion: The Movement for a Limitation of Armaments to 1907* (New York: Macmillan, 1942).

2. Inis L. Claude, *Swords into Plowshares* (New York: Random House, 1971), p. 298. The complete abolition of armaments, said Litvinov, is "the only real means of guaranteeing security and affording a guarantee against the outbreak of war." For Litvinov's statement and further analysis, see Robert W. Lambert, *Soviet Disarmament Policy 1922–1931*, Research report 64–2 (Washington, D.C.: United States Arms Control and Disarmament Agency, 1964), p. 156.

3. Salvador De Madariaga, *Disarmament* (1929; reprint ed., New York: Kennikat Press, 1967), p. 56.

2

The Pre-Atomic Charter: Security, Disarmament, and the Nuclear Factor

As one who was at San Francisco in the spring of 1945, I can say with confidence that had the delegates at San Francisco known we were entering the age of atomic warfare, they would have seen to it that the Charter dealt more positively with the problems thus raised.[1]

John Foster Dulles

If the United Nations cannot produce an Atomic Charter that will work, then the United Nations Charter will not work, either.

New York Times, editorial
June 14, 1946

A principal characteristic of United Nations operations in the field of disarmament lies in the fact that at the time the United Nations Charter was agreed upon, its framers could not have been aware of the most revolutionary change in military power in the post–World War II era. While they were ironing out their last differences on the draft Charter at San Francisco in June 1945, work on the atomic bomb was proceeding in the greatest secrecy. The first atomic bomb was exploded (at a test site) three weeks after the Charter was signed, and on August 6, 1945, six weeks after the termination of the San Francisco Conference, the bomb fell on Hiroshima.

As soon as it came into being, the United Nations was doomed to function under the "Sword of Damocles" of a nuclear catastrophe. Immediately, the newborn international body, whose Charter starts from the commitment "to save succeeding generations from the scourge of war," was confronted with unprecedented military and political challenges. Symbolically, the first resolution of the United Nations General Assembly was to establish an Atomic Energy Commission (UNAEC) with the urgent task of making specific proposals for the elimination from national armaments of atomic weapons and of all other major weapons of mass destruction.[2] However, this resolution remained symbolic indeed, for the United Nations Atomic Energy Commission was paralyzed from the beginning by irreconcilable differences.

The commission's members last met on July 29, 1949, and when the Soviets exploded their first atomic bomb in September 1949, UNAEC's failure was sealed.[3] The commission was finally dissolved on January 11, 1952, by a United Nations General Assembly resolution, which created the Disarmament Commission.[4] This chapter will address two major questions: Was the United Nations Charter a document that envisaged and designated an important role for disarmament efforts? Could the United Nations Charter provide a resonable framework for an international control system and ultimately the elimination of the threat of nuclear catastrophe?

It would be unfair and misleading to attribute the shortcomings in the Charter's provisions on disarmament solely to its pre-atomic character. The reasons are more fundamental and grew out of the special historical background and intellectual environment under which the United Nations founding fathers developed their concept about a postwar security organization. It is important, therefore, first to examine this historical context and then to proceed to analyze the United Nations' first major treatment of the issue of nuclear disarmament.

THE CHARTER AND THE COVENANT

"International organization," writes Inis Claude, "is fundamentally, even though not exclusively, a reaction to the problem of war."[5] In the twentieth century, the urge to avoid war has been the major impetus for establishing international organizations that were, in most cases, set up following world wars. Both the League of Nations and the United Nations were organizations designed to maintain international peace and security in order "to save succeeding generations from the scourge of war." However, the nature of these organizations was, in considerable measure, determined by the intellectual environment of their founders. Some major differences between the United Nations Charter and the League of Nations Covenant suggest that the drafters of the two documents approached the problem of international security and its links with disarmament differently. It is clear that the Charter of the United Nations by no means echoes the general approach and the specific provisions of the Covenant on issues relating to the maintenance of international peace and security and disarmament measures.

The different approaches taken in drafting the two documents can be illustrated by the striking differences in their treatment of the concept of security. The word *security* appears only once in the Convenant—and only in a very general and vague form—in the preamble, in reference to the purpose of the league "to promote international cooperation and to achieve international peace and security." Thereafter, the term *security* does not reappear, and the Covenant confines itself to terms such as peace, peace of nations, and peace of the world.

In the United Nations Charter, however, the concept of security is dealt with as the centerpiece of the organization, and the phrase "international peace and security" appears thirty-two times. In addition, the supreme and most powerful body envisaged in the Charter is the Security Council. This organ is referred to numerous times, often in conjunction with the specific duties of maintaining international peace and security.

The concept of collective security, which is the cornerstone of the Charter, grew out of the League's failure to stop the deterioration of security and the effects of the unilateral disarmament of the democratic powers during the thirties, when the Axis states had heavily armed themselves.[6] It is clear, therefore, that the notion of collective security, particularly as an instrument of peace enforcement, had a direct impact on the Charter's approach to the issue of disarmament. The law enforcement measures in the Charter (Articles 39, 41, 42) go far beyond anything the Covenant of the League contemplated.

As the first article of the Charter indicates, collective security is based on the belief that the most effective way to maintain peace and security is for the international community to mobilize strong collective countermeasures "for the prevention and removal of threats to the peace, and for the suppression of acts of aggression or other branches of the peace." By definition, to enforce the law against the law breaker requires readily superior military power. That is why the system of peacekeeping and enforcement measures envisaged by Chapter 7 of the Charter was predicated upon the continued existence of strong national armies, navies, and air forces as an integral part of collective security.

This straightforward interrelationship between the concept of collective security and disarmament was in the back of the minds of those involved in the preparations for the new international organization. As early as 1942, it was clear to the men involved in the preparatory work in the U.S. Department of State that the problem of the enforcement of peace was "the most difficult problem to resolve in planning a new international institution that would be able to use force when necessary to keep the peace."[7]

Analysis of official documents indicates that the approach in the United Nations Charter to the idea of peace enforcement was a convergence, on one hand, of President Franklin Roosevelt's ideas on a postwar international order based upon the "Four Policemen" (the four major Allies of World War II), and, on the other, of the more modified approach of the State Department, which was thinking more in terms of the previous international organization, the League of Nations.[8] Official documents and records released by the State Department reveal how the ideas of postwar security, gradually developed during the war and thereafter, led to the concept of peace enforcement and the new role of the Security Council in the United Nations.[9] This had direct effects on the Charter's treatment of disarmament.

President Roosevelt and Secretary of State Cordell Hull were committed to establishing a general international organization and were determined, at the same time, to avoid President Wilson's disillusioning experience with the League of Nations. The widespread public support in the United States for the establishment of a new international organization during and after World War II was a departure from the refusal to join the League of Nations a generation earlier, and it encouraged American leaders to play a prominent role in it.[10] Roosevelt himself envisaged an international order based on the "Four Policemen" concept, whereby the four great powers (the United States, the Soviet Union, Great Britain, and China) would patrol the world for the benefit of all peaceloving nations. This view of postwar security problems was based on the belief that, under conditions of modern warfare, the majority of small nations were incapable of defending themselves against powerful aggressors. Consequently, the police power of the world should reside in the hands of the few powerful nations, who would assist the weaker members of the international community. Roosevelt expressed these ideas to Stalin as early as May 1942, and reiterated them in their summit meeting in Teheran.[11]

After the United States joined the war against the Axis, postwar planning activities in the State Department entered their most intensive and important stage. Within the department, early in 1942, a new Advisory Committee on Postwar Foreign Policy, with an elaborate system of subcommittees, was established. The committee considered ideas for a postwar organization that came from a wide range of private organizations. Most of the committees' personnel were co-opted from outside from both the public and private sectors.[12] The role of the new international organization in the fields of security and disarmament was discussed primarily in the Special Subcommittee on International Organization and the Subcommittee on Security Problems.

Naturally, in 1942, the issues of armaments and disarmament were clouded with uncertainty. The members of the subcommittee on international organization faced a clear dilemma:

On one hand, the relation between armaments and postwar security was clear; on the other hand, general demand to curtail expenditures in this field was likely. The regrettable effects of the drain upon budgets in practically all states caused by armaments pointed toward great reduction, but the need had also to be met for the maintenance of armaments at a level that would permit the discharge of international obligations respecting the enforcement of peace and security. The successful aggressions of the enemy against weak neighbors and the attack by Japan upon Pearl Harbor were lessons in the danger of weakness that could not be forgotten if peace and security were not to be imperiled. A *minimum* level for *some states* and a *maximum* for *others* was envisaged in the tentative views developed.[13]

Similar questions were discussed in the Subcommittee on Security. It was understood that enforcement measures for peace necessitated armaments, and therefore the question was: Would not these armaments have to come from nations?

Thus, in the course of these preparations, in accordance with Roosevelt's view, the seeds of the "discriminatory" approach to disarmament were planted: "a minimum level for some states and a maximum for others." Indeed, the problem of discrimination in the field of security and disarmament would be revived later, after three decades, at the United Nations within the framework of the North–South confrontation on disarmament (see Chapters 5–6).

Though it was agreed that there should be a reduction from the wartime level of armaments, the League experience taught that "the armaments of peace-loving states in the future would have to be maintained at a level sufficient to enforce the peace."[14] Accordingly, at the Dumbarton Oaks Conference of the major Allies in August 1944, the participants concentrated their efforts on the security provisions of the emerging Charter.[15] The concept of enforcement also raised profound questions concerning sovereignty and equality among the large and small states cooperating for maintenance of peace.[16] It seems that in the process the drafters of the Charter abandoned the issues of disarmament and sovereignty in order to give priority to security issues. It became clear that the security system envisaged by the Charter would require all states to maintain domestic order.[17] As a result, it was agreed among experts on international law that the enforcement of peace was the most radical innovation to be written into the Charter, which also offered the most marked contrast to the provisions of the Convenant.[18]

In order to understand even better the link between a particular concept of security and disarmament, it is interesting to review the statement of the Covenant of the League on disarmament. The members of the League of Nations were convinced, as the Covenant says, that the maintenance of peace requires a major effort to reduce "national armaments to the lowest point consistent with national safety and the enforcement by common action of international obligations." Their conviction was influenced by the belief that the race in armaments between the major powers in Europe had been largely responsible for World War I. Their approach was a ramification of the deterministic theory supporting disarmament, which views arms races as self-propelling processes in which armament breeds counterarmament, leading to an inexorable march to the violent climax of war.[19] This was, as one observer puts it, the fallacy of the direct approach to disarmament, which regarded armaments in themselves as the main source of insecurity among nations; therefore, disarmament would automatically bring an easing of international tensions.[20] As F. P. Walters indicates, when the League was created there were great expectations within international public opinion that the new organization "would put an end to the burden and danger of great national armaments." Rightly or wrongly, disarmament was regarded then:

not only as the test of the League's success, but as almost the principal object of its existence. Men had looked forward, year after year, to the day when the signature of the first general Disarmament Treaty should concentrate and consolidate the peaceful organization of the modern world.[21]

As a result, disarmament received high priority in the Covenant of the League of Nations. Already in its first article, "arms regulations" was a stipulation under which every new member that joins the League had to "accept such regulations as may be prescribed by the League in regard to its military, naval and air forces and armaments."

Article 8 of the Covenant is, as a matter of fact, a specified framework of guidelines and agreed principles on disarmament:

1. The members of the League recognize that the maintenance of peace requires the reduction of national armaments to the lowest point consistent with national safety and the enforcement by common action of international obligations.
2. The Council, taking account of the geographical situation and circumstances of each State, shall formulate plans for such reduction for the consideration and action of the several Governments.
3. Such plans shall be subject to reconsideration and revision at least every ten years.
4. After these plans shall have been adopted by the several Governments, the limits of armaments fixed shall not be exceeded without the concurrence of the Council.
5. The members of the League agree that the manufacture by private enterprise of munitions and implements of war is open to grave objections. The Council shall advise how the evil effects attendant upon such manufacture can be prevented, due regard being had to the necessities of those Members of the League which are not able to manufacture the munitions and implements of war necessary for their safety.
6. The Members of the League undertake to interchange full and frank information as to the scale of their armaments, their military, naval and air programmes and the condition of such of their industries as are adaptable to war-like purposes.

Article 9 provides the establishment of a permanent commission to advise the League's Council "on the execution of the provisions of Articles 1 and 8 on military, naval and air questions generally." The commitments to carry out a "reduction and limitation of armament" were continuously in the forefront of the aims and activities of the League, and the efforts culminated in the Disarmament Conference convened at Geneva in 1932.

If World War I was followed by a deep disillusionment with the arms race, World War II led to disillusionment with disarmament. Edward Teller, who fled from Nazi Europe before the war to become a leading nuclear scientist in America, gives an indication of the international climate at that time: "there can be little doubt that World War II was caused by an uncontrolled race for disarmament. The peace loving nations disarmed, thereby they gave one lawless government a chance to bid for world domination."[22]

The same opinion, with extended application to the nuclear age, is expressed by a prominent scholar on the United Nations, Inis Claude:

An arms race in the 1930's might have prevented the greatest war yet recorded. Such peace as the world had known since 1945—and, for all its imperfections, the records of statesmanship in this period does include the notable achievement of the nonoccurrence of World War III—may conceivably owe more to the same arms race than to any other factor.[23]

For the United Nations' founding fathers, all assumptions of the new security organization started from the recognition of the existence of a state of war.[24] They were not just disillusioned with disarmament but also aware of the special circumstances at that time. The final negotiations on the Charter at San Francisco, in the spring of 1945, took place while the war was still raging and the real problem facing the Allies was "not one of reducing armaments but of producing them."[25] The Allies were striving to increase their military might in order to win the war. Under these circumstances, any attempt to discuss and formulate specific disarmament measures "would have been distracting at best."[26] It would be inconceivable, moreover, to expect direct criticism such as that contained in the Covenant, in Article 8, on weapons manufacture by private enterprises.

Not surprisingly, the United Nations Charter's statement on disarmament was relatively weak, with only a vague reference to possible measures to be taken. Unlike the Covenant of the League, the Charter does not obligate the members of the United Nations to reduce their armaments. It is a curious fact that Articles 1 and 2 of the Charter setting forth the purposes and principles of the organization contain not a single reference to disarmament. Only in Article 11 does the provision appear that the "General Assembly may consider the general principles of cooperation in the maintenance of international peace and security, including the principles governing disarmament and the regulation of armaments."[27]

The Charter's understated reference to disarmament can be further illustrated by reviewing its provisions on the functions of the General Assembly in other fields (economic, social, health, etc.). In these cases the Charter uses firmer and clearer language (Article 13, and Chapters 9 and 10 contain an extensive list of provisions on international economic and social cooperation and composition, functions, and powers of the Economic and Social Council of the United Nations). In a word, the Charter's low-key approach to disarmament is not accidental; it is an integral part of its philosophy.

The United Nations Charter subscribes to a particular philosophy concerning the link between international security and disarmament. As Ruth Russell points out, implicit in the Charter one can identify the so-called French thesis, which linked national disarmament together with the development of a system of international military sanctions. According to this view, which was most strongly promoted by France during the League period, there is an interdependence between the reduction of national armaments, which would weaken the capacity of national protection, and the development of a system of international military sanctions, which would safeguard the countries' vital interests. Though the "French thesis" is not spelled out in the Charter, its bearing can be found both on the overall approach of the Charter to international security and in its missing provisions on disarmament. It has been recognized that a number of principal features from the French thesis have been embodied in the Charter and, thus, hailed by many as making it an instrument superior to the Covenant for maintaining international peace and security.[28] The fact that the Charter's provisions for security are more definite than those of the Covenant highlights even more the former's vague reference to disarmament. The drafters of the Charter did not subscribe to the deterministic logic that, since men fight because they have arms, elimination of weapons will make fighting impossible. Weapons were treated as the result and not as the cause of insecurity and, moreover, as a necessary evil to prevent war. The interwar experiences of the United Nations' founding fathers, as indicated by Nicholas, suggested that armaments per se did not cause war; rather, "armaments in the wrong hand" led to that condition.[29]

Philosophically speaking, the founding fathers of the United Nations were realists who regarded peace as a political situation that would allow disarmament to take place as a natural by-product of a conflict resolution but not an effective method to tackle international conflicts. Accordingly, they have listed disarmament as one of a variety of optional measures (the "general principles of international cooperation") that the General Assembly "may consider." Disarmament, thus, was envisaged as an option, not as a prerequisite. It has been argued correctly that, as far as disarmament is concerned, "the Charter was an unfinished document."[30]

THE ATOMIC CHALLENGE

It is clear that the nuclear age created a new pattern of security problems that could not have been foreseen when the United Nations Charter was negotiated. The Charter, it was argued, was inadequte since it "furnished no clue as to the appropriate method for dealing with the control of atomic energy.[31] Ironically, the United Nations Charter, which was from the beginning an unfinished document for conventional disarmament, was the only accepted framework to tackle the dangers of the emerging nuclear age.

It is against this background that the American plan for international control of nuclear energy, better known as the Baruch Plan, was submitted to the newly created United Nations Atomic Energy Commission. A lot has been written on the "lost opportunity" and the epic failure of the Baruch Plan. Though there are different interpretations of the reasons for the failure, one thing should be clear: the Baruch Plan introduced a different philosophy of international order for the specific purpose of nuclear energy. Unlike the United Nations Charter, the Baruch Plan was perceived, and correctly so, as another prescription for world government, "in the sense that it envisaged an international agency with functions and powers cutting deeply into the traditional preserves of national sovereignty."[32] It provided for a sweeping change in the priorities so carefully established in the Charter on the delicate triangular relationship among international security, disarmament, and sovereignty. In terms of the "French thesis," it was a major leap forward toward a total submission of national security in the nuclear field to an international authority. Collective security under the terms of the Baruch Plan required that every sovereign state surrender its prerogative of acquiring the most powerful of all weapons and submit to a supranational authority in nuclear matters. But the world of 1946 was not ripe yet to update its law and order to the new requirements of the nuclear age.

It has to be noted that what came to be known as the Baruch Plan was a result of an intensive and extensive process of policy-making starting as early as August 1945, a few days after Hiroshima. At the beginning of November 1945, President Truman, British Prime Minister Attlee, and Canadian Prime Minister King met in Washington and agreed on the need for international action under the auspices of the United Nations to ensure the use of atomic energy for peaceful purposes only, to outlaw atomic weapons and other weapons of mass destruction, and to provide for inspection safeguards. Another diplomatic effort brought about a Soviet agreement to cosponsor, with the United States and the United Kingdom, the first United Nations General Assembly resolution on the establishment of a commission on atomic energy.[33]

In the meantime, a committee consisting of high officials, scientists, and industrialists had met under the leadership of Dean Acheson, then under secretary of state, to formulate the substantive American position on the subject. Later, the committee was enlarged to include a Board of Consultants headed by David Lilienthal. The "Acheson-Lilienthal Report," made public in March 1946, carried out the Three-Power Declaration proposing a supranational International Atomic Development Authority, which would hold a monopoly over all phases of nuclear research and development.

In an effort to make the Acheson-Lilienthal recommendations more palatable to a skeptical Congress,[34] Truman and his secretary of state, Byrnes, chose to entrust Bernard M. Baruch, the banker and former adviser to presidents, with the task of presenting the American proposal to the UNAEC, which was scheduled to meet that summer. Truman and Byrnes hoped that Baruch's prestige and previous record would assure the anxious members of Congress that the Truman administration would not be duped into an international control plan that would only distribute atomic secrets to the Russians.[35] Baruch added to the Acheson-Lilienthal Report the enforcement measures that were not to be subject to veto in the Security Council.

On June 14, 1946, Baruch outlined the American plan at the first meeting of the new twelve-nation United Nations Commission. The language was dramatic and apocalyptic, directed at his fellow citizens of the world: "we are here to make a choice between the quick and the dead. . . . Let us not deceive ourselves; we must elect World Peace or World Destruction."[36] The immediate reaction was enthusiastic and overwhelmingly favorable.[37] The *New York Times* ran a huge headline on its front page proclaiming "The World at Crossroads" and applauded the plan in its editorial: "For the first time in history a nation possessing a unique and destructive weapon has offered to make the essential facts about the weapon generally available, and then to put a stop to its use."[38]

Yet the response from the Soviet representative to the UNAEC, Andrei Gromyko, was: "So far matters are going smoothly."[39] Smoothly, however, for only a few more days. It took only five days for Gromyko to indicate that the formal East–West tug of war of disarmament negotiations had begun.

At the second meeting of the commission, on June 19, 1946, Gromyko, without mentioning the Baruch proposal, introduced what was almost the exact opposite of the American plan.[40] The Soviet counterplan raised the chief issue of all subsequent disarmament negotiations: Which comes first? The commitment to disarm or the control measures to ensure the implementation and observance of commitments?

The American plan was proposed to be put into effect stage by stage. First, a control mechanism would be established providing effective safeguards, after which the United States would carry out its obligation for the elimination of its existing bombs and hand over to the authority its complete scientific knowledge. The Soviet Union called for the prohibition and "destruction" of weapons at the outset, with the machinery to ensure observance set up at a later date. Not only did the USSR demand the reversal of American priorities, it also rejected the comprehensive list of the envisaged control mechanism. Gromyko proposed an international agency that would have been subordinated to the Security Council, lacking authority to own, operate, and license atomic facilities. The control function was vaguely defined with limited competence to inspect national atomic establishments. For the Soviets, the enforcement of the outlawing of atomic weapons remained on the declaratory level without any concrete measures. It was on the same moral plane as the Briand-Kellogg Pact of 1928, which outlawed war as a serious crime against humanity.[41] In other words, the Soviet plan really proposed that each state assume the responsibility for its own atomic energy industry and see to it that there would be no violations: "Each state was to operate on its own—and serve as its own policeman."[42]

For the first period, lasting from January 1946 until December 1948, United Nations deliberations on disarmament were characterized by a relatively detailed and precise discussion, which for a long time thereafter was not repeated.[43] The UNAEC was divided into committees and subcommittees that dealt with the general proposals, control questions, and legal and scientific aspects. On the basis of its findings, the commission recommended in its first report to the Security Council on December 30, 1946, the creation of a strong and comprehensive international system of control and inspection by an international treaty. Despite the evident difference between the American and Soviet ideas, the commission went through "intensive activity" throughout 1947.[44] In the course of these negotiations, the superpowers elaborated and modified their proposals, but the fundamental differences remained intact. Simultaneously, as a result of a Soviet initiative, a United Nations Commission for Conventional Armaments was established by the Security Council, but its meetings resulted in no measurable progress.

As the cold war mounted in intensity, the exchanges deteriorated, regardless of the technical feasibilities that were discussed at the United Nations. There was really very little left to do, and the debate became a "parallel monologue."[45]

The deadlock was officially acknowledged in the commission reports, which pointed out that an impasse had been reached.[46] On November 4, 1948, a modified version of the Baruch Plan was finally approved by the General Assembly by an overwhelming majority of forty to six, with five abstentions (Res. 191, III), but the lack of agreement between the superpowers made it a hollow victory. In 1949, the meeting of the commission immediately degenerated into petty haggling and propaganda harangues.[47] The commission reported that the "differences are irreconcilable at the Commission level, and that further discussion in the Atomic Energy Commission would tend to harden these differences and would serve no practical or useful purpose."[48]

THE FAILURE OF THE BARUCH PLAN

The failure of the Baruch Plan was critical, since it demonstrated the inability of the parties to adjust the rules of international conduct and the provisions of collective security to the new requirements of the nuclear age. From then, there has been a long stalemate over disarmament discussions at the United Nations and outside. For the purposes of this study, it does not matter whether the Baruch Plan was a bold initiative[49] or just shrewd diplomatic gamesmanship.[50] Those who criticize the provisions of the plan as being part of an alleged American "atomic diplomacy"[51] fail to understand that the major weakness of the Baruch Plan was not so much in its style and technicalities as in the philosophy it represented. "The Acheson-Lilienthal-Baruch proposal," writes Claude, "seemed to be in conformity with the requirements of technical reality, but it did not adequately reflect the conditions of political reality."[52]

Unlike the Soviet proposal, as Ruth Russell points out, the Baruch Plan was both detailed and free of propaganda broadsides.[53] It reflected the intellectual strains in American thinking in the aftermath of Hiroshima and Nagasaki. Scientists shared a feeling of guilt, and the theme of editorials was that time was running out on mankind. On December 15, 1945, the first issue of the *Bulletin of the Atomic Scientists* was published, and its cover carried a clock set at a few minutes to twelve (still the theme of the publication today). Americans doubted whether the international order envisaged by the United Nations Charter was compatible with atomic weapons. One leading commentator wrote:

It is no reflection on the [UN] Charter, to say it has become a feeble and antiquated instrument for dealing with the problems of an Atomic Age. . . . Time today works against peace . . . once the nature and imminency of the peril are clearly understood by the peoples of the world their differences will not be a bar but an incentive to common government.[54]

It should be noted that the leading atomic scientists in the United States regarded an international authority with inspection powers as critical to prevent nuclear holocaust. The original ideas were those of Robert Oppenheimer from the Manhattan Project and were incorporated in the Acheson-Lilienthal Report.[55]

In developing the plan, Acheson had already pointed out the centrality of inspection at the expense of national sovereignty.[56] It was assumed by scientists that openness, friendliness, and cooperation with the Soviets were essential.[57] Already on April 25, 1945, the American secretary of war, Henry Stimson, wrote to President Truman on the control over nuclear weapons:

No system of control heretofore considered would be adequate to control this menace [of atomic weapons]. Both inside any particular country and between the nations of the world, the control of this weapon will undoubtedly be a matter of the greatest difficulty and would involve such thorough-going rights of inspection and internal controls as we have never heretofore contemplated.[58]

In an article that appeared on June 1, 1946, in the *Bulletin of the Atomic Scientists*, Edward Teller made a sweeping proposal for an open society with free communication jointly guaranteed by the United States and the Soviet Union. The Americans would declassify all atomic secrets, and an Atomic Development Authority would be established as a supranational body to inspect activities in the nuclear field. The inspectors would be nominated and responsible only to the authority and would have "the right freely to inquire into any activity which may seem to them directed against their own country, or against world peace."[59]

There is no doubt that the Baruch Plan was designed to revise the Charter, or as the *New York Times* entitled its editorial on the eve of Baruch's speech, "Toward an Atomic Charter."[60] Public figures in the West called for far-reaching political conclusions and a complete readjustment of all international relations to prevent atomic war. It was clear that people thought in terms of sweeping changes in international order: "If world government cannot save us, the world as we know it is lost."[61]

In the memoranda submitted by the United States to the UNAEC in July 1946, the Baruch Plan had been developed and elaborated reflecting also an intellectual soul-searching. In dealing with the functions and powers of the proposed authority and its relations to United Nations organs, the Americans emphasized that the plan aimed "to fill an existing gap since the question of control and development of atomic energy was neither considered nor dealt with in the framing of the Charter of the United Nations." It was clear that the Baruch Plan was designed to update the Charter:

If the Charter is to survive, it must be susceptible of adaptation to meet new needs dictated by new conditions...even if the Charter could be construed to provide for a subsidiary organ created by collective action of several of the existing organs and possessing an aggregate of powers delegated by each of them, such subsidiary organ would not have adequate powers under the Charter. Accordingly, the authority, as a new organ, should be established by treaty granting it all necessary powers and defining its relation with the existing organs of the United Nations.[62]

As Michael Mandelbaum explained, the Baruch Plan was a liberal proposal, bearing three distinct liberal trademarks: it was sweeping in scope; it was presented to the United Nations; and it included provisions for the dilution of national sovereignty for the sake of a supranational government.[63] It was part and parcel of what Mandelbaum terms "liberal diplomacy," born out of optimistic belief in human progress, political reform, and the abolition of national sovereignty, "foreseeing a world government drawn along the lines of the political institutions of the liberal state."[64]

In this respect, the plan marked a major departure from the vision and arrangements of the United Nations Charter. In order to achieve nuclear disarmament, the plan regarded as a prerequisite the need to strengthen an international authority at the expense of national sovereignty. These proposed revisions of the Charter were totally unacceptable to the Russians and were rejected out of hand.

Those who today still accuse the Baruch Plan of being part of the American "nuclear diplomacy" against the Russians fail to examine closely this intellectual trend in the United States toward demanding changes in the United Nations Charter for the nuclear age. Similarly, they fail to criticize, at least equally, the counterplan presented by the Soviets.[65] The Soviet response made it clear that the gap was fundamental and philosophical. The Soviet Union had enjoyed for a couple of months the advantage of prior knowledge of the American approach as it found its expression in the Acheson-Lilienthal Report already in March 1946. The speed with which Gromyko responded to Baruch at the United Nations (within five days at the second meeting of the UNAEC) and the fact that his response contained no specific references to Baruch's statement made it seem likely that the fundamental Soviet approach had been formulated in Moscow well before Baruch introduced his controversial amendments. Apparently, Gromyko had come to the United States with a comprehensive statement of the Soviet Union's minimum conditions regarding international atomic energy control. They were thoroughly irreconcilable even with the Acheson-Lilienthal plan (before Baruch suggested abolishing the veto).

Similarly, from a military point of view, it is hard to believe that the Baruch Plan was part of a grand strategy based on "nuclear diplomacy." It is a fact that, at the time, no American strategy was devised for employing the nuclear options as a bargaining instrument. Officials in Washington had no intention of actually using the bomb to compel Moscow's cooperation.[66] Moreover, the fact of the matter is that, despite the plan's failure, in the period between 1945 and 1949 the Americans did not go anywhere in their atomic program. They did not expand their production of uranium or of fissionable materials to any appreciable extent, nor did they proceed on any reactor program.[67] In 1949, for instance, the Canadians were far ahead in the use of heavy water for certain types of nuclear reactors. As one American nuclear scientist said, "We just seemed to be sitting by and doing nothing."[68]

The Baruch modifications of the Acheson-Lilienthal Report should also be viewed against the background of the growing distrust of the Soviet Union by Americans in 1946. U.S. policy, hence, was based not only on what the Russians might accept but also on what Congress would not condemn,[69] under the special circumstances at that period. Historically, the United States and its allies were engaged at that time in unilateral conventional disarmament, and the Baruch Plan implied giving up the only weapon that made it superior without similar provisions for the reduction of conventional forces.

Some historians assert in retrospect that the American monopoly at that time, paradoxical as it sounds, debilitated rather than helped U.S. foreign policy. As Adam Ulam explains, a huge democracy like the United States is prone in peacetime "to indolence and procrastination in international affairs." The bomb, he concluded, encouraged a Maginot Line psychology.[70] Nevertheless, many have believed that the supremacy of the United States in atomic weapons served as a main defense of Western Europe and therefore should not be given up without adequate guarantees. Winston Churchill said in March 1949: "It is certain that Europe would have been communized like Czechoslovakia and London would have been under bombardment some time ago but for the deterrent of the atomic weapon in the hands of the United States."[71]

Though the veto issue created the greatest attention at that time, it is widely agreed that Baruch's insistence on abolishing it did not in itself wreck prospects for international control. According to Bechhoefer, who was a member of the U.S. delegation to the UNAEC, the veto was an unnecessary element that permitted the Soviet Union to reject the whole plan for the wrong reason. The issue has camouflaged the essence of the Soviet rejection: "It was desirable that failure to agree should rest firmly on Soviet unwillingness to permit sufficient penetration of its iron curtain to ensure observance of its commitments."[72]

Baruch himself regarded the veto issue as secondary in the Soviet rejection. He told Lilienthal that the real reason for Soviet opposition was not the veto "but rather the whole idea of permitting their country to be subjected to the inspection from outside."[73] Even Lieberman, who doubted the sincerity of the Baruch Plan, admits that the Soviets would have rejected it regardless of the veto element.[74] It is clear that for the Soviet Union the first and foremost barrier in every plan of new international authority was the limits that it put on their national sovereignty and their control over internal affairs in the Communist system. While there is no doubt that the presence of foreign inspectors was a minimum condition of any reasonable plan for international control of atomic energy, it is also clear that the idea ran against the grain of the entire Soviet political system. As William Frye explains, in the days of Stalin, the Soviet Union was "a closed shop, utterly barred to foreigners. Comprehensive international inspection, puncturing the Iron Curtain, was anathema to Stalin."[75] At about the time the United Nations was discussing the Baruch Plan, Soviet authorities were refusing to allow a handful of Russian women married to Britons and Americans during the war to leave the Soviet Union: "If what those few women could tell about life in Russia was considered to be a danger justifying this extraordinary inhumanity and pettiness, what of inspection of bomb installations and research facilities?"[76]

Richard Barnet, who professed a critical view of American security policies in the postwar era, admitted that for the Soviet Union virtually every form of on-site inspection would be unacceptable. "Secrecy," says Barnet, "has been regarded historically as a diplomatic asset in Russia's dealing with other nations."[77] Foreign inspection, he continues, puts a challenge to the exclusive claim of the ruling Communist party to power. In addition, the Soviets do not need much inspection in the West since they get a large amount of information from Western open societies anyway.[78]

The Soviets made no secret of their complete rejection of any form of control authority and international inspection. In his speech to the Security Council in March 1947, which lasted an hour and a half, Gromyko gave a surprisingly explicit expression of Soviet fears of political and ideological contamination. For Groymko the idea of the control authority was "incompatible with state sovereignty," and he described it as "thoroughly vicious and unacceptable." He indicated forcefully:

Unlimited control would mean an unlimited interference in the economic life of the countries on whose territories the control would be carried out and interference in their internal affairs. The Soviet Union and probably not only the Soviet Union cannot allow the fate of its national economy [to be turned] over to this organ.[79]

Gromyko's arguments with regard to sovereignty and interference in internal affairs underscore that it would be misleading to attribute the Soviet–American struggle at the United Nations as only over priorities: control versus disarmament. At the root of the dispute was a struggle concerning the very nature of the new international order in the emerging nuclear age.

It is against this background that the Soviets also rejected Baruch's proposal to abolish the veto power. The issue of the veto was simply a ramification of the contending approaches to the broader issues of national sovereignty and international control. The American memorandum pointed out that the controls would be ineffectual if the enforcement could be prevented by the veto. It would render the entire principle of veto ridiculous: "It is intended to be an instrument for the protection of nations, not a shield behind which deception and criminal acts can be performed with impunity."[80] Similarly the *New York Times* explained: "In the final analysis no plan will work or be acceptable to the United States unless it provides the guarantees essential to safeguard the world against an ambush. That calls for an agency of international control with authority beyond any veto power."[81]

The Russians rejected any idea of change in world order. For them, both concepts of national sovereignty and the veto granted to the major powers were integral parts of the international order agreed upon when the United Nations Charter was drafted. Mr. Gromyko, in his reaction to the American memorandum (No. 3), emphasized: "When the Charter of the United Nations was prepared by the conference at San Francisco, the question of sovereignty was one of the most important questions considered.''

This principle of sovereignty, he said, is one of the cornerstones on which the United Nations structure is built. If this were touched, the whole existence and future of the United Nations would be threatened. Similarly, Gromyko said, it was unacceptable to deny the rights of the Security Council under the Charter, as the American memorandum suggested. The position of the Soviet government was that "the power, authority, and prestige of the Security Council should not be undermined in connection with the problem of atomic energy.''[82]

Once more, in March 1947, in the speech that put an end to all optimism for an international control on nuclear energy, Gromyko indicated why the veto was so central. The Soviet position was that nothing had changed in the world that would have justified abolition of the veto:

What other principle can be proposed to us by those who are sick of the principle of unanimity of the Great Powers, for the solution of all the important questions involved in the maintenance of peace, including the question of sanctions? What substitute can they propose for the veto? Don't they want to draw us back to the ruins of the League of Nations?[83]

Of course, from the Soviet point of view, at stake also was the challenge of an unacceptable balance of power. It was not merely the fear of foreign inspectors spying on its society but rather its giving up the race for atomic power. It could not forgo the opportunity to obtain a position of power, equal to that of the United States, with a nuclear capacity of its own. As early as April 1946, immediately after the Acheson-Lilienthal Report was made public, the State Department was informed by its envoy in Moscow that the Soviets had no interest in a workable international control system. The U.S. ambassador, Walter B. Smith, explained that the Soviet Union was counting on producing its own bombs, relying in the meantime on domestic political constraints within the United States to keep the Truman administration from employing "atomic blackmail." The only control system that Moscow would accept, according to Smith, would be one that furnished Soviet scientists with full technical data on development of the bomb, with no restrictions as to the use of such information.[84]

THE RIGHT OF SELF-DEFENSE

Besides the elementary issues of collective security, national sovereignty, veto, and the realities of power politics, there was another issue which, though almost unnoticed in the literature, highlights the pre-atomic nature of the United Nations Charter: the right of self-defense. Self-defense is an inherent right in customary international law, arising from the existence of a threat to the state defending itself, the lack of any alternative course of action in the prevailing circumstances, and the use of proportionate action to counter the threat. Article 51 of the United

Nations Charter confirms the existence of this customary right as "the inherent right of individual or collective self-defense" in the event of "an armed attack."

The primary responsibility for dealing with acts of aggression resides in the Security Council, and member states of the United Nations are obligated to report their responses to attack to the Security Council but are not required to wait for effective United Nations action before taking measures in self-defense. In effect, Article 51 stipulates that insofar as a violation of international law takes the form of an armed attack against a state, the law enforcement system is decentralized. The injured nation, or other nations in "collective self-defense," are allowed to enforce international law against the law breaker. One problem with the concept is that a major power, by ignoring the obligation to report individual or collective self-defense measures to the Security Council, or by the use of veto in the Security Council, may nullify the role of the United Nations and proceed to handle the situation independently. The problem becomes more complicated when one attempts to apply the provisions of Article 51 to a possible military use of nuclear energy.

Several leading jurists have indicated that developments in the nature, technology, and effectiveness of modern weaponry require a consequential, interpretative adjustment to the notion of a threatened or actual armed attack. These developments in warfare technology added new dimension to the anticipatory right for self-defense, under which the factual circumstances inherent in preparations for atomic warfare is a factor seen by jurists as an "armed attack" within the meaning of Article 51. Professor Derek Bowett of Cambridge University, in his authoritative work *Self-Defense in International Law*, states: "No State can be expected to await an initial attack which, in the present state of armaments, may well destroy the state's capacity for further resistance and so jeopardize its very existence."[85]

The memorandum submitted by the United States to the UNAEC in 1947 reflected the fear that the right of self-defense may take an entirely different form in the nuclear sphere. Referring to the proposed treaty on the International Atomic Development Authority, the United States called for a redefinition of the term *armed attack* in Article 51 to fit the requirements of atomic weapons:

"Armed attack" is now something entirely different from what it was prior to the discovery of atomic weapons. It would therefore seem to be both important and appropriate under present conditions that the treaty define "armed attack" in a manner appropriate to atomic weapons and include in the definition not simply the actual dropping of an atomic bomb, but also certain steps in themselves preliminary to such action.[86]

In retrospect it seems interesting how the Americans had envisaged in 1946 the peculiar logic and the delicate nature of nuclear deterrence. Yet, the Russian reply to the American observations was unequivocal. Gromyko contended that, in general, the American paper had raised "many important political questions, not just legal ones." The Soviet focus remained political, and regardless of the new strategic-military dimension, the proposal, which would "change entirely the meaning of Article 51 of the Charter," was totally unacceptable to the Soviets. The Soviets did not regard the discovery of atomic weapons as a change that requires some adjustments in the legal field, particularly in respect to the right of self-defense. For the Soviets the Charter and existing organs of the United Nations were adequate and empowered to deal with control of atomic energy: "Since the United Nations Charter contained general provisions, there was no reference to particular arms of aggressors. Nevertheless the Charter conferred upon the Security Council full power to control atomic energy, as it was a problem relating to peace and security."[87]

Sir Humphrey Waldock, who was the president of the International Court of Justice, has further observed on the need to broaden the meaning of self-defense in light of the technological progress in both conventional and nuclear weapon systems:

To cut down the customary right of self-defense beyond even the Caroline doctrine does not make sense in times when the speed and power of weapons of attack has enormously increased. Indeed, in the Atomic Energy Commission [Document A.E.C/18/Rev.1, p. 24] it has been suggested that—assuming atomic weapons to be controlled by Convention— preparations for atomic warfare in breach of the Convention would in view of the appalling power of the weapon, have to be treated as an "armed attack" within Article 51. But even without atomic weapons modern developments in warfare lend force to the inter- pretation of that Article which has just been put forward.[88]

The legal implications of modern conventional and nuclear weapons could not be resolved by international jurists. Similarly, there is nothing in the records of the United Nations in the almost four decades that have elapsed since the Baruch Plan that indicates renewed interest on the subject. Among scholars who have discussed the issue, some have pointed out that a serious dilemma still exists. Moreover, as Morton Kaplan and Nicholas Katzenbach indicated, Article 51 of the Charter is inadequate for contemporary problems in the field of armed attack and the right of self-defense. In *The Political Foundations of International Law*, Kaplan and Katzenbach said the following:

The only serious defect of Article 51 is the limitation to an "armed attack," a limitation that may be both naive and futile in an atomic age, or, for small states, in an age of jet planes and fast tanks.

Must a state wait until it is too late before it may defend itself? Must it permit another the advantages of military build-up, surprise attack, and total offense, against which there may be no defense? It would be unreasonable to expect any state to permit this— particularly when given the possibility that a surprise nuclear blow might bring about total destruction or at least total subjugation, unless the attack were forestalled. Even though Article 51 permits collective self-defence and even though Article 52 has been interpreted to permit supranational defensive blocs such as NATO, the Charter restriction of self-defence to cases of armed attack undoubtedly is not fully adequate to defense problems of the present age.[89]

The Cuban missile crisis in October 1962 served as a reminder of the fragility of existing legal definitions and interpretations on issues relating to Article 51 of the United Nations Charter. The crisis started after the intelligence services of the United States provided hard evidence that the Soviet Union was secretly building offensive missile bases in Cuba. The crisis, which was the climax of rising tensions between the superpowers in 1961–1962, was the first "eyeball-to-eyeball" confrontation between the two great nuclear powers. It was a seminal event for which history offers no parallel. According to President John F. Kennedy, the odds on disaster—a nuclear war—were estimated "between one out of three and even."[90]

The thirteen days of the crisis have symbolized the character of the mutual deterrence on which international stability and security is largely based. The inadequacy of the provisions of Article 51 were obvious: while Soviet actions in Cuba could not be dealt with by traditional yardsticks of "armed attack" and the right of "self-defense," for American planners it was a classic dilemma of deterrence strategy. No declaration of war was made and no shot was fired during the crisis, but for the leaders of the United States the deployment of Soviet missiles in Cuba was a violation of the status quo that would have given the Soviets an important military advantage and significantly upset the mutual strategic balance between the superpowers.

The United States responded with a naval quarantine of Soviet shipments to Cuba. The blockade against missiles, which were not yet operational, in foreign territory has also dramatized another legal aspect that is central to the complex relationship between world order and disarmament: the issue of national sovereignty. As pointed out by Myres McDougal, the notion of self-defense should be broadened to include issues related to the nature of intentions and the structure of the state posing the threat:

The explicit and consistent public utterances of its official spokesmen, the totalitarian character of its internal structures of authority and monolithic character of its demanded system of world public order raised grave questions about the genuineness of the...dedication by the state concerned to the basic principle of minimum order, that violence and coercion are not to be used as instruments of expansion across state lines.[91]

In addition, McDougal continues, a state has to take into consideration the fact that under existing world order it would be impossible to wait for appropriate international action: "Given the continuing ineffectiveness of the general community organization to act quickly and certainly for the protection of states, no other principle could be either acceptable to states or conducive to minimum order."[92]

*   *   *

On the second anniversary of the nuclear bomb, the editors of the *New York*

Times said that the ultimate protection against it can only be the abolition of war itself. The *Times* suggested again that the final success of these efforts could be realized only in an ultimate world government. The debate over the Baruch Plan and the later deadlock over nuclear disarmament within the United Nations demonstrated that an entirely different constitutional foundation is required for dealing with international security in the nuclear age. The United Nations Charter was drafted on the basis of several specific assumptions of international order and within a specific intellectual environment concerning the approach toward disarmament and security. In one blinding flash, science and technology seemed to have outdated international realities and political institutions. The challenge that members of the United Nations faced was whether to update the constitutional arrangements of world order in the light of the new circumstances or to continue clinging to previous understandings not anchored in the bedrock of international security.

NOTES

1. John Foster Dulles, "United Nations Charter Review," Speech before the Subcommittee of the Senate Foreign Relations Committee on the UN Charter, January 18, 1954, Series 5, No. 3 (Washington, D.C.: Department of State).

2. General Assembly Resolution 1(1), January 24, 1946. For background, see *The United Nations and Disarmament 1945–1970* (New York: United Nations, 1970), pp. 11–12.

3. Michael Mandelbaum, *The Nuclear Question: The United States and Nuclear Weapons, 1946–1976* (Cambridge: Cambridge University Press, 1979), p. 25.

4. General Assembly Resolution 502(VI). The Soviets voted against it. See *UN and Disarmament 1945–1970*, p. 41.

5. Claude, *Swords*, p. 215.

6. Ruth B. Russell, *The United Nations and United States Security Policy* (Washington, D.C.: The Brookings Institution, 1968), p. 51.

7. Ruth B. Russell, *A History of the United Nations Charter—The Role of the United States: 1940–1945* (Washington, D.C.: The Brookings Institution, 1958), p. 227.

8. Ibid., Chap. 10, esp. p. 228.

9. *Postwar Foreign Policy Preparations* (Washington, D.C.: Department of State, 1949).

10. Leroy A. Bennett, *International Organizations: Principles and Issues* (Englewood Cliffs, N.J.: Prentice-Hall, 1980), p. 42.

11. Russell, *History of the UN Charter*, pp. 43, 96–97, 154.

12. Bennett, *International Organizations*, pp. 40–42.

13. *Postwar Foreign Policy Preparations*, pp. 113–14.

14. Ibid., p. 210.

15. Bennett, *International Organizations*, p. 45.

16. Ibid., p. 129.

17. Russell, *History of the UN Charter*, p. 239.

18. Ibid., p. 228; see also Leland M. Goodrich, "From League of Nations to the

United Nations," in *The Strategy of World Order*, vol. 3, *The United Nations*, ed. Richard Falk and Saul H. Mendlovitz (New York: World Law Fund, 1969), p. 31.

19. See James T. Shotwell and Marina Slavin, *Lessons on Security and Disarmament—from the History of the League of Nations* (New York: Carnegie Endowment for International Peace, 1949), p. 10; Ruth B. Hening, ed., *The League of Nations* (New York: Barnes & Noble, 1973), p. 63; Claude, *Swords*, and his criticism on this view, pp. 288–92.

20. Bennett, *International Organizations*, p. 218.

21. F. P. Walters, *A History of the League of Nations*, vol. 2 (London: Oxford University Press, 1952), p. 500. Disarmament, explains Walters, was "continuously in the forefront of the aims and activities of the League." The world in general and the members of the League were convinced that the armaments race that preceded World War I "had been the greatest single element in making disaster inevitable." Ibid., vol. 1, p. 217. In particular, British public opinion was impatient in its expectations for immediate disarmament leading to recovery and prosperity in England. The British plan for disarmament submitted to the League by Lord Esher was an extreme example of the "direct method of arms reduction which starts from the conviction that disarmament in itself promotes security." Ibid., pp. 220–21.

22. Edward Teller, "The Feasibility of Arms Control and the Principle of Openness," in *Arms Control, Disarmament and National Security*, ed. Donald G. Brennan (New York: George Braziller, 1961), p. 122.

23. Claude, *Swords*, p. 292.

24. Russell, *The UN and U.S.*, p. 49.

25. Russell, *History of the UN Charter*, p. 685.

26. Russell, *The UN and U.S.*, p. 49.

27. Article 26 makes a vague reference to a plan "for the establishment of a system for the regulation of armament" to be submitted by the Security Council to the United Nations members. Article 47 provides for a "Military Staff Committee" that will advise the Security Council on its "military requirements for the maintenance of international peace and security, the employment and command of forces placed at its disposal, the regulation of armaments and possible disarmament." The Military Staff Committee has never become effective. See also Hans Kelsen, *The Law of the United Nations* (London: Stevens & Sons, 1950), p. 10.

28. Walters, *History*, p. 502; Russell, *The UN and U.S.*, pp. 50–52. France had pushed for its plan since the early days of the drafting of the Covenant. It was presented to the Disarmament Conference in Geneva in 1932 by André Tardieu, the minister for war.

29. H. G. Nicholas, *The United Nations as a Political Institution* (London: Oxford University Press, 1959), p. 27.

30. Claude, *Swords*, p. 80.

31. James T. Shotwell, "The United Nations Atomic Commission," *International Conciliation*, no. 432 (September 1946): 314.

32. Claude, *Swords*, p. 303.

33. On December 27, 1945, the foreign ministers of the United States, the United Kingdom, and the Soviet Union met in Moscow and agreed upon sponsoring the resolution. For review and background, see Francis O. Wilcox and Thorsten V. Kalijarvi, *Recent American Foreign Policy—Basic Documents 1941–1951* (New York: Appleton-Century-Crofts, 1953), pp. 51–53; Arthur M. Schlesinger, Jr., ed., *The Dynamic of*

World Power—A Documentary History of the United States Foreign Policy 1945–1973 (New York: Chelsea House, 1973), vol. 5, *The United Nations*, ed. Richard C. Hottelet. Additional sources are listed below in the following notes.

34. John Lewis Gaddis, *The United States and the Origins of the Cold War 1941– 1949* (New York: Columbia University Press, 1972), p. 332.

35. Joseph I. Lieberman, *The Scorpion and the Tarantula: The Struggle to Control Atomic Weapons 1945–1949* (Boston: Houghton Mifflin, 1970), p. 410.

36. *Official Records of the Atomic Energy Commission*, First Year, No. 1, 1st meeting, June 14, 1946, p. 7.

37. Shotwell, "The United Nations," p. 321, says there was almost no debate on the details of the Baruch Plan. The proposal to get rid of the veto power in the Security Council "won ardent support among the advocates of world government"; Gregg Herken, *The Winning Weapon: The Atomic Bomb in the Cold War 1945–1950* (New York: Alfred A. Knopf, 1980), p. 173.

38. *New York Times*, editorial, June 15, 1946.

39. Ibid.

40. *Official Records of the AEC*, First Year, No. 2, 2nd meeting, June 19, 1946.

41. Shotwell, "The United Nations," p. 332.

42. John W. Spanier and Joseph L. Nogee, *The Politics of Disarmament: A Study in Soviet–American Gamesmanship* (New York: Praeger Publishers, 1962), p. 75.

43. Bernard G. Bechhoefer, *Postwar Negotiations for Arms Control* (Washington, D.C.: The Brookings Institution, 1961), pp. 124, 562.

44. *UN and Disarmament 1945–1970*, p. 15.

45. Richard J. Barnet, *Who Wants Disarmament* (Boston: Beacon Press, 1960), p. 22.

46. *Official Records of the AEC*, Third Year Special Supplement, May 1948.

47. Lieberman, *The Scorpion*, p. 393.

48. *Official Records of the AEC*, Fourth Year, Special Supplement, July 29, 1949.

49. Willim R. Frye, "Characteristics of Recent Arms Control Proposals and Agreements," in *Arms Control, Disarmament and National Security*, ed. Donald G. Brennan (New York: George Braziller, 1961), p. 71.

50. Spanier and Nogee, *Politics of Disarmament*, p. 57.

51. The case has been developed by Gar Alperovitz, *Atomic Diplomacy: Hiroshima and Potsdam* (New York: Simon and Schuster, 1965); see also Herken, *The Winning Weapon*, a modern version of revisionist history.

52. Claude, *Swords*, p. 306.

53. Russell, *The UN and U.S.*, p. 68.

54. Norman Corwin, *Modern Man Is Obsolete* (New York: Holt and Co., 1945), pp. 41–42.

55. Lieberman, *The Scorpion*.

56. Richard J. Barnet, "Inspection: Shadow and Substance," in *The Strategy of World Order*, vol. 4, *Disarmament and Economic Development*, ed. Richard Falk and Saul H. Mendlovitz (New York: World Law Fund, 1969), p. 383.

57. Stanley A. Blumberg and Gwin Owens, *Energy and Conflict: The Life and Times of Edward Teller* (New York: G. P. Putnam's Sons, 1976), p. 339.

58. Henry L. Stimson and McGeorge Bundy, *On Active Service in Peace and War* (New York: Octagon, 1974), pp. 35–36.

59. Edward Teller, "A Suggested Amendment to the Acheson Report," *Bulletin of the Atomic Scientists* 1, no. 12 (June 1, 1946): 5.

60. *New York Times*, June 14, 1946.

61. Sir Arthur Salter, "The United Nations and the Atomic Bomb," *International Conciliation*, no. 423 (September 1946): 41.

62. *Official Records of the AEC*, First Year, July 1946, Special Supplement, annex 5, pp. 106–7.

63. Mandelbaum, *The Nuclear Question*, pp. 27–28.

64. Ibid., p. 16.

65. Herken, *The Atomic Bomb*, is a typical example: the author dedicates only one paragraph to the Soviet plan in a factual review, without any word of criticism (p. 174). On the other hand, he is extremely critical of Bernard Baruch: "Thus the Baruch Plan did not differ in substance from an ultimatum the United States might have given Russia to forswear nuclear weapons or be destroyed" (p. 173). Herken develops the theory that U.S. diplomacy and strategy was based on the fallacy that the American nuclear monopoly could be retained for a long time. It was, he says, a false belief in the "winning weapon"— a "deadly illusion" of enduring nuclear monopoly (pp. 338–42). However, when he comes to the Soviet side he has to admit, though just in passing—in one sentence—that there is no way to prove that an altogether different policy on the bomb "would have avoided the cold war or could have lessened subsequent Soviet–American enmity" (p. 340). Herken, like the other revisionists of the 1960s, does not make a strong case that different U.S. policies would have led to a radically different situation.

66. Gaddis, *The United States*, p. 246.

67. Blumberg and Owens, *Energy and Conflict*, p. 202.

68. Ibid., p. 20.

69. Gaddis, *The United States*, p. 332.

70. Adam B. Ulam, *The Rivals: America and Russia Since World War II* (New York: Penguin Books, 1977), pp. 103–4.

71. John Foster Dulles, *War or Peace* (New York: Macmillan, 1950), p. 116.

72. Bechhoefer, *Postwar Negotiations*, p. 60.

73. David E. Lilienthal, *The Journals of David E. Lilienthal: The Atomic Energy Years, 1945–1950* (New York: Harper & Row, 1964), p. 74.

74. Lieberman, *The Scorpion*, p. 111.

75. William R. Frye, "The Quest for Disarmament since World War II," in *Arms Control—Issues for the Public*, ed. Louis Henkin (Englewood Cliffs, N.J.: Prentice-Hall, 1961), p. 21.

76. Ulam, *The Rivals*, p. 37.

77. Barnet, "Inspection," p. 390.

78. Ibid., p. 392.

79. *Official Records of the Security Council*, Second Year (22), March 5, 1947.

80. *Official Records of the AEC*, First Year, July 1946, Special Supplement, annex 5, p. 110.

81. *New York Times*, June 21, 1946.

82. Summary Records of the meeting in *Official Records of the AEC*, pp. 117–18. See also the *New York Times*, July 24, 1946.

83. *Official Records of the Security Council*, Second Year (22), March 1947.

84. Gaddis, *The United States*, p. 335.

85. Derek Bowett, *Self-Defence in International Law* (New York: Praeger Publishers, 1958), pp. 191–92.

86. *Official Records of the AEC*, First Year, pp. 109–10.

87. Ibid., pp. 108–17.

88. H. Waldock, "The Regulation of the Use of Force by Individual States in International Law," *81 Recueil des cours* 2 (1952): 489; see also M. McDougal Feliciano, *Law and Minimum World* (New Haven: Yale University Press, 1961), p. 238, who observes: "The second major difficulty with a narrow reading of Article 51 is that it requires a serious underestimation of the potentialities both of the newer military weapons systems and of the contemporary techniques of non-military coercion."

89. Morton A. Kaplan and Nicholas de B. Katzenbach, *The Political Foundations of International Law* (New York: John Wiley & Sons, 1961), pp. 212–13.

90. Theodore Sorensen, *Kennedy* (New York: Harper & Row, 1965), p. 705.

91. Myres S. McDougal, "The Soviet–Cuban Quarantine and Self-Defense," *American Journal of International Law* 57 (1963): 601.

92. Ibid., p. 599.

3

United Nations Activities and Mechanism in Disarmament

There seems to be at present a tendency in the thinking of the West which I find worrying.... If the disarmament control were to be lifted out of the UN...the result would be a weakening of international cooperation all around as the UN would be robbed of a main part of its substantive content without new and really viable substitutes being created.[1]

Dag Hammarskjold, secretary general
of the United Nations, in a letter
to Christian Herter, U.S.
secretary of state, March 1959

In the disarmament field, UN debates continue to have little impact outside the United Nations.... Everyone understands that UN debates have little leverage in the "real world" of disarmament talks. None, therefore, gets terribly excited about "irresponsible" resolutions or debates in the General Assembly.[2]

Charles William Maynes,
shortly before taking office
as assistant secretary of
state for international
organizations, 1976

It is true that already from the beginning disarmament has been the source of more continuous effort and debate than any other single item on the United Nations agenda.[3] Perhaps there are few, if any, items in the United Nations agenda on which more resolutions have been passed than on disarmament.[4] However, it is misleading to attribute the functions and deliberations of the United Nations on disarmament, as some people at the United Nations try, to the fact that "disarmament is one of the main objectives of the United Nations under the Charter'' or even to regard disarmament as a ''prerequisite for the effectiveness of the system of world order outlined in the Charter.''[5] As demonstrated in the previous chapter, the fact of the matter is that deliberately, and in sharp contrast to the Covenant of the League of Nations, little attention was given by the drafters of the Charter to disarmament matters. The United Nations Charter places no obligation on the General Assembly or the Security Council to achieve disarmament. Accordingly it makes no promise that disarmament is to be regarded as a goal of the organization. Moreover, the founding fathers produced a relatively weak and vague reference to disarmament in the Charter simply because they believed in an international system of collective security under which the maintenance of national armaments, particularly in the hands of the big powers, is a prerequisite to permitting the discharge of international obligations respecting the enforcement of peace and security. War is to be prevented, as the Charter implied, not by disarmament but by regulating and controlling the *use* of armed force.

Thus, it should be said that the United Nations has intensified its debates in the field of disarmament not because of the Charter's objectives but, quite to the contrary, despite the limits and constraints of the Charter. There is no doubt that one of the most compelling reasons for United Nations activities in the field was the world-wide alarm at the horrific dimensions and possibilities of the nuclear arms race that were introduced after the signing of the Charter.

In this respect, United Nations deliberations on disarmament served different factions. For the superpowers, and particularly during the cold war period, it provided a major forum for introducing disarmament proposals as part of East–West psychological maneuvers. For the smaller nations it could provide a consciousness-raising forum to express their fears and concerns over the perils of the nuclear arms race. For their part, members of the United Nations Secretariat, such as former Secretary General Dag Hammarskjold, were convinced that, if the United Nations wants to be relevant to international politics, disarmament ''must remain a central preoccupation of the United Nations.''[6] In a similar vein, Secretary General U Thant regarded disarmament as the most important problem of our time, which together with the other two ''Ds'' (development and decolonization) are the three main tasks of the organization.[7]

There would be little point in undertaking a detailed survey of United Nations debates in the field of disarmament. There is no need for it, since the broad outlines of much future disarmament and arms control discussions were laid down at the beginning of the United Nations debate. The fundamental differences between the superpowers in their first major confrontation on the problem of international atomic control indicated the pattern of disagreements and the ''parallel monologue'' for future disarmament discussions for the first fifteen years of the United Nations and beyond.[8] We shall, therefore, examine just some highlights of these debates. In this chapter, disarmament deliberations at the United Nations will be examined in relation to three questions: (1) What was the pattern of differences between East and West in disarmament discussions?

How did it reflect their different outlook on international order? (2) What was the role of the United Nations in the arms control agreements that were achieved during the 1960s and the 1970s? (3) What is the United Nations machinery for disarmament, and how does it operate today?

Our review of some of the highlights of the debate reveals that the fundamental gap between East and West was not as much on disarmament as on the conception of world order. With a continuing deadlock over disarmament at the United Nations, the superpowers had decided to move away from the organization and started to negotiate a series of arms control agreements without altering the existing international order. Being hollowed out of its activities in the field of arms control, the United Nations was left with the unworldly role of playing bureaucratic and procedural games with its machinery for disarmament.

PATTERN OF DIFFERENCES

It became apparent that with the lack of a common approach to a system of international order, superpower initiatives on disarmament were doomed to fail. In addition, the cold war enhanced the propagandistic tendencies of United Nations debates, making a serious exchange on disarmament impossible. But even in this propaganda battle one could identify in each side's proposal the philosophical ingredients that constituted their basic approach to international order. It is true, as Inis Claude puts it, that the proposals were formulated with a view to their unacceptability.[9] Yet they represented a consistent pattern of differences in their approach to the link between disarmament and world order.

From the beginning, following their rejection of the Baruch Plan, the Soviets were consistent in their proposals. In a variety of proposals for reduction of armaments (1946–1957),[10] the primary object was always defined as the prohibition of atomic weapons, leaving the control issue in rather general and vague terms. While the West called for "effective international control" and went on to specify what was meant by it (describing in detail the various measures of disclosure, inspection, and verification on a continuing basis with a special international control organ to carry out those duties), the Soviets have referred instead to "strict international control" without providing too much detail. This was also the case in the much celebrated Russian initiative of May 10, 1955, which Philip Noel-Baker regarded as "the moment of hope." Even then the contol provisions fell short of Western proposals. The British proponent of disarmament himself admitted that in the Soviet plan "the proposals about inspections and control left some points obscure."[11] The control organ in the Soviet plan raised the same problems of decision-making and enforcement which had frustrated all efforts since 1945, since the Soviets rejected the idea of enforcement and sanctions and insisted on maintaining their veto right.

The pattern has repeated itself in the field of conventional weapons. Always in Western proposals on reduction of armaments the "first and indispensable step" was disclosure and verification.[12] For instance, a French–Belgian draft resolution (1948) proposed that first the Commission for Conventional Armaments should devote its attention to "formulating proposals for the receipt, checking and publication, by an international organ of control within the framework of the Security Council, of full information to be supplied by Member States with regard to their effectives and their conventional armaments."[13]

Here, in the course of the debate, it was revealed that Soviet opposition to effective international control was *conditio sine qua non*. In this case, unlike in the Baruch Plan, the Soviet veto was guaranteed ("within the framework of the Security Council") and the issue under consideration was conventional forces in which the Soviets enjoyed superiority. Nevertheless, the Soviets and their allies voted against the proposal, adding to their reservations the argument that the resolution endorsed the theory that security must precede disarmament.[14]

Even when the Soviets incorporated the idea of inspection in their plan, they never spelled out the meaning of what they called "permissible inspection." The nature of their political system could not afford on-site inspection (see Chapter 2), and, thus, these insertions in their proposals could not but be dismissed by observers, such as Ruth Russell, as probably a propaganda ploy. The gap, she explains, was fundamental:

What seems a reasonable precaution to Americans as well as the sine qua non for any arms control for reduction agreements—that the fulfillment of any undertaking should be verified by inspection—has been consistently resisted by Soviet officials as an attack in disguise on the heart of their closed system.[15]

The pattern of irreconcilable differences reemerged also on the highest level when the heads of state tried to impress world public opinion with dramatic initiatives. President Eisenhower introduced in 1955 the "open skies" proposal: reciprocal aerial inspection of the United States and the Soviet Union and an exchange of the blueprints of U.S. and Soviet military establishments. It was a limited measure of inspection, marking the beginning of the arms control orientation in strategic thinking, in that it was intended to establish an effective warning system to lessen fears and dangers of surprise attack. The Soviets responded that aerial surveillance should not be permitted until the last stages of a comprehensive disarmament process (disarmament before control). Similarly, when Premier Nikita Khrushchev launched the new Soviet offensive on "General and Complete Disarmament" he told United Nations delegates that only by complete disarmament (and not through control) could the possibility of a state gaining military advantages be eliminated.[16]

On September 20, 1961, there was an impression of a narrowing of the gap between the parties and of an increasing likelihood of agreement. John J. McCloy and V. A. Zorin, who represented the United States and the Soviet Union, respectively, in the negotiations, managed to put together a Joint Statement of Agreed Principles for Disarmament Negotiations. The Joint Statement presented a sweeping view of what general and complete disarmament would be like and listed its characteristics, quite specifically setting disarmament by stages. At the United Nations, some regarded it as a "turning point" and as the "most important landmark and guide to disarmament negotiations."[17] But in reality the progress was illusory. Obviously, the Joint Statement itself cannot tell the whole story. In order to understand the differences, one has to scrutinize the documents that preceded the compromise formula. In the less known exchange of letters between the Soviets and the Americans, the parties made it clear that the gap was substantial and not just another quibbling over details of control methods. In fact, the Joint Statement had been reached only after the parties agreed not to agree on the issue of control and the United States reluctantly withdrew its insistence on specifying the measures of verification. The omitted sentence read: "Such verification should ensure that not only agreed limitations or reductions take place but also that retained armed forces and armaments do not exceed agreed levels at any stage." The United States indicated in its letters, issued on the same day as the Joint Statement, that it agreed reluctantly to this omission on the grounds that the Soviet Union had not accepted it.[18]

Once again, the Soviets indicated that the idea of a broad control system runs against the raison d'être of their Communist regime. In his letter to the secretary general of September 22, 1961, Foreign Minister Andrei Gromyko reaffirmed the arguments that he had already delivered in the first debate in the mid-1940s. Even in their declaratory policy, the Soviets would agree merely upon a vague concept of control restricted to disarmament measures only. In other words, international control could be exerted only over those weapons that were destroyed and dismantled but not over existing stockpiles or other possible sources of violations. The Soviet representative emphasized: "While it advocated effective control over disarmament, the Soviet Union is emphatically opposed to control over armaments.... Any control unrelated to disarmament measures would evolve into an international system of legalized spying.... What is important is disarmament, not control."[19]

The accompanying exchanges revealed what the joint statement concealed, that the gap between the parties was even more fundamental, touching upon the issue of national sovereignty and world order. The United States, consistent with its previous proposals, maintained that parallel to the implementations of measures leading to total disarmament it is essential to create effective peacekeeping machinery. Moreover, the Americans reiterated their philosophical assertions about the inadequacies of current international arrangements:

The United States believes firmly that nations must be prepared to moderate gradually the exercise of unrestricted sovereignty and to abide by the decisions and judgements of tribunals and other bodies, even if such decision at times may not meet with a particular nation's approval.[20]

Correctly, the Soviet Union regarded these ideas as amounting to an attempt to change the existing world order. Therefore it went on to oppose the idea of a new peacekeeping force as an "evasion of the Security Council," and to reject the demand "for the abolition of the unanimity rule provided in the Charter,"[21] namely, their veto right.

From the beginning of the negotiations at the Ten Nation Conference in Geneva in 1960, there was a deadlock between East and West on this issue of peace enforcement in the course of a disarmament process. The Eastern bloc contended that Western ideas sought to supplant the United Nations in the field of peace and security and objected to this tampering with the role of the Security Council and the General Assembly as provided in the Charter. The Western powers insisted that the new peace machinery would remain within the framework of the United Nations but it should be strengthened so it could not be frustrated and rendered impotent by the actions of a single power or group of powers. Here, on these questions of international order, the most telling reply came from both Poland and the USSR, which questioned the emphasis placed by the West "on armed coercion in a disarmed world with widespread controls."[22]

These fundamental differences were often overlooked by some disarmament specialists, even those who were close observers of the scene. The tendency to read selectively superpowers' declaratory statements on disarmament was highlighted again a few months later in March 1962, when the Soviet Union and the United States submitted their draft treaties for general and complete disarmament. The drafts, submitted to the newly convened Eighteen Nation Disarmament Conference, may have created an appearance of basic understanding between the parties since some observers expressed satisfaction that both plans had formal resemblances, with many elements almost identical. Alva Myrdal, for instance, emphasized this resemblance: "The two programs were not only very similar as to their general structure, but set great store on a control and verification system to guarantee the security of nations once the complete disarmament was achieved."[23]

But the resemblance was deceiving. Myrdal failed to point out that at their roots the two approaches were irreconcilable. Speaking of the American concern for control, Myrdal dismissed it as "overzealous." In fact, as pointed out by other observers, there were fundamental differences in the two plans on several major issues of the disarmament program.[24] Typically, the two parties could not even agree upon what appears as innocent a phrase as the insertion in the preamble by the United States that general and complete disarmament could realistically take place only "in a peaceful world." The Soviet Union consistently demanded to drop this phrase since, in their view, it implied a need to establish some political arrangements before the GCD, which was in sharp contrast to their approach that "the way to disarm is to disarm." As pointed out elsewhere, this Soviet–American skirmish over a phrase in the preamble was nothing but their traditional controversy on what should come first: disarmament or control.[25] In this regard the differences were as sharp as ever.

At issue were again the different outlooks on the relationship between disarmament and world order. Hedley Bull, who compared the plans of 1962, emphasized the permanent nature of their differences:

The difference between the conception of the enforcement of disarmament in the two plans is rooted in a fundamental disagreement about the kind of international order it would be the purpose of the plan ultimately to create—a disagreement that was already manifest at the time of the debate over the Baruch Plan in 1946. The Soviet plan is based squarely on the idea of the maximum possible disarmament, without providing for any other changes of a far-reaching sort in the organisation of international relations. The U.S. plan attempts to link the disarmament of states with the concentration of military power in the hands of a *central authority*; and it regards both as inseparable from changes in the organisation of international relations that involve *much more than disarmament* itself and that are unlikely to be capable of compression into a timetable laid down in a treaty.[26]

The parties failed to agree on the nature of peace in a disarmed world and what would be required to change in the existing arrangements to guarantee such a peace. Robert E. Osgood and Robert W. Tucker explain that the comprehensive disarmament proposals, which are limited to the disarmament process itself (the Soviet proposals), presuppose the continuation of the order of the present world. They assume the retention of the paramount position of the nation-state international system as well as the central role of the great powers within it. In this regard the 1962 Soviet proposal is addressed almost entirely to the disarmament process itself, whereas its peacekeeping measures scarcely go beyond a reaffirmation of the United Nations Charter. The Soviets are committed to the existing international order with its conflicts of interest and with the traditional freedom of action retained by the superpowers, including their right of veto in the Security Council. Philosophically, the Soviet approach implies that states in a disarmed world will continue to rely upon the traditional instruments of diplomacy (including military force) and possibly may "always break the disarmament covenant and rearm."[27] All this, of course, they add, is based on a very large assumption that the Soviets offer in their draft a reliable system of verification.

The American approach, on the other hand, assumes that in a world without a very large and all-powerful centralized force the risks of disarmament would be inordinately great. In essence, their peacekeeping provisions envisaged disarmament "within a transformed—and, ultimately, a radical transformed—system of international security."[28] It presumes the establishment of a workable and effective system of collective security in which a central authority with the monopoly over legitimate force (similar to government in domestic societies) has replaced the existing institutions of self-help. Self-help, as defined by Robert Tucker, is "the right of the state to determine when its legitimate interests are threatened, or violated, and to employ such coercive measures as it may deem necessary to vindicate those interests."[29]

It is interesting that, despite these deficiencies, the McCloy–Zorin principles and the notion of GCD provided a source for abundant rhetoric in disarmament discussions in many years to come. People would continue to ignore the fundamental problems of world order even after realizing that it was impossible to translate the principles of the apparent "Joint Statement" of the superpowers into mutually acceptable programs of disarmament. The lessons seemed to be forgotten in 1978, when, at the General Assembly Special Session on Disarmament (SSOD), under the initiative of the Third World, the same approach of "joint statement" was adopted in the form of a multilateral document adopted by all member states of the United Nations. Indeed, the Final Document of the SSOD can be regarded as an elaboration, to a large extent, of the Joint Statement of 1961.

A closer look at the proposals submitted to the SSOD reveals that, notwithstanding the Final Document, the basic divergences between the superpowers remained. The Soviets submitted a proposal calling for a complete ban on nuclear weapons ("ban the bomb"), cessation of production and development of all kinds of weapons. Typically, nothing in the Soviet paper was said about methods and implementation of inspection. Gromyko even went out of his way to deplore the term *control* as meaningless.[30] Conversely, the West continued to stress control on weapons as a major condition. Vice President Mondale in his statement to the SSOD offered no new substantive proposals for disarmament but announced another measure of control. The United States, he said, is prepared to offer countries serial and underground monitoring devices that would detect the presence of nearby weapons systems. These "eyes and ears of peace," he said, could "help create the confidence" necessary to make mutual arms reductions agreements between countries workable.[31] Other Western countries submitted proposals involving verification measures and strengthening the United Nations peacekeeping machinery.[32]

THE UNITED NATIONS' ROLE IN DISARMAMENT

The record of disarmament debates at the United Nations demonstrates that its forums could not promote a businesslike approach to negotiations. In the first fifteen years from 1946 to 1960, the political climate of the cold war dominated disarmament deliberations at the United Nations.[33] The public forum character of the United Nations with its democratic concept of open diplomacy made it suitable to promote a public relations campaign. The General Assembly became a forum for proposals that were part of the East–West propaganda warfare rather than serious overtures to negotiations.[34] Spanier and Nogee describe these "politics of disarmament" as cynical gamesmanship:

The essence of this game of disarmament is for each side to pose as the representative of virtue and to picture its opponent as the offspring of the devil. And this is accomplished by including in every disarmament plan a set of proposals calculated to possess wide popular appeal. But every such set of proposals and counter-proposals has also included at least one feature—a ''joker''—that has been unacceptable to the other side, thereby compelling it to reject the opponent's plan.[35]

It was during this period that nuclear specialists concluded that United Nations debates on disarmament, being entangled in cold war politics, are divorced from real strategic concerns and cannot contribute to agreements in the field. Political analysts concluded that the United Nations has proven to be an ineffective instrument for ''either the forging or the implementation of disarmament policies.''[36] Inis Claude's views were formulated in the 1950s and have remained apt since then:

International organization has become a great promoter of sheer diplomatic loquacity and has provided an exceptional opportunity for the exercise of propagandistic skill: disarmament debates provide as good example as one might seek of speeches for the record only, and proposals formulated with a view to their unacceptability.[37]

It seems that the great powers had reached similar conclusions. While realizing that prevention of nuclear war requires cooperation amid competitive efforts, they understood that the open forum of the United Nations cannot provide the necessary setting for this kind of businesslike approach. As a result, after 1957, major negotiations on disarmament moved outside the United Nations to ad hoc bodies established by agreement of the major powers. These bodies have had ''only a tenuous connection with the United Nations.''[38]

The trend toward negotiating disarmament outside the United Nations angered members of the United Nations Secretariat. Secretary General Dag Hammarskjold was dismayed by what he regarded as ''great-power elitism'' and ''irresponsible'' attempts to create new machinery for disarmament. Protesting the Western proposal to establish a new separate international disarmament organization, Hammarskjold wrote to the U.S. secretary of state that it ''would hollow out of the United Nations one of its main fields of activity.''[39] However, this protest did not impress the great powers. Even later, when the superpowers enlarged their East–West Ten Nation Disarmament Committee to include eight nations of the Third World in the new Eighteen Nation Disarmament Conference (ENDC), they did not mean to strengthen the United Nations' role. The major aim was to create a forum ''where the Soviet Union and the United States could meet outside the highly charged political atmosphere of the United Nations.''[40]

It is clear that whenever the parties concerned were genuinely interested in pursuing a particular arms control agreement they would move their negotiations away from the United Nations. Even the staunchest supporters of the United Nations had to recognize the fact that the organization has never been a primary organ for negotiation of specific arms control agreements. With its parliamentary character, it cannot treat arms control in a businesslike manner, freed of other political considerations. With 157 (in 1983) member states, it is also too huge a forum for the complex technical issues of arms control.

Nevertheless, some arms control agreements are sometimes misleadingly attributed to the United Nations. Particularly in two cases—the Partial Test Ban Treaty (1963) and the Non-Proliferation Treaty (1968)—some analysts are inclined to regard the United Nations' role as influential and effective.[41] The fallacy stems from the failure to understand that, while the United Nations was indeed debating for several years some similar initiatives (in fact, United Nations resolutions usually encompass almost everything in disarmament), actually the agreements were reached outside United Nations forums. Moreover, it is misleading to assume that because the superpowers were exposed to unpleasant criticism at the United Nations they moved to iron out their differences and reached arms control agreements. Today it becomes apparent that denunciation of the superpowers at the United Nations on the lack of progress in their negotiations is to no avail.

Basically, these two treaties, like most other arms control agreements, should be viewed against the backdrop of the superpowers' shift to arms control dialogue in the aftermath of the Cuban missile crisis of October 1962. Only after this "shock treatment" of the thirteen fearful days teetering on the brink of world holocaust were both leaders in the United States and the Soviet Union compelled to look into the nuclear abyss to see how narrow the escape route is. It was a bloodless "eyeball-to-eyeball" confrontation that changed dramatically the entire complexion of the cold war and ushered in a period of a series of arms control negotiations and agreements. As a result of the crisis, the common interests of the two powers have become more explicit and closely defined, the aim being to prevent an uncontrolled nuclear race.

As a realistic approach that acknowledges the limits and constraints of the international system, arms control is designed to develop a political framework that will maintain international stability and security by the skillful management of weaponry. The agreements were to reduce the risk of nuclear war through accidents and to provide regulators and safety valves for the emerging mutual deterrence. In this process leading toward arms control agreements, three stages can be identified. First came the establishment of some "confidence-building" agreements (hot-line), in order to avoid miscalculated risks. Second, the superpowers moved to secure their monopoly by creating a "non-proliferation regime" (based on the NPT) to prevent smaller powers from acquiring nuclear weapons capability. Finally, they began to stabilize a state of deterrence between themselves, at least for the present, on the mutual understanding that each side will retain a second-strike capability. During this period of SALT I and SALT II, the superpowers demonstrated how mutual deterrence is their pre-eminent concern.

Unlike the previous exchanges on disarmament at the United Nations, arms control negotiations were not intended to alter international order. To the contrary, arms control relies primarily on the existing balance of power and aims to make the military competition between the superpowers safer in order to mitigate the dangers of the nuclear age. The PTBT and the NPT were, thus, an integral part of the emerging new pattern of relations between the superpowers.

The issue of international control was no longer dealt with in the framework of revisions in the United Nations Charter or the establishment of new international organs. In addition, technological progress has reduced in some limited respects the control problem by making some verification possible without formal inspection. The Partial Test Ban Treaty of 1963 became possible only when the United States began to launch surveillance satellites, which enabled it to detect and verify violations of the ban in the three environments covered.[42] Soon it became apparent that both the PTBT and the NPT reflected the particular interests of the superpowers and failed to take account of the wishes and the interests of the United Nations majority. Let us examine the role of the United Nations in the achievement of these treaties.

United Nations deliberations on a test ban are in effect the most prolonged of all arms control efforts, going back to the early 1950s. In 1954, as a result of an American thermonuclear testing in the Bikini Atoll in the Pacific, voices were raised at the United Nations to deal with nuclear testing as an urgent measure separate from the general issue of disarmament. Already in 1955, the United Nations decided to set up a scientific committee on the effects of atomic radiation. In 1959, for instance, four resolutions were passed by overwhelming majorities at the General Assembly urging a moratorium on nuclear tests. The Soviets, having initiated the moratorium that went into effect in 1958 and was maintained for three years, shocked the world with its decision (August 30, 1961) to resume testing, crowning the new series with a fifty-megaton blast in the atmosphere. The United States followed suit and also resumed nuclear testing.

In these years the United Nations played a role that can be viewed as similar and equal to other movements that expressed grave concern over radioactive fallout, notably the scientists and the intellectuals of the Pugwash movement. Moreover, even the multilateral bodies that dealt with the technical problems of the test ban did not constitute United Nations machinery: the Conference of Experts on Detection of Nuclear Tests (Geneva, 1958), the Conference on the Discontinuation of Nuclear Weapons Tests (Geneva, 1958–1962), the Ten Nation Committee on Disarmament (established in 1960, Geneva) and enlarged later (1962) to the Eighteen Nation Committee on Disarmament, and particularly the Tripartite Moscow Test Ban Negotiations (Moscow, 1963). All these bodies were established as a result of U.S.–USSR agreements in which the two countries, in effect, invited the others to participate. Technically they were not United Nations bodies, though some of them were endorsed by the General Assembly and submitted reports to the United Nations.

But even these bodies, in hundreds of meetings, did not finalize the Partial Test Ban Treaty. The agreement was reached only when the superpowers saw it as their common interest: "Suddenly, in the summer of 1963, the superpowers switched the test-ban negotiations from multilateral talks in Geneva to trilateral talks in Moscow. There, within weeks, a partial ban was produced."[43] From the superpowers' point of view, the treaty reflected a compromise between the traditional three strands: the Americans could be satisfied, since aboveground tests could be controlled; the treaty did not ban underground tests, which necessitated verification of a kind unacceptable to the Soviets; it also reflected the emergence of the new superpowers' common interest: weapons research could be satisfactorily carried on by them with underground tests, an option that was unfeasible for less technologically advanced countries. In addition, the treaty served their new common propaganda function against the emerging anti-superpowers front of the non-aligned nations. Arthur Lall, representing the Third World's view, wrote in a somewhat frustrated tone about the ineffectiveness of multilateral machinery for disarmament negotiations: "The United Nations, the Test Ban Conferences, the Eighteen Nation Disarmament Committee, all discussed the test ban for some nine years, but when a partial agreement was reached it was, in fact, reached bilaterally."[44]

Soon it also became apparent that the treaty, which was hailed at the time as the first significant breakthrough in efforts to limit the nuclear arms race, was never intended as a measure to curtail weapons development. Its critics, disillusioned by the superpowers' negotiations in the field, call it rather a public health measure,[45] since it has reduced radioactivity in the atmosphere. Or in another version, "a clear air bill, a victory for the environmentalists rather than the arms controllers."[46] As Ruth Russell explains, the PTBT "formalized rather than changed in any significant way the existing situation between the parties." The treaty did not disturb the military balance between the superpowers, and by restricting its application "to the three environments where international verification was not necessary the thorny issue of inspection was avoided."[47]

The role played by the United Nations machinery in the conclusion of the nuclear Non-Proliferation Treaty was different only in the procedural sense. Here the United Nations forum was more instrumental, since the NPT necessitated the active participation of the majority of the non-nuclear weapons countries. Also, an important role was envisaged for the United Nations International Atomic Energy Agency (IAEA) in supervising the implementation of the treaty. Nevertheless, the NPT was discussed at the United Nations for years, but it became possible only when the United States and the Soviet Union wanted it:

The tremendous power they [the superpowers] wielded and their worldwide interests and commitments could be challenged and endangered if additional and smaller powers acquired nuclear weapon capability. International diplomacy and the exercise of political influence would become much less manageable.[48]

Since with the NPT the superpowers were mostly engaged in "selling" activities and their potential "buyers" were the non-nuclear nations, the United Nations became a major vehicle to promote their ideas. Naturally this involved more multilateral negotiations in larger forums in order to obtain almost universal commitment to maintain, in effect, the existing distribution of world power. The United Nations machinery was therefore a major instrument in the hands of the big two, and the last stage of the struggle for the United Nations' endorsement of the draft treaty (1968) was marked by a United States–Soviet Union partnership all the way.[49] In a few years the NPT would be viewed by the majority of its parties as a discriminatory measure designed to promote only the interests of nuclear weapon states at the expense of the rest of the world (see Chapter 6).

Other arms control agreements that the superpowers submitted to the Geneva Committee, such as the Sea-Bed Treaty and the Biological Convention, are considered less significant. They followed the same procedure as the NPT, first submitted separately but in identical drafts by the superpowers and later introduced as their joint draft treaty text.[50] As Michael Sullivan explains, both treaties may be considered quite insignificant as disarmament measures. Since the real threat from underwater missiles comes from highly mobile submarines and not from stationary emplacements, the superpowers regarded the ocean bed as unfeasible for their nuclear deterrence policies. Similarly, the Biological Convention prohibited only those bacteriological agents and toxins that were so noxious and dangerous that their value was doubted.[51] So far attempts to extend the scope of previous limited agreements by the Comprehensive Test Ban (CTB) and the Chemical Weapons Treaty (CW), have failed, in part because of the inspection issue.

The record of the 1970s demonstrates that whenever the parties concerned were really interested in arriving at an agreement on arms limitation, or in discussing specific issues of arms control, they immediately moved away from the United Nations. This was also the case in two regional agreements: the Denuclearization of Latin America (Tlatelolco, Mexico, 1967), and the Conference on Security and Cooperation in Europe (Helsinki Agreement, 1975). In the 1970s the superpowers held a series of bilateral negotiations on a variety of disarmament issues—the SALT talks, chemical and radiological weapons, comprehensive test ban (with the United Kingdom), Indian Ocean arms limitation, international arms trade. Since 1973, countries of the NATO and Warsaw military pacts have been holding periodic talks on force reductions in Central Europe (MBFR). Especially in SALT, the Americans and the Soviets established an elaborate, formalized, permanent machinery outside the United Nations and the CCD framework. For its first four years the forum was rotated between Vienna and Helsinki, "almost as if to emphasize its independence from the United Nations-related organs at Geneva and New York."[52]

Be that as it may, the striking fact is that at the United Nations and its other related forums disarmament deliberations had little impact on the "real world" of the superpowers. In sharp contrast to their deadlock at the United Nations over the implications of disarmament measures on world order, the superpowers were able, outside the organization, to develop their framework of achievable arms control agreements that conformed to the existing international order and balance of power. Stripped of any role in the arms control process, the United Nations could deal only with its own store: creating and recreating various organs of disarmament.

THE UNITED NATIONS' MACHINERY IN DISARMAMENT

A United Nations publication concluded correctly: "from the very beginning, it was not the lack of machinery that stood in the way of disarmament agreements."[53] Indeed, in light of the United Nations' record in the field of machinery for disarmament, it can be argued that almost every possible structural and functional option was explored and exhausted. Numerous bodies with a variety of functions and different procedures have been established, enlarged, merged, reformed, dismantled, and revived. Composed of from two nations to the full United Nations membership, these bodies have held thousands of meetings, and their proceedings are recorded in an immense United Nations documentation. The extent to which organizational proliferation and bureaucratic growth influenced the substance of disarmament exchanges remains an open question. It seems, and this will be elaborated later, that sometimes organizational reforms were initiated simply as cosmetic maneuvers to compensate for the lack of real progress. Later, with the growing assertiveness of Third World nations, reforms in the United Nations machinery for disarmament were carried out with the deliberate aim to challenge and undermine the delicate framework of arms control agreements negotiated and achieved between the superpowers (Chapter 5).

Gradually the so-called negotiating forum in Geneva has grown from its nucleus in the Ten Nation Disarmament Committee of 1960, through the ENDC (eighteen nations) and CCD (twenty-six nations in 1969 and thirty-one in 1975), to the new Committee on Disarmament (CD) with forty members (1979). At the Special Session on Disarmament (SSOD), the leadership of the Third World countries succeeded, in what Dag Hammarskjold said failed, to strengthen the link between the CD and the United Nations and to abolish its superpower cochairmanship. This paved the way for the participation of the two remaining nuclear weapon states: France and China. In addition, the SSOD revived the United Nations Disarmament Commission (UNDC), a plenary body to which every United Nations member belongs.

The movement to shake up and reform the disarmament negotiating forum dates back to the early 1970s.[54] The CCD at Geneva has come increasingly under criticism, primarily for not producing results—new and significant treaties. United Nations members were irritated by "bilateralism rampant"—the tendency of the superpowers to negotiate alone and their "condominium" in the CCD, under which they determined the agenda, pace of discussions, working methods, etc. This situation was sharply at variance with the rising power of the Third World bloc within the United Nations system and the demand for greater equality of all states.[55] Third World delegates pointed out that the CCD was often being dismissed as an irrelevant talking-shop and called for a reform that would democratize the forum, taking into account the many changes that had taken place in the world since 1961.[56] As a result, one of the major goals of the 1978 SSOD was to reevaluate and reform the existing United Nations machinery for disarmament. While the Final Document has recognized that lack of political will

Table 1

The Vicissitudes of the International Disarmament Machinery

UN Machinery		Linked, but not UN
1946 -Atomic Energy Commission (11 members)		
1947 -Commission for Conventional weapon (11 members)		
1952 -The two aboved merged into the Disarmament Commission (12 members)		
1954 -Subcommittee of the DC in London (Canada, France, U.S., USSR, U.K.)		
1957 -Disarmament Commission enlarged with another 14 members		
1958 -DC enlarged to include all UN members	1958	-Discontinuance of Nuclear weapons tests (US, U.K., USSR)
Since 1958 the DC has held only two session in 1960 and in 1965, until it was revived by the SSOD.		-Experts on Prevention of Surprise Attack (Geneva; West 4, East 4)
		-Experts on Detection of Nuclear Tests (Geneva: West 4, East 4)
	1959	-Ten Nation Committee on Disarmament (Geneva: West 4, East 4)*
1979 -UN Disarmament Commission revived: includes all member states	1962	-Eighteen Nation Committee on Disarmament (Geneva: West 5, East 5, Non-aligned 8)*
	1970	-Conference of the Committee on Disarmament (CCD)* (Geneva: West 7, East 7, Non-aligned 12)
	1975	-CCD enlarged to 31 members* (Geneva: West 8, East 8, Non-aligned 15)

1979 - Committee on Disarmament (Geneva) under rotated chairmanship, with stronger ties to the UN (40 members)

* Under superpowers' co-chairmanship.

was a significant obstacle on the way toward disarmament, it also expressed the belief that improvements in the machinery are important:

Although the decisive factor for achieving real measures of disarmament is the political will of States, and especially of those possessing nuclear weapons, a significant role can also be played by the effective functioning of an appropriate international machinery designed to deal with the problems of disarmament in its various aspects.[57]

The struggle over United Nations' machinery for disarmament during the SSOD revealed the gap between the majority of the General Assembly and the united front of the superpowers. As the annotated version of the draft final document demonstrates, both superpowers rejected the non-aligned idea of putting the CCD "under the auspices of" the United Nations. The Soviets emphasized the voluntary nature of the links between the CCD and the United Nations, while the non-aligned insisted upon a variety of proposals to strengthen the link.[58] Soviet bloc countries expressed more preference than the West, including the Americans, for continuing the cochairmanship structure at the CCD. They explained that cochairmanship never prevented equality in reaching decisions; on the contrary, the close collaboration of the two cochairmen had saved the committee from lengthy discussions.[59] However, at the SSOD, the superpowers, unwilling to budge on substance, agreed to let the Third World have a face-saving achievement in the form of bureaucratic reforms. As a result, superpowers' cochairmanship in the Geneva Committee was eliminated, its membership was expanded, and its links with the United Naitons were strengthened (see Chapter 5).

Nevertheless, even those who were interested in strengthening the role of the United Nations in the process of disarmament had to recognize its limits. The non-aligned, which obviously prefer the huge forums where they enjoy a majority, agreed—particularly those of them in the CCD—on the need for some permanent multilateral negotiating machinery smaller than the annual General Assembly deliberations.[60] In their working papers and statements to the SSOD, they explicitly recognized that there must be a separate body, smaller in size and representation, in order to conduct negotiations. Therefore, it was for the first time at the SSOD that an official distinction between two different types of disarmament machinery was drawn and incorporated into United Nations practice and terminology. From then on, United Nations' machinery was organized around two pillars: deliberative and negotiating bodies.[61]

A *deliberative* body is usually large in number and strives to develop general guidelines and principles. At the United Nations, deliberations usually involve all member states and deal primarily with general policy (the G.A. and Committees, the United Nations Disarmament Commission, the NPT review conferences, etc.).

A *negotiating* body is usually limited in size, and in it the professionals and the experts deal with the specifics and technicalities of agreements and treaties

Table 2

Membership of Successive Geneva Disarmament Committees

	Ten-Nation Disarmament Committee 1960	Eighteen-Nation Disarmament Committee (ENDC) 1962-69	Conference of the Committee on Disarmament (CCD) 1969-74	(CCD) 1975-78	Committee on Disarmament (CD) 1979-?
Soviet Union	**	**	**	**	*
United States	**	**	**	**	*
Britain	*	*	*	*	*
Bulgaria	*	*	*	*	*
Canada	*	*	*	*	*
Czechoslovakia	*	*	*	*	*
France	*	(*)	(*)	(*)	*
Italy	*	*	*	*	*
Poland	*	*	*	*	*
Romania	*	*	*	*	*
+Brazil		*	*	*	*
+Burma		*	*	*	*
+Egypt (formely as UAR)		*	*	*	*
+Ethiopia		*	*	*	*
+India		*	*	*	*
+Mexico		*	*	*	*
+Nigeria		*	*	*	*
+Sweden		*	*	*	*
+Argentina			*	*	*
Hungary		*	*	*	*
Japan			*	*	*
Mongolia			*	*	*
+Morocco			*	*	*
Netherlands			*	*	*
+Pakistan			*	*	*
+Yugoslavia			*	*	*
Federal Republic of Germany				*	*
German Democratic Republic				*	*
+Iran				*	*
+Peru				*	*
+Zaire				*	*
+Algeria					*
Australia					*
Belgium					*
China					*
+Cuba					*
+Indonesia					*
+Kenya					*
+Sri Lanka					*
+Venezuela					*

** Superpowers'Chairmanship;   + The Group of 21 non-aligned countries;
(*) France did not ocuppy its reserved seat.

(SALT, MBFR, the trilateral meetings on CTB with the United States, Soviet Union, and United Kingdom).

These distinctions were incorporated in the resolutions of the United Nations SSOD and were translated into practice in the follow-up machinery. In the words of the SSOD Final Document:

For maximum effectiveness, two kinds of bodies are required in the field of disarmament— *deliberative* and *negotiating*. All member States should be represented on the former, whereas the latter, for the sake of convenience, should have a relatively small membership....The General Assembly has been and should remain the main *deliberative* organ of the United Nations in the field of disarmament....The Disarmament Commission shall be a *deliberative* body, a subsidiary organ of the General Assembly....The Assembly is deeply aware of the continuing requirement for a single multilateral disarmament *negotiating* forum of limited size taking decisions on the basis of consensus...the Committee on Disarmament in Geneva.[62]

It remained questionable, however, whether any United Nations organ that by definition is subordinate to a representative body of the General Assembly can serve as an effective negotiating body. The record of the CD since 1979 is not encouraging in this regard.

THE COMMITTEE ON DISARMAMENT SINCE 1979

The opening of the new negotiating forum—the Committee on Disarmament—in Geneva on January 24, 1979, attracted a lot of media attention. The Algerian foreign minister became the first chairman of the CD under the new monthly alphabetical rotation system. The French foreign minister was there also (together with four other foreign ministers) to mark the return of his country to the negotiating forum. But, as some observers indicated, the impressive gathering with so much fanfare did not affect the substance of the discussions.[63] The French maiden address to the CD was a ringing reminder to the delegates of how France's priorities do not coincide with those of the CD's other members. There was no mention, in the French speech, of a nuclear test ban, which has been the chief priority (and still is) of the majority in the Geneva organ.[64] Ironically, both newcomers to the CD, France and China (which joined the CD in February 1980), are the traditional dissenters among the five nuclear-weapon states. They did not join the major arms control treaties: PTB, NPT, Sea-Bed Treaty, and the Biological Weapons Convention. How could so many hope that the entrance of France and China to the CD would strengthen United Nations disarmament efforts?[65] It was, once more, a failure to understand that as long as there are no common grounds on the issues related with the framework of world order, a real breakthrough in disarmament would be impossible. Both China and France, particularly in their arms control and disarmament policies, have always been the *enfants terribles* among the Big Five and did not accept the basically bipolar "arms control regime" that the superpowers had begun to elaborate since the early 1960s (see Chapter 5). It should have been clear to specialists in the field that it would be an illusion to expect this fundamental gap to be narrowed by petty reforms in the disarmament mechanism. Actually, the net result of these reforms would be to enhance the gap between the deliberations at United Nations forums and the real world of arms control outside.

The Chinese maiden speech a year later (February 5, 1980) was even worse from the point of view of disarmament supporters. Delivered by the Chinese vice foreign minister, the speech was dominated by accusations and recriminations, expostulations and reply (he was interrupted twice by the Soviet ambassador), which are unusual even at the United Nations regular disarmament deliberative bodies. The Chinese charged Moscow with engineering wars by proxy and staging *coups d'état* and sending its own troops abroad while masking its true motives with "fraudulent rhetoric." China did not identify the Soviet Union by name but made it clear which country it meant by a reference to the Soviet "armed intervention in Afghanistan."[66] One may conclude that the entrance of France and China did not mark any change in their attitudes and approaches toward the fundamental problems of disarmament but rather reflected a tactical decision to make use of the negotiating forum for national purposes.

Soon it was realized that the reform in the CD had created some new problems in the actual conduct of negotiations. The increase in participants meant simply a substantial increase in the workload—mainly for the purposes of deliberations, with more countries issuing statements during the general debates in the plenary and more discussants on agenda items. In addition to the differences between North and South on disarmament (see the next chapters) and the new aspects of friction introduced by China and France, the CD has witnessed a deterioration in the cooperation between the superpowers. In 1981, the Soviet Union introduced the subject of the "neutron bomb" to the CD discussions with the knowledge that it would be defeated immediately because of the required approval by consensus in the committee. The Soviet initiative, seconded by all other Communist countries in the CD, demonstrated the decline of the organ into another United Nations deliberative body.[67] It may be argued that, had the cochairmanship of the superpowers remained at the CD, it would have been impossible for the Soviets to get the required American approval for injecting an "East–West" issue to the negotiating forum. As Richard Hass of the International Institute for Strategic Studies pointed out, already in 1979, the reforms in the CD may have had the unexpected result of further complicating the activities of the body, thereby accelerating the trend against using it for serious negotiations.[68]

Gradually, therefore, the Committee on Disarmament, designated as a negotiating forum, was getting closer and closer to being another United Nations deliberative forum. Practically, there have been no negotiations at the CD since its establishment. The protocols of the meetings reveal that the participants are delivering almost identical speeches to what they say in the other deliberative forums: the First Committee of the General Assembly and the UNDC. Similarly, as revealed by the agenda of the CD, by working papers submitted to it, and by the indexes of statements by country and subjects, the CD represents not just some overlap with United Nations deliberations but rather virtually repetitions of the same positions, proposals, and even mutual recriminations. One can find hardly any difference between the discussions and elaborations on the "comprehensive progammme of disarmament" in the United Nations Disarmament Commission (one of the deliberative forums) and the CD (supposedly a negotiating forum).[69] The Soviet ambassador to the CD, himself active in introducing the new divisive issues, admitted that the organ for negotiations has failed during its first three years to work out a single, even very modest, agreement in limiting the arms race.[70]

Moreover, even in its organizational structure the CD is becoming more a forum for deliberations than a multilateral negotiating forum. The CD's major achievement in its first year of operation, as heralded by the Mexican representative, Alfonsu Garcia Robles, often referred to as the "dean of Geneva" or the "godfather of disarmament,"[71] was the adoption of rules of procedures.[72] Further hindsight on the issue reveals that from the point of view of negotiations this achievement might be a Pyrrhic victory. As indicated by the representative of the Netherlands, Richard Fein, rules of procedures belong to the United Nations deliberative bodies but were deliberately avoided in diplomatic conferences that met to negotiate treaties. By introducing rules of procedure and other procedural devices, "the fundamental difference between a deliberative body and a negotiating conference" was blurred.[73]

In 1980, the "Group of 21" in the CD (the Third World countries) proposed the establishment of ad hoc working groups on five agenda topics as "the best available machinery for the conduct of concrete negotiations within the Committee."[74] This was, in effect, an admission of the difficulties of carrying on negotiations in the enlarged CD. Similarly, Garcia Robles emphasized that the new CD procedures still allow the nuclear powers, when they consider it necessary, "to carry out bilateral agreements they considered to be important."[75] This was an attempt to salvage the newly reformed organ before it became completely irrelevant, as have other United Nations organs, to the arms control process outside the United Nations. Hence, the Third World had to recognize that the superpowers still may consider, on a bilateral level, some of their arms control issues.

The reformed United Nations' machinery for disarmament did not bring any breakthrough in disarmament. The annual reports of the "deliberative forum" (DC) reveal that the members are able to agree only on reporting their differences.[76] Thus, the extensive deliberations and negotiations in these organs, instead of harmonizing views and approaches to disarmament, have sharpened and emphasized disagreement. As shown, the SSOD created terminological confusion in its attempt to formalize and institutionalize the distinction between negotiating and deliberative forums. Ironically, at the CD there are complaints about the deliberative tendencies and the inability to negotiate in the enlarged forum. On the other hand, when the United Nations Disarmament Commission wants to create at least the appearance of progress and to issue something close to a consensus report, it has to dedicate *most* of its work to an informal meeting, thus becoming a negotiating body.[77]

In 1981 it became apparent that the CD could not function anymore as a negotiating forum. This represented not just a temporary failure due to some transitional developments in international relations but in essence a collapse of the whole notion that structural and procedural reforms can help to reconcile diametrically opposite outlooks and philosophies on issues such as international stability and world order (see next chapters).

It became obvious that the real debate in the United Nations on disarmament items is not on how to limit or control the arms race but rather on whether to change the international order by means of disarmament. In 1981, for the first time in the history of the disarmament negotiating forum in Geneva, the CD report to the United Nations General Assembly included several paragraphs that raised criticism of the superpowers' doctrines of nuclear deterrence. The Geneva organ, which according to the SSOD resolutions should "conduct its work by consensus," became in its third year of operation a kind of panel of experts, or an international seminar on nuclear strategy and international peace and stability. Besides its formal deliberations on these issues, which are, after all, part and parcel of an existing world order, the CD has dedicated special informal meetings on the "complex character" of issues "involving security concerns and strategic doctrines."[78]

In these informal meetings, as reported by the CD to the General Assembly:

the group of 21 put forward the view that doctrines of nuclear deterrence, far from being responsible for the maintenance of international peace and security, lie at the root of the nuclear arms race and lead to greater insecurity and instability in international relations. The group rejected the existing superpower deterrence as politically and morally unjustifiable.[79]

Though the report also states the views of the socialist states and members of the Western alliance, it still remains an unprecedented document for a negotiating forum that relies upon consensus among its members. It seems also inconceivable that countries with such divergent interests as Sweden and Iran, or regional rivals such as Brazil and Argentina, or India and Pakistan, or the United States and Cuba, would be able to iron out their differences and offer a workable proposal on disarmament.

MECHANISM AND WORLD ORDER

The early debates, during the cold war period, between East and West were marked by the failure to revise the international order in order to accommodate it to the requirements of the nuclear age. The Baruch Plan, whether it was naive or shrewd, was consistent with the official U.S. view at that time that the prospects of a nuclear arms race were too dangerous to be dealt with, in the words of President Truman, "in the framework of old ideas" of national sovereignty.[80] The failure of the Baruch Plan has established the pattern of differences between East and West that characterized the long impasse in United Nations activities in the field of disarmament.

With the failure of the United Nations to provide a conducive atmosphere for arms control negotiations, the superpowers began to discuss their matters outside the international organization. The public forum of the United Nations, with its inherent tendencies toward propaganda warfare, made it impossible for the superpowers to negotiate limited measures of arms conntrol without altering the world order. As shown in this chapter, all agreements on arms control during the 1960s and 1970s were reached outside the United Nations and always after bilateral negotiations between the superpowers. The various treaties were submitted, then, to the United Nations organs as *faits accomplis*. The only choice left for the disarmament community at the United Nations (diplomats and staff members) was to indulge in a Parkinson-type of bureaucratic aggrandisement.

The reforms and innovations in the United Nations' machinery for disarmament reached new records in the SSOD of 1978. According to a report by the secretary general of the United Nations prepared by a group of experts, the number of disarmament bodies in the United Nations has almost tripled in a period of three years since the SSOD. During the three-year period 1974–1976, there was a total of fifteen disarmament bodies that met for 46 sessions; in the three-year period 1979–1981, about forty committees, commissions, conferences, expert groups held approximately 140 sessions.[81] The CD itself, as a "negotiating" body, has more than doubled its activities in its first two years (1979–1980) in terms of meetings and the production of working papers and other documents.[82] The SSOD brought about an unprecedented expansion of United Nations involvement in research and studies in the field of disarmament. In three years (1979–1981) the United Nations Centre on Disarmament produced sixteen different studies on disarmament.[83] Some of the studies had a clear political bias on controversial issues, threatening to politicize the role of the organization (see Chapter 5).

The result is an endless, vicious cycle of bureaucratic activities aimed apparently at compensating for the lack of real influence of the United Nations in the field of disarmament. First the majority of the Third World calls for strengthening and consolidating the role of the United Nations in the field of disarmament. Then it adopts resolutions that establish new organs and orders new reports and studies. Finally, the secretary general, with the help of governmental experts, reports that the "growing disarmament agenda" and the "increasing complexity of the issues" and the "more active participation" of member states in the new and expanded bodies "create increasing demands on the United Nations in the field of disarmament."[84] No wonder the next step is a further expansion, with more financial implications, of the United Nations' machinery for disarmament.

It seems that the United Nations is creating a bureaucratic monster that would not necessarily serve as the institutional framework for the joint exploration of approaches to disarmament. This process gives rise to an illusion that the problem of disarmament can be dealt with through organizational innovations instead of by tackling the political roots of the issues involved. The tendency, as in many complex organizations, "to keep doing what you are doing" may lead to complacency among disarmament observers and overreliance on the structural apparatus of the disarmament machinery. In the SSOD, for instance, the issue of the machinery of disarmament has overwhelmed many other aspects of the debate—matters related directly to the substance of disarmament. The proliferation of organs, sessions, studies, and reports since the SSOD has underscored the trend toward an indiscriminate approach of organizational and bureaucratic experiments instead of dealing with the real political matters. Experience has shown that organs dedicated to disarmament can be easily transformed into an arena for the conduct of international political warfare, or can serve as an instrument for the advancement of the political objectives of a particular state or group of states (see next chapters). Machinery as such cannot generate its own supply of leadership, inspiration, and the required political will; the danger is that it may become a substitute for these qualities.

NOTES

1. Brian Urquhart, *Hammarskjold* (New York: Alfred A. Knopf, 1972), p. 325.

2. Charles William Maynes, "A UN Policy for the Next Administration," *Foreign Affairs* 541 (Winter 1975–76/July 1976): 805.

3. Urquhart, *Hammarskjold*, p. 315.

4. Leland M. Goodrich, Edward Hambro, and Anne Simmons, *United Nations Charter: Commentary and Documents* (New York: Columbia University Press, 1969), p. 120.

5. Urquhart, *Hammarskjold*, p. 315.

6. Ibid., p. 332.

7. William Epstein, *Disarmament—Twenty-five Years of Effort* (Ontario: Canadian Institute of International Affairs, 1971), p. 4.

8. See Hedley Bull, *The Control of the Arms Race* (New York: Praeger Publishers, 1965), introduction; Claude, *Swords*, p. 301; Frye, "The Quest for Disarmament," p. 21; Mandelbaum, *The Nuclear Question*, p. 33. For an extensive account of East–West propaganda warfare of disarmament proposals, see Spanier and Nogee, *The Politics of Disarmament*.

9. Claude, *Swords*, p. 296.

10. See, for instance, the following Soviet drafts in General Assembly Official Records: A/C.1/87, November 29, 1946; A/723, November 17, 1948; DC/4/Rev.1, March 19, 1952; DC/SC.1/Rev.2, May 10, 1955; A/C.1/793, September 20, 1957.

11. Philip Noel-Baker, *The Arms Race* (New York: Oceana Publications, 1960), p. 20.

12. See, for instance, in GAOR: A/C.1/89, December 2, 1946 (United States); A/1943, November 7, 1951 (France, the United Kingdom, the United States); DC/87, July 3, 1956 (Canada, France, the United Kingdom, and the United States).

13. Adopted as General Assembly Resolution 192(III), November 19, 1948.

14. *UN and Disarmament 1945–1970*, p. 31.

15. Russell, *The UN and U.S.*, p. 91; also in Louis Henkin, *Disarmament*, The Hammarskjold Forums of the Association of the Bar of the City of New York (New York: Oceana Publications, 1964), p. 19.

16. GAOR, Fourteenth Session Plenary Meetings, 799th meeting, September 8, 1959.

17. Epstein, *Disarmament*, pp. 14–15.

18. The United States insisted also that verification should start from the beginning and regarded the Soviet position as too ambiguous, which "would make any disarmament plan a sham." GAOR, Sixteenth Session, Annexes, agenda item 19, Document A/4880.

19. Ibid., Document A/4887.

20. Ibid., Document A/4880.

21. Ibid., Document A/4887.

22. *UN and Disarmament* 1945–1970, p. 83.

23. Alva Myrdal, *The Game of Disarmament: How the United States and Russia Run the Arms Race* (New York: Pantheon Books, 1976), p. 298.

24. William Epstein, *The Last Chance—Nuclear Proliferation and Arms Control* (New York: Free Press, 1976), p. 16.

25. Trevor N. Dupuy and Gay M. Hammerman, eds., *A Documentary History of Arms Control and Disarmament* (New York: R. R. Bowker, 1973), p. 482.

26. Bull, *The Control of the Arms Race*, p. xx. See also James E. Dougherty, "Soviet Arms Control Negotiations," in *Detente—Cold War Strategies in Transition*, ed. Eleanor Lansing Dulles and Robert Dickson Crane (New York: Praeger Publishers, 1965), pp. 179–200.

27. Robert E. Osgood and Robert W. Tucker, *Force, Order, and Justice* (Baltimore: Johns Hopkins Press, 1967), pp. 334–35 n.14.

28. Ibid., p. 336 n.17.

29. Robert W. Tucker, *The Inequality of Nations* (New York: Basic Books, 1977), p. 4. The feature of self-help, Tucker suggests, may be the distinguishing feature of the legal equality between sovereign and independent states. In practice it highlights the essential inequality of states "since the utility of a right of self-help is of necessity dependent upon the power at the disposal of those exercising this right." Similarly, "the balance of power itself formed the principal political expression of self-help" (p. 6).

30. GAOR, A/S-10/PV.5, May 26, 1978.

31. GAOR, A/S-10/PV.3, May 24, 1978.

32. The Federal Republic of Germany submitted proposals concerning "seismological verification of a comprehensive test ban" and "chemical-weapon verification" (A/S-10/AC.1/12-13). The United States and other Western countries introduced proposals on "confidence-building measures" and peacekeeping by the UN (A/S-10/AC.1/24,26).

33. Epstein, *The Last Chance*, p. 11.

34. John G. Stoessinger, *The United Nations and the Superpowers* (New York: Random House, 1977), p. 162; Ralph Townley, *The United Nations: A View from Within* (New York: Scribners, 1968), p. 95; Barnet, *Who Wants Disarmament*, p. 23.

35. Spanier and Nogee, *The Politics of Disarmament*, p. 52.

36. Alfred Paul Brainard, *The United Nations and the Question of Disarmament 1950–1955*. A Ph.D. dissertation, University of Washington, 1960 (Ann Arbor, Mich.: University Microfilms, 1961), p. 232.

37. Claude wrote it first in 1961 and has maintained it in his revised edition of 1971. *Swords*, pp. 295–96.

38. Goodrich, Hambro, and Simmons, *United Nations Charter*, p. 120.

39. Urquhart, *Hammarskjold*, p. 325.

40. Michael J. Sullivan, III, "Conference at the Crossroads: Future Prospect for the Conference of the Committee on Disarmament," *International Organization* 29, no. 2 (Spring 1975): 394.

41. See Bennett, *International Organization*, pp. 230–34; a similar role to the United Nations is implied in a SIPRI publication: *Agreements for Arms Control*, by Jozef Goldblat (London: Taylor & Francis, 1982), p. 39.

42. Russell, *The UN and U.S.*, pp. 82, 92.

43. Myrdal, *The Game of Disarmament*, p. 93.

44. Arthur Lall, "The Superpowers, the UN and Disarmament: A View from the Third World," in *Soviet and American Policies in the United Nations*, ed. Alvin Z. Rubinstein and George Ginsburg (New York: New York University Press, 1971), pp. 57–58.

45. Myrdal, *The Game of Disarmament*, p. 95.

46. Elizabeth Young, *A Farewell to Arms Control* (Harmondsworth: Penguin Books, 1972), p. 86.

47. Russell, *The UN and U.S.*, p. 82.

48. Epstein, *The Last Chance*, pp. 102–3.

49. Stoessinger, *The UN and the Superpowers*, p. 176.

50. Epstein, *The Last Chance*, pp. 71–72.

51. Sullivan, "Conference at the Crossroads," pp. 399–400. Also Frank Barnaby, the director of SIPRI, told the delegates of the UN SSOD:

The arms control Treaties now in force have had little or no effect on the military potential of States. The choice of measures adopted has been haphazard. In several cases the outlawed activities have never even been seriously considered as methods of war. It is now obvious that the method of negotiating small, unrelated steps cannot produce meaningful arms reductions. Insignificant restraints are bound to lag behind the rising levels of armaments and advances in military technology. (GAOR, A/S-10/AC.1/PV.8, p. 47, June 13, 1978)

52. Sullivan, "Conference at the Crossroads," p. 396.

53. *The UN and Disarmament 1945–1970*, p. 3.

54. Sullivan, "Conference at the Crossroads," p. 396.

55. See, for instance, Nicholas A. Sims, *Approaches to Disarmament* (London: Quaker Peace & Service, 1979), pp. 12–20; William Epstein, "UN Special Session on Disarmament, How Much Progress?" *Survival* (November–December 1978): 251; Homer A. Jack, *Disarmament Workshop—The UN Special Session and Beyond* (New York: World Conference on Religion and Peace, 1979), pp. 89–91; Philip Towle, "The UN Special Session on Disarmament—Retrospect," *World Today* 35, no. 8 (May 1979): 212.

56. Nigeria, *Documents of the Conference of the Committee on Disarmament*, CCD/PV.769, 1978. For a summary of CCD debates on the issue, see the *Report of the Conference of the Committee on Disarmament 1978*, GAOR, Thirty-Third Session, Supplement No. 27 (A/33/27), pp. 77–90.

57. GAOR, SSOD Final Document, Tenth Special Session Supplement, No. 4, A/S-10/4, article 10.

58. Annotated document, see Jack, *Disarmament Workshop*.

59. Report of the CCD (1978), p. 81. These debates provided another opportunity for

Romania to assert its independence on disarmament matters by joining the non-aligneds' demands for reform of the CCD. Ibid., p. 85.

60. Sullivan, "Conference at the Crossroads," p. 395.

61. The concepts have been known quite before but were formalized at the SSOD. See ibid., p. 395 n.4; Sims, *Approaches*, p. 12.

62. SSOD Final Document, articles 113, 115, 118(a), p. 120.

63. *Disarmament Times*, February 28, 1979.

64. *Report of the Committee on Disarmament*, Appendix 4, Vol. 1, CD/PV.2, January 24, 1979.

65. See SIPRI, *World Armament and Disarmament, SIPRI Yearbook 1979* (London: Taylor & Francis, 1979), pp. 18, 520; *New York Times*, July 5, 1978; *Christian Science Monitor*, June 28, 1978.

66. CD/PV.2, February 5, 1980.

67. The Soviets submitted to the CD papers that are nothing but sheer propaganda. There is no attempt on their part even to pretend that they are in a "negotiating forum." On August 17, 1981, they circulated in the CD a long statement by TASS, the Telegraphic Agency of the Soviet Union, which refers to the "cynical disregard" of the U.S. president for "the wishes and interests of the peoples of the world" in deciding to produce the "barbarous device for the mass destruction of human beings." The article was circulated as a document in the CD, CD/216, August 17, 1981.

68. Richard Hass, reviewing *Opportunities for Disarmament* in *Survival* (July–August 1979): 188.

69. See Report of the Committee on Disarmament, GAOR Thirty-Fifth Session, Supplement No. 27 (A/35/27), 1980, pp. 56–60. The repetition is best illustrated in the UN disarmament yearbooks of 1979 and 1980, which provide systematic coverage on each disarmament subject at the UN General Assembly, the DC, and the CD.

70. "Soviet Ambassador Issraelyan Criticizes Geneva Forum," *Disarmament Times* 4, no. 4 (September–October 1981).

71. See, for instance, the statement by Richard Fein from the Netherlands, GAOR, A/C.1/34/PV.12, October 23, 1979.

72. Garcia Robles, GAOR, A/C.1/34/PV.4, October 16, 1979.

73. GAOR, A/C.1/34/PV.12, October 23, 1979.

74. "Statement of the Group of 21," Document CD/64, February 27, 1980, on the establishment of working groups on items on the annual agenda of the Committee on Disarmament in 1980, also in CD/139/Appendix II/Vols. I and II, 1980.

75. GAOR, A/C.1/34/PV.4, October 10, 1979.

76. *Report of the Committee on Disarmament*, GAOR, Thirty-Fifth Session, Supplement No. 27 (A/35/27); and Thirty-Sixth Session, Supplement No. 27(A/36/27), 1981.

77. Most of the meetings of the UNDC in its 1979 and 1980 sessions were closed meetings (unusual for a deliberative forum) and consultations within working groups. See "Comments," *Disarmament Times* 2, no. 7 (June–July 1979).

78. *Report of the Committee on Disarmament*, GAOR, Thirty-Sixth Session, Supplement No. 27 (A/36/27), 1981.

79. Ibid., para. 70.

80. Osgood and Tucker, *Force*, p. 180 n.45.

81. "Study of the Institutional Arrangements Relating to the Process of Disarmament," Report of the Secretary General, GAOR, A/36/392, September 11, 1981, p. 10.

82. Frank Barnaby, "United Nations Center for Disarmament," *Bulletin of the Atomic Scientists* (January 1982): 6.

83. "Study of the Institutional Arrangements," p. 10.

84. Ibid., p. 6

4

The Third World and Disarmament: The New Context

When two elephants get together, whether to fight or to make love, the grass and shrubs always get crushed.[1]

Sri Lankan proverb

The pursuit of disarmament is at the same time the pursuit of development by all nations....It is an integral part of the process of creating a new international order.[2]

The Foreign Minister of Sri Lanka
speaking on behalf of the
non-aligned nations.

The proliferation and expansion of the United Nations machinery of disarmament and the new North–South type of confrontation in disarmament debates were the culmination of a revolutionary process that took place within the United Nations over two decades. Since it was founded in 1945, the United Nations has changed dramatically; from the 51 that signed the Charter, the United Nations tripled its membership to 158 in 1983. By the 1960s, as a result of the liquidation of the colonial empires, the birth of new nations became virtually a monthly event. By the 1970s, about one hundred new nations from the Third World enjoyed an absolute arithmetic majority in the General Assembly. Within only one generation the United Nations totally changed in character and became an important political vehicle for its newcomers.

While the two superpowers have moved outside the United Nations to consolidate their framework of achievable arms control agreements, the Third World has emerged as the master of proceedings in the General Assembly. Third World countries, most of which came into existence within the last thirty years, introduced a revolutionary element to the post–World War II balance of power within the United Nations framework. These changes had direct effects on the agenda, confrontations, and substance of United Nations debates on disarmament. The overall record of the General Assembly makes it clear that the major political controversies have shifted during the 1960s from an East–West to a North–South axis.

From the beginning of this transition the primary problem for the Third World has always been economic: the demand to reallocate resources from the rich to the poor countries in the framework of the so-called New International Economic Order (NIEO). Gradually, within the framework of the economic struggle, the Third World realized that disarmament is closely linked to their major collective goal, the new economic order. It became apparent that while the economic and social gap between the rich and the poor countries was not being narrowed, but in fact was widening, military expenditures continued to increase in absolute figures. Hence, disarmament became the next logical field to tackle in connection with a new world order. This chapter will examine the different phases in the evolution of the Third World approach to disarmament and how disarmament became a corollary of their NIEO politics.

In this chapter, as in other chapters, the terms *non-aligned* and *Third World* are used interchangeably, as in many publications.[3] *Third World* is a rather more general term that has less rigor than does *non-aligned*, which denotes a political movement with members and institutions. Since *Third World* has become widely accepted and utilized mostly by the developing countries in the United Nations to generate a new sense of common identity and purpose,[4] it is legitimate to refer to it as a bloc of nations sharing some common interest. Moreover, it is within the United Nations system that this bloc was institutionalized as the so-called Group of 77, representing 120 members in 1981 (see Table 3). Experience has shown that Third World nations adopt in most cases the general approach and basic principles of disarmament as agreed upon by the non-aligned movement, which comprises the bulk of the Group of 77 (90 states out of 120).

THE INITIAL EMPHASIS ON DISARMAMENT

There is no doubt that increased tensions between the superpowers had a large influence on the origins of the non-aligned movement. In fact, the meeting that is referred to as the first non-aligned meeting took place in New York, in September 1960, in response to another outburst of the cold war between the Americans and the Russians. For this get-together, during the General Assembly's Fifteenth Session, Nehru of India, Nkrumah of Ghana, Sukarno of Indonesia, and Nasser of Egypt came to the Yugoslavian mission to the United Nations upon the invitation of Tito.[5] The predominant concern of these leaders was how to reduce tension between the superpowers and to move forward toward disarmament.

As Robert Mortimer explains, the role of Tito is important to understanding the beginning of the non-aligned movement. Unlike his colleagues in Africa and Asia, Tito represented a special case of a country from Europe with a fierce desire for independence from both superpowers. For this reason he sought allies in Asia and Africa while calling into question the geographic rationale of Bandung, which excluded Yugoslavia from Third World diplomacy. The intensification of the cold war in the period 1960–1962 gave Tito the opportunity to seize upon the concern about another world war, as he argued that the fundamental interest of the developing states was "to act against the bloc system."[6] Tito shared the views of Nehru, who believed more than anybody else that the menace of nuclear war between the superpowers was the overriding problem that all states faced,[7] and the non-aligned movement was established on a strong disarmament platform.

When the founding fathers of the non-aligned movement gathered at Belgrade in 1961 for their first summit conference, disarmament was the most important issue in their discussions. Interestingly enough, as it seems from the 1980s vantage point, during the first decade economic demands were played down. It is striking today to realize that in the first non-aligned summit conference (1961) six of the twenty-seven points were devoted to disarmament, while only three and a half dealt with economic matters. The heart of the final declaration of Belgrade was the issue of world peace; economic matters were discussed vaguely and in noncommittal language. Expressing a growing concern over the threat of an atomic confrontation between the superpowers, the leaders also recommended that the United Nations General Assembly convene either a special session of the United Nations on disarmament or a World Disarmament Conference (WDC) under United Nations auspices.[8]

It is precisely this new focus on problems of world peace that marks the departure of the Belgrade Conference from previous Afro-Asian conferences. The Belgrade Conference was unique not only because it was without China (and with the addition of Yugoslavia and Cuba—both outside Afro-Asia) but because of the new theme under which the non-aligned countries had gathered. In the Afro-Asian conference of Bandung (1955), the accent had been placed on geographical solidarity and on problems of the emerging countries of Asia and Africa. Though there was a reference to world peace, disarmament was not on the agenda and was not discussed as a separate item at the Bandung Conference. At Belgrade, on the contrary, the focus was on world affairs, war and peace, and disarmament issues. The literature on the subject seems to gloss over the fact that by definition the Bandung Conference could not be a meeting for non-alignment[9] since two military allies of the United States participated there: Turkey (member of NATO) and Japan. In addition, Iraq and Pakistan, which also attended the Bandung summit, were, in 1955, members of the Central Treaty Organization together with Iran, Thailand, and the Philippines.

At Belgrade the line of Nehru and, to a lesser degree, of Tito and Nasser prevailed against the view of Sukarno and Nkrumah, who wanted decolonization before disarmament.[10] There was a great deal of talk at the conference on the need to serve as the conscience of the world and to stand between the two world giants and save the universe from mass destruction by preventing a head-on collision between them. The leaders added a special statement to the final declaration on the "Danger of War and an Appeal for Peace" and a special message to President Kennedy and Premier Khrushchev, urging them to resume the stalled superpowers negotiations. High-level emissaries went to Moscow and Washington to bring the letters to the leaders of government personally.[11] The debates and documents of the Belgrade meeting demonstrate that the non-aligned focused their campaign on disarmament, regarding themselves as first and foremost acting to prevent global war by trying to mediate between the superpowers. It is quite revealing that a comprehensive study on the non-aligned movement written in 1964 did not regard economic issues as an important concern of the movement. In its index, there is no reference whatsoever to terms such as *economy* or *development* (just rare references to foreign aid). Instead, a whole chapter (among seven), is dedicated to disarmament and the United Nations, calling it "the topic at the forefront" of the non-aligned and adding: "As with one voice, proponents of non-alignment have echoed the view of Prime Minister Nehru that disarmament is an 'urgent and vital problem' and a prerequisite for the creation of an effective world order."[12] At that time, as one observer put it, the non-aligned conceived their role as a "golden bridge" between East and West on disarmament issues.[13]

It is understandable, therefore, that seventeen years after Belgrade, when the United Nations convened a Special Session on Disarmament (SSOD), some writers would conclude that it was a logical outcome of consistent policies of the non-aligned for almost two decades.[14] Similarly, many leaders of the movement have emphasized in their speeches to the SSOD that the session was a result of their continuous effort since the first summit of non-aligned leaders in 1961 at Belgrade. In his concluding remarks to the SSOD, the representative of Sri Lanka, speaking on behalf of the non-aligned movement, reiterated once more: "I think we would not be wrong in saying that this special session on disarmament was the realization of a non-aligned initiative launched as far back as 1961."[15]

It is clear that the dreams of Nehru and his Third World colleagues could not have materialized without the dramatic shift in power in the General Assembly of the United Nations. In the late 1970s, the United Nations was under the full control of the Third World.[16] Sometimes United Nations meetings were just a replica of or rubber stamp for the non-aligned conferences: resolutions adopted at non-aligned summits have become actual guidelines of United Nations General Assemblies. At the end of the 1970s it was agreed that "the new nations have taken over the United Nations, imbuing it with values and cutting it to their cloth. It become their major platform, the place where they express their aspirations and frustrations and where they mobilize world opinion."[17]

It is also true that for twenty-seven years the idea of an international conference for dealing with disarmament has been periodically raised by various countries, for different purposes. The SSOD came into being after the Third World succeeded in regaining the initiative from the Soviets and moved to reformulate it according to their objectives and interests. In this regard, the convening of the session was itself a victory of the non-aligned over the superpowers, which agreed to it reluctantly; it was testimony indeed to the power transformation that had taken place at the United Nations.

However, it would be simplistic and even misleading to view the SSOD as the natural offspring of non-aligned endeavors since 1961. To do so would be to ignore some significant and dramatic developments during this period. One cannot conclude from the fact that the non-aligned pressed for the SSOD in 1978 that they still professed the same objectives as in 1961. It was not only the United Nations that had been changed; the non-aligned approach to disarmament had grown in complexity and sophistication. Gradually, with the emergence of new practical concerns and increasing conflicts of interest, disarmament, as a policy goal for the non-aligned, began to decline.

CHANGING ATTITUDES TOWARD DISARMAMENT

The demise of disarmament issues within the framework of the non-aligned movement was gradual and had several causes. It was affected not only by international developments but also by changes within the non-aligned group. The second summit conference of the non-aligned, in Cairo in 1964, for example, was held in different circumstances from those of Belgrade. There had been a rapprochement between the superpowers in the wake of the Cuban missile crisis. With the Sino–Soviet split and the independent policy of France, the division of the world into two opposing world blocs had become less pronounced. The death of Nehru before the conference probably also accounts for the fact that there was less talk there on disarmament and world peace. Anti-colonialism returned as the major theme, following the more militant approach of Nkrumah and other Africans: "As long as oppressed classes exist there can be no such thing as peaceful coexistence between opposing ideologies."[18]

The military attack of China on India, and the consequent humiliation of the latter, was a supreme test for non-alignment. India discovered painfully that the invocation of the concept of non-alignment and the so-called spirit of Bandung among its participants could not in itself provide national security. It was then discovered that non-alignment was no substitute for national defense. The Indians, in spite of the pacifist heritage of Gandhi, realized that the notion of non-alignment had to be "refined" and "purified," to the extent that "there was no incompatibility between adherence to non-alignment and a condition of military preparedness."[19]

In a parallel development, Third World countries began to share the feeling that detente between the great powers, as characterized, for example, by the Moscow test-ban treaty of 1963, could have an adverse effect on them, both in the domain of great-power aid and in the role they would be able to play in the international arena. With growing skepticism for the tenets of "peaceful coexistence" expressed at the Cairo Conference, some leaders were convinced that the non-aligned should strive for "equal strength" in their struggle with the "imperialist states."[20] The general atmosphere, thus, was not favorable anymore for maintaining the Belgrade emphasis on disarmament.

It seems that sometimes the non-aligned approach toward disarmament reflected their perceptions of and attitudes toward the role and goals of their movement. The focus on and devotion to disarmament matters by the non-aligned at Belgrade was an expression of their desire to provide their "good offices" as a third party to the superpowers in order to bring about world peace. At the Cairo conference of 1964, although disarmament was still an important issue in the final communique, it did not dominate the agenda. It was probably an expression of the continued struggle between the approach of Tito, who emphasized "non-alignment" and wanted a second Belgrade, and Sukarno with others, who wanted in effect a second Bandung in order to press the more parochial interests of Afro-Asians.[21] Some authors even maintained that non-alignment did not live beyond 1961, and its second conference in Cairo was an Afro-Asian and not a non-aligned conference.[22] According to Ashok Kapur, Indian neutralism and non-alignment after 1962 may be described as post-neutralism.[23]

The second half of the sixties was a period of decline and disappointment for the non-aligned.[24] It seemed as if detente between the superpowers was hurting the very foundations of non-alignment; they could not pursue the policy of "playing one bloc against the other and gaining aid from both."[25] There was a common feeling of powerlessness, enhanced by internal divisions between radicals and conservatives, Arabs and Africans, and so forth.[26] In addition, there was a psychological crisis of confidence in the once new policies hailed as an alternative to traditional power politics, especially as several founding fathers of the movement (Ben Bella, Nkrumah, and Sukarno) were ousted by military coups. There was even some speculation that the non-aligned group might gradually disappear from the international scene.[27]

It was particularly in the field of disarmament that the new international circumstances diminished the potential role of the non-aligned. At the United Nations, where Third World power was rising, cold war–type confrontations were replaced by new issues and actors. The growing cooperation between the superpowers on issues of international security took place on the basis of their own self-interest, as if to demonstrate that there was no need for a third party to mediate and find compromise formulas. Ironically, the non-aligned, who had consistently pressed for a superpower dialogue, began to feel that the way it had been handled by the big two had some adverse effects on their interests.

As the non-aligned had realized earlier, in the course of the negotiations for the Partial Test Ban Treaty (PTBT) and to a greater extent for the Nuclear Non-Proliferation Treaty (NPT), the superpowers largely ignored their views. They discovered too that in the superpower "strategic dialogue" the two elephants shared similar views about the role of the grass and the shrubs in the bipolar hierarchy of the international system. The NPT negotiations, which by nature encompassed all nations on earth, quickly developed into a two-sided dialogue, with the two superpowers on one side and the non-nuclear powers on the other. The superpowers negotiated with such dexterity that it has been described by one of the American negotiators as the "greatest con game of modern times."[28] The feeling of many United Nations delegates at that time was that the super-powers in their Geneva talks "had become so addicted to the club-like atmosphere of their private negotiations that they had forgotten the political arts of multilateral United Nations diplomacy."[29]

It was perhaps around this period that the non-aligned realized, as the new version of the Sri Lankan proverb suggests, that it is in the common interest of the grass to reject not just the fighting between the elephants but also their love affairs. Robert W. Tucker has pointed out that, however persistent many Third World governments had been in their criticism of the cold war, they have be-nefited from the attention they received as a result of that conflict. The cold war provided them with a psychic confirmation of independence and gave them a much needed sense of importance and worth.[30] Detente, therefore, which was reflected also in arms control efforts by the superpowers, was seen by the non-aligned already in the early 1970s as "no boon for the Third World."[31]

In sum, a comparison of non-aligned attitudes and pronouncements on dis-armament in 1961 and the late 1960s reveals how the significance of the issue declined and how the approach to it had grown more complex over the decade. The component of disarmament within the ideology of non-alignment has clearly declined "from a near pacifist crusade at the beginning of the decade to being only of secondary importance at the end of the decade."[32] This dramatic decline can be illustrated in the formulation of the final documents at the non-aligned summits. At the third conference of non-aligned heads of states in Lusaka in 1970, the term *peaceful coexistence* and the idea of general and complete dis-armament had disappeared from the agenda. Instead there was just a reference to "problems of disarmament," which have received relatively little attention. Moreover, the Lusaka Conference introduced for the first time a militaristic theme for non-alignment: "To safeguard international peace and security through the development of social, economic, political and military strength of each country."[33] With the new explicit emphasis on *military strength*, this declaration markes the end of what was once the moral and internationalist approach of the non-aligned toward disarmament issues.

THE REVIVAL OF THE NON-ALIGNED MOVEMENT

Against this background, it was all the more surprising that the non-aligned states actually recovered from their setbacks and came to life again in the sev-enties as an organized force in the international system. There seem to be two basic reasons for this revival. One is of an organizational nature, and the other involves the real character of the movement. Organizationally, the democratic nature of the United Nations allowed the Third World to become a major political force. It is only at the United Nations that the developing countries can link up together and create a force in international relations whose weight, by far, exceeds the sum of their power as individual states. As one delegate from the Third World commented on the significance of the United Nations: "This is where we little fishes can talk like whales."[34] In this regard the United Nations, which initially was established as a security instrument of the great powers, was transformed into a forum in which new states began to press their claims for changes in the international system.

But the major reason for their revival was the non-aligned shift from political to economic matters, which provided the movement with new unity and cooperation in international forums. This shift marked also the "beginning of a particularly active phase of the non-aligned movement."[35] Basically the Third World argument was that the political decolonization that had been achieved by no means entailed liberation from their compelling economic ties with the rich countries. On the contrary, they said, the gap between rich and poor countries kept widening. Gradually, from the beginning of the 1970s, the non-aligned became preoccupied with one overriding issue: the call for economic reforms on an international scale, namely the creation of a New International Economic Order (NIEO).[36] In the words of the former prime minister of Jamaica, Michael Manley: "The NIEO represents increasingly the primary focus of the Non-aligned Movement and the meeting ground that unites all members of the Third World."[37]

The politics of the NIEO cannot be understood without reference to the oil factor. There is no doubt that the dramatic success of the oil cartel of the Organization of Petroleum Exporting Countries (OPEC) gave birth to the widespread belief in the Third World that a major shift in the existing international economic order is possible. The world energy crisis created by the 1973 oil embargo and the subsequent fourfold increase in oil prices brought about the "sudden and unexpected rise of Third World economic and political power."[38] As the Brandt report on the North–South confrontation maintains, the OPEC success "marked a major turning point in North–South relations. . . . For the first time a group of countries outside the circle of the industrialized world was able to exert its own powerful economic pressure. . . . This gave the whole North–South dialogue a new impetus."[39]

The OPEC success was seen by its supporters in the Third World as the beginning of a new chapter in world history. Third World leaders, such as Michael Manley, proclaimed that OPEC along with other economic cartels "have changed the fundamental equations of economic power as decisively as did the Industrial Revolution."[40] For the purposes of our analysis it does not matter whether the expectations that were generated by OPEC have a solid basis in economic reality. The significance lies in the manner in which the oil cartel has been perceived by the Southern states and the expectations this perception has engendered into United Nations' discussions between the North and the South. Some observers regarded oil power as a source for rearmament in order to facilitate the change in international order. According to this logic, military buildup in itself may be viewed as a measure for disarmament. Authors such as

Ali Mazrui believe that "militarization" and even "nuclearization" of oil power may create new ground rules for international disarmament efforts.[41] Here, around this new theme of change in the world order, the Third World approach to disarmament was consolidated.

The NIEO declarations, which burst upon the international scene in April 1974 after the United Nations Special Session, have had a very broad scope. Hardly an area of global economic concern escaped the recommendations of the Third World for radical reform. The declarations call for a comprehensive change in the international economic order, in all crucial areas of North–South relations— trade and commodities, financial matters, science and technology, and industrialization.[42]

It is generally agreed that the new focus on the NIEO saved the movement from anticipated disintegration after the upheavals of the 1960s.[43] At the United Nations, the establishment of the NIEO has become a high-priority item on the international agenda,[44] and the North–South confrontation was added to the divisiveness in the world. The issue has dramatically affected the Third World bloc to the extent that it has been viewed as the "evolution of the Non-aligned Movement into a pressure group for the establishment of the NIEO."[45] As a result, any analysis of non-aligned behavior in the 1970s must begin with the premise that the NIEO has become the overriding issue of the movement.

THE NIEO AND DISARMAMENT

To repeat, against this background of changes within the non-aligned movement it would be simplistic and even misleading to regard the SSOD as a natural offspring of their policies since Belgrade 1961.[46] First and foremost it must be recognized that disarmament and world peace became issues of secondary importance in the new agenda of the non-aligned.

As William Sweet explains, the SSOD came about at a time "when disarmament has moved to second spot on the Third World agenda, and when the coalition favoring world disarmament shows signs of internal collapse."[47] For the Third World it was not just a change in focus. The economic dimension has introduced a new way of looking at disarmament in the first place, by completely subordinating it to the NIEO struggle. From the Third World point of view, right on the eve of the SSOD, the question of priorities never arose:

It is generally recognized that the current platform of the Southern world will continue to be the demand for a New International Economic Order. The developed world has grudgingly come to the view that whatever the merits of this demand and the chances of its realization, the NIEO will provide the main arena for interaction, be it by dialogue or confrontation between the developed and the developing world. . . . It is within this context that the UNSSOD must be viewed. . . . The primary task for Southern strategists is to postulate a credible and attainable field theory organically linking disarmament to the main collective task of the South—the New International Economic Order.[48]

The focus on disarmament during the SSOD did not modify Third World minds. This an Indian official wrote after the SSOD:

For the Third World countries the most pressing problem is the widening gap between the rich and poor nations of the world, and therefore, further economic dislocation at the international level and human decay at the national level. For most Third World countries hunger and poverty are aggravated by the pressures to divert their resources to armaments.[49]

The politics of the NIEO have changed dramatically the substance of the debates in the United Nations. Thus, disarmament has not been approached as a political issue with direct bearing on international security but rather as an instrument for the reallocation of economic resources. In their summit meeting in Colombo in 1976, the non-aligned made clear that their major preoccupation is the NIEO and that disarmament is just a means to achieve it:

The conference declared that the arms race is inconsistent with efforts aimed at achieving the New International Economic Order in view of the urgent need to divert the resources utilised for the acceleraton of the arms race towards socio-economic development, particularly of the developing countries.[50]

In their working paper submitted to the SSOD, the non-aligned reiterated, in six different references, the links between disarmament and development, concluding that the spiraling arms race is incompatible with the goal of the NIEO.[51] To be on the safe side, the non-aligned immediately made sure that possible failure in disarmament will not affect their predominant economic concerns and proclaimed that despite the link, progress in one area "should not be contingent upon progress in the other."[52]

With their influence in the General Assembly, the Third World succeeded in getting almost a universal consensus to their view on the link between disarmament and the NIEO. In the Final Document of the SSOD, adopted by consensus, this causal link was elaborated several times and was taken for granted in the opening declaration that disarmament is essential for the achievement of the NIEO. Moreover, the concept of the Comprehensive Program of Disarmament (CPD) has become in the Final Document another vehicle in the NIEO struggle. The document proclaimed explicitly that the CPD should encompass all measures that will ensure disarmament in a world "in which the international economic order is strengthened and consolidated."[53]

THE LINK BETWEEN DISARMAMENT AND DEVELOPMENT

In numerous United Nations resolutions and reports a so-called link between disarmament and development was established and, as a result, taken for granted.[54]

In light of the objectives of the NIEO this trend is understandable, but its acceptance by United Nations majorities does not make it scientifically valid. The mere fact, as stated by a United Nations study on the subject, that disarmament and development are the issues that have most preoccupied the attention of the international community since World War II[55] does not mean that these two concepts have much in common. The tremendous gap between the resources devoted to armament world-wide and those allocated to development purposes contributes to rising expectations and demands based on a link between the two. In United Nations debates it is fashionble, and indeed dramatic, to argue that the elimination of a single aircraft carrier can release funds to be used to eradicate some diseases and alleviate human sufffering in the Third World or to describe how with the cost of two stategic bombers UNESCO could launch a world-wide literacy campaign.

Soon it became apparent that the focus on the disarmament–development link within the framework of the NIEO diluted attention, in United Nations deliberations, to the security dimensions of disarmament (see Chapters 5, 6, 7). Moreover, there is a danger that United Nations deliberations and activities may create an illusion of a political–economic process that is considered by many authorities as unrealistic and unfeasible. Even United Nations officials such as Bradford Morse, the administrator of the United Nations Development Programme (UNDP), cautioned member states on the tendency to oversimplify, in his words, the linkages between disarmament and development. Practically, he said, one cannot guarantee that resources saved by disarmament among developed countries would be converted into resources to support development.[56] Moreover, one may add, experience has shown that it would be difficult to assume that the regimes of the developing countries would use this transfer of resources for economic and social purposes and not, for instance, for their own growing military programs (see Chapter 7).

The "establishment" of a link between disarmament and development by the United Nations General Assembly serves as a case study in the politicization of the secretary general's reports by the numerically powerful majority of the Third World. First the General Assembly passed in 1977 a resolution (32/88-A) that enunciated this link and called for a study on the subject. Later, the SSOD Final Document spelled out the terms of references and guidelines of the mandate of the group of experts for the study. The link was taken as a foregone conclusion: "In view of the relationship between expenditure on armaments and economic and social development. . ." In what the document called a "forward-looking and policy-oriented" study on the reallocation of resources, the mandate of the experts had determined and prejudged the outcome with specific instructions: "The study should further be made in the context of how disarmament can contribute to the establishment of the new international economic order."[57]

These guidelines followed other foregone conclusions in the document, which simply stated that there is "a close relationship between disarmament and development,'' and ''progress in the former would help greatly the realization of the latter,'' and further assertions about reallocation of resources that would bridge the economic gap between developed and developing countries.[58]

For three years (1978–1981) a group of twenty-seven governmental experts appointed by the secretary general (on the recommendation of member states) studied the relationship between disarmament and development. Their conclusions were not unexpected in light of the mandate:

This investigation suggests very strongly that the world can either continue to pursue the arms race with characteristic vigor or move consciously and with deliberate speed toward a more stable and balanced social and economic development within a more sustainable international economic and political order. It cannot do both. It must be acknowledged that the arms race and development are in a competitive relationship, particularly in terms of resources but also in the vital dimension of attitudes and perceptions.[59]

Here, in an official report by the secretary general, it is openly declared that the NIEO means change in the world order in both economic and political terms. It is not just an interpretation of linkages between disarmament and development but rather a quest for a change in world order through disarmament. The chair of the group of experts, Inga Thorsson of Sweden, reiterated the economic and political aspects of the NIEO, emphasizing the role of ''disarmament in a dynamic economic environment.''[60] It should be noted that certain members of the group of experts, those from Western countries, have submitted some reservations on the report, particularly on the paragraphs dealing with the establishing of a new international economic order.[61]

For the purposes of this analysis it is not important to establish the degree to which there is a link between disarmament and development. What matters, however, is the clear attempt to introduce biased interpretations in a policy-oriented report of the United Nations secretary general. The report amounts to promotion of a partisan ideology of the NIEO with a special emphasis on *attitudes* and *perceptions* regarding a new *political* and economic order. These conclusions should be disturbing, particularly in light of the fact that a review of the academic literature suggests that the relationship among military expenditures, economic growth, and social development in the Third World is not yet well understood. A study by Emile Benoit on ''Defence and Economic Growth in Developing Countries,'' for example, concludes that military spending can stimulate civil economic activities and that economic growth more than offsets the fact that these resources could have been put to directly productive use.

The Benoit study is admitted to be the most ambitious statistical survey undertaken on the relationship between Third World defense expenditure and economic growth. Benoit found that countries with high growth rates tended to have high defense burdens, and vice versa. His statistics suggested that defense programs directly contribute various useful inputs into civil economies in developing countries. In some cases an increase in defense expenditures by a developing country may take no resources out of civilian investment at all but even increase such investment and further contribute to development. As a result, Benoit rejects what he calls as "a strong intuitive and common-sense impression" that defense expenditures are inherently wasteful or that defense programs necessarily have adverse effects on Third World economies.[62]

The Third World campaign for a link between disarmament and development is understandable in light of the political character of disarmament debates in the United Nations. One may even agree that when arms races reach the "over-kill" level it is proper to reconsider national policies of defense expenditures. It is questionable, however, whether by subjecting the disarmament debate to NIEO politics the Third World enhances the understanding of their plight in the industrialized countries. It is hard to believe that the developed countries would be forthcoming to the transfer of resources to a group of nations committed to a radical change in the world order, especially at a time of recession and unemployment at home. Ironically, from the Third World point of view, disarmament also means less military consumption of scarce goods such as oil, bauxite, chromium, and copper and so would lead to a lowering of the demand for such goods. Several producers of these raw materials in the Third World might suffer as a result. Another aspect that is also neglected in the debate is the role of military organization and military life in some underdeveloped countries as a social institution.[63]

It is evident that many experts, even those who are known to be sympathetic to Third World economic problems, are aware of the complexities involved in reallocating resources. Gunnar Myrdal, one of the outstanding scholars on development, has pointed out:

All general and speculative theories about the relations between economic progress of underdeveloped countries and peacefulness are utterly void of true knowledge and of relevance for the problem of peace and war between countries, as well as peace or rebellion within the countries.[64]

It was recognized, a long time before North–South confrontations dominated the agenda of the United Nations, that the transfer of resources is not a panacea for international upheavals. Already in 1951 Charles Malik of Lebanon, who served also as the president of the United Nations General Assembly, concluded on the same problem: "The poor, the sick, the dispossessed, must certainly be done justice to. But to suppose that there will be peace when everybody is materially happy and comforted, is absolute nonsense."[65]

The link between disarmament and development is questionable also in light of the experience of many developing countries. Except for most Latin American countries, in all other regions in the Third World many states are devoting a larger proportion of their national budget to military expenditures than they are to health and education.[66] In contrast, the developed Western countries, including the United States, tend to spend more on health and education combined than they do for military purposes. It should be noted that, in terms of military expenditures per capita or per soldier, the oil-producing countries of the Middle East—all of which are members of the non-aligned movement—are today the top spenders in the world, providing the greatest single boost to international arms sales in the last decade.[67] Finally, the United Nations treatment of the disarmament–development link deliberately ignores other views on the morality as well as on the practicality of the linkage concept. An important school of thought in the field rejects the link as well as the whole notion of the NIEO. The NIEO, according to its critics, does not offer a more egalitarian world or more justice in international relations. They argue, contrary to what NIEO proponents suggest, that peace and prosperity in the international system is not dependent at all upon the massive transfer of resources from the North to the South.[68]

Notwithstanding all these reservations, the link between disarmament and development is treated at the United Nations as a matter of fact as an integral component of the NIEO. No wonder that the study by the group of experts was welcomed by the overwhelming majority of NIEO supporters at the United Nations. These representatives found in the report what they wanted. As one delegate from Ghana stated with satisfaction: "The report . . . has established that arms race and development are incompatible." Since we live in a world of interdependence, he continued, the reallocation of resources to the Third World is "no longer a moral issue but an inescapable international obligation." Therefore, the African delegate concludes, "Lasting peace and security can be attained through general and complete disarmament and the equitable redistribution of resources within the framework of the new international economic order."[69]

DISARMAMENT, DEVELOPMENT, AND WORLD ORDER

With the politics of the NIEO in the background, the disarmament confrontation between the South and the North became more and more identified with issues concerning world order. As Charles Maynes has explained, the NIEO is not just about the transfer of resources from industrialized countries to the Third World but rather a political struggle. The North–South confrontation is over the Third World attempt "to integrate dissatisfied powers into the central management of the international system."[70] Development, as seen in the South, is not just an economic phenomenon but rather a multitude of problems: economic, political, social, legal, and institutional.[71] Third World spokesmen at the United Nations such as Algerian Ambassador Mohammed Bedjaoui, who was elected in 1982 as a judge to the International Court of Justice, do not conceal the objectives of the NIEO: to change the international power arrangements negotiated at Yalta in 1945 between the two superpowers and the international economic arrangements based on the Bretton Woods agreement of 1944. It is a struggle to get rid of the "law of the great powers" through the establishment of a new international legal order.[72]

Essentially, the NIEO is a struggle over power in its traditional sense. The NIEO, concluded George C. Abott, is "about power, political and economic power, how to get more of it, and how to use it effectively in the pursuit of national goals."[73] The character of this power struggle was reflected also in the institutionalization of the various organs of the Third World in their campaign against the North. The new leaders of the non-aligned movement, for instance, had different views on their role and began to reject the notion that non-alignment "was created to avoid involvement in bloc politics."[74] No doubt, the new attitude marked a departure from the Nehru–Tito legacy on the "golden bridge" role of the non-aligned in war and peace matters. As a result, some writers argue, "There is as little reason to define the Non-Aligned in relation to the Cold War as there is to say that the members of the North Atlantic Treaty Organisation are the countries that catch fish around Iceland."[75] In September 1973, alluding to the Algiers summit of the non-aligned, Secretary of State Henry Kissinger spoke testily of the "alignment of the non-aligned," which was assuming in his words "the characteristics of a bloc of its own."[76]

While they reestablished their sense of solidarity around the new themes, the non-aligned began also to develop the features of a formal institution. The previous practice of rather informal summit conferences has been replaced by more structured and carefully prepared summits held on a regular basis every three years. Preparatory committees discuss and formulate the agenda of the summit meetings in advance. Usually, very lengthy documents, encompassing almost every single aspect of international affairs, are issued at the conclusion of these meetings. Since 1970, the summit meetings have had a chair, the head of state or government of the respective host country, who serves also as the coordinator and official spokesman of the movement for the following three-year period. Since 1973, the movement has had a Co-ordination Bureau, which operates on the foreign minister level, and ambassadors to the United Nations meeting at least once a year and once a month, respectively.[77] By the end of 1977, the non-aligned movement had succeeded in mobilizing most developing countries in setting up a highly structured organization and in establishing a close network of lines of communication for intensive interaction among its members.[78] Gradually the United Nations headquarters in New York became the "de facto headquarters of the non-aligned movement."[79]

The United Nations system provided a major vehicle for the non-aligned to expand and strengthen their grip over the Third World, particularly under the mantle of the Group of 77. The Group of 77 has managed to become the major actor in the United Nations system, despite the fact that they did not have headquarters, secretariat, staff, or bureau of their own.[80] Through the United Nations Conference of Trade and Development (UNCTAD), which was founded in 1964, the Group of 77 was able to coordinate the divergent interests of its members into a single platform for international action. UNCTAD had for practical purposes fulfilled the functions of a secretariat for the Group of 77 and helped to bring in to the non-aligned movement most Latin American countries.[81]

With this process of institutionalization the non-aligned movement or for our purposes the Third World bloc in the United Nations (see Table 3), was trying to exert its influence in international forums.

As radical leaders of the movement maintained, the bloc has reached a stage at which it has a definite strategy in its struggle against the "North"—the rich countries. According to this interpretation, the non-aligned have progressed "from the formulation of disconnected grievances to the definition of a combat strategy designed to transform international economic relations." At this stage, however, these spokesmen do not confine themselves to the economic arena but rather speak about a "new international order," which "embraces the political social and cultural fields annd goes beyond eliciting claims of the developing countries in the economic sphere."[82]

In adopting this combat strategy, disarmament got a special connotation in Third World parlance. When the foreign minister of Sri Lanka rose to speak on behalf of the non-aligned countries, he told the SSOD delegates:

We hold that disarmament is not only a political question, but also an integral element in the new international order, and its co-relationship with development is an extremely close and critical one. We are firmly convinced that the pursuit of disarmament is at the same time the pursuit of development by all nations. This is an aspect of disarmament that should not be minimized, misinterpreted or misunderstood. It is an integral part of the process of creating a new international order.[83]

Although the foreign minister of Sri Lanka opened by saying that disarmament is not a political problem, he meant political in a very narrow sense. His following elaborations demonstate that the corelationship between disarmament and development relate to the broader process of establishing a new international order. Interestingly enough, the spokesman of the non-aligned made it clear that his bloc strives for a new international order, not just an economic order. This approach was manifested in a meeting of scholars and officials from the Third World in New Delhi before the SSOD, where these separate strands were tied together: "Disarmament, Development and a Just World Order." Their working paper called on the Third World countries to "take initiatives for halting the arms race and changing the present structure of inequity and domination in global power relations."[84]

Disarmament, thus, when it is dealt with within the framework of development and the NIEO, means a restructuring of world power. In the words of another Third World thinker at an international seminar on disarmament sponsored by Pugwash, the developing countries "should engage in a radical movement to change the international system."[85] Others, such as Ali Mazrui, were more explicit, indicating that the Third World should rearm itself in order to achieve a "new international military order" as one of the prerequisites of the NIEO.[86] According to this point of view, disarmament means simply disarming the powerful while the Third World continues its military buildup in order to bridge the

Table 3

Third World Grouping: The Group of 77 and the Non-Aligned

Afghanistan - N,B	Ivory Coast - N
Algeria - N,CD	Jamaica - N
Angola - N	Jordan - N,B
Argentina - N,CD	Kampuchea - N,B
Bahamas	Kenya - N,CD
Bahrain - N	Kuwait - N
Barbados	Laos - N,B
Bangladesh - N	Lebanon - N,B,
Benin - N	Lesotho - N
Bhutan - N	Liberia - N,B
Bolivia - N	Libya - N,B
Botswana - N	Madagascar - N
Brazil - Nob, CD	Malawi
Burma - B,CD	Malaysia - N
Burundi - N	Maldives - N
Cape Verde - N	Mali - N
Central - N	Malta - N
African	Mauritania - N
Republic	Maurituis - N
Chad - N	Mexico - Nob, CD
Chile	Morocco - N, CD
Colombia - Nob	Mozambique - N
Comoros - N	Nepal - N,B
Congo - N	Nicaragua - N
Costa Rica - Nob	Niger - N
Cuba - N, CD	Nigeria - N,CD
Cyprus - N	Oman - N
Djibouti - N	Pakistan - N, B,CD
Dominican	Panama - N
Republic	Papua New Guinea
Ecuador - Nob	Paraguay
Egypt - N,B,CD	Peru - N,CD
El Salvador	Philippines - Nob,B
Equatorial - N	Qatar - N
Guinea	Romania - CD
Ethiopia - N,B,CD	Rwanda - N
Fiji	Saint Lucia - N
Gabon - N	Saint Vincent
Gambia - N	and the Grenadines
Ghana - N.B	Samoa
Grenada - N	Sao Tome &
Guatemala	Principe - N
Guinea - N	Saudi Arabia - N,B
Guinea- - N	Sengal - N
Bissau	Seychelles - N
Guyana - N	Sierra Leone - N
Haiti	Singapore - N
Honduras	Solomon Islands
India - N,B,CD	Somalia - N
Indonesia - N,B,CD	Sri Lanka - N,B,CD
Iran - N,B,CD	Sudan - N,B
Iraq - N,B	Suriname - N

Table 3 (continued)

Swaziland	- N	Upper Volta	- N
Syria	- N,B	Uruguay	
Thailand	- N	Venezuela	- Nob,CD
Togo		Vietnam	- N,B
Trinidad &	- N	Yemen	- N,B
Tobago		Yemen Dem.	- N
Tunisia	- N	Yugoslavia	- N, CD
Uganda	- N	Zaire	- N,CD
UN. Arab	- N	Zambia	- N
Emirates		Zimbabwe	- N
Un. Rep. of	- N		
Cameroon			
Un. Rep. of	- N		
Tanzania			

* The republic of Korea (South) and the Democratic Peoples Republic of Korea (North) are not Member States of the United Nations. However South Korea belongs to the Group of 77 and North Korea to the Non-aligned Movement. The South West African People Organization belongs to the Non-Aligned and the Palestine Liberation Organization belongs to both the Non-Aligned and the Group of 77. Burma, a participant at the conference in Bandung (1955) and a founding father of the Non-Aligned, withdrew from the movement in 1979. China participated in the Bandung conference but did not join later the non-aligned movement for the Group of 77.

Legend:

Group of 77 - The list of the members in the Group of 77 is seldom published but it is available at the Hammarskjold Library at UN Headquarters in New York.

N - The Non-Aligned movement. Its Conference of Foreign Ministers held in February 1981 at New Delhi, India, drew 90 member states of the UN, one state which is an observer state at the UN and two liberation organizations. Seven states attended as observers (Nob). (See UN Document A/36/116, 6 March, 1981).

B - Bandung, Indonesia. (a second conference was never consummated). A total of 28 states attended (in addition to the states listed, China, Turkey, Japan and South Vietnam also participated).

CD - Members in the Committee on Disarmament in Geneva. The listed states are members of the Group of 21 non-aligned and independent states in the CD (Romania is not member of the Group since it joined the CCD under the East-West packages). Sweden which is not member of the Group of 77 is a member of Group of 21.

gap. The positions of Third World countries in the United Nations on issues such as nuclear non-proliferation and the conventional arms race (Chapters 6, 7) demonstrate that these militant views reflect a prevailing attitude among the developing countries.

As a correspondent at the United Nations concluded, disarmament conferences are viewed by the non-aligned as "a bargaining chip in the larger context of the North–South dialogue."[87] By giving the United Nations a larger voice in disarmament, the Third World hoped to be able to achieve greater influence in world affairs toward achieving their ultimate goal of a new international order.

NOTES

1. "Elephant Superpowers Crush Our Grass." Interview with A.C.S. Hameed, foreign minister of Sri Lanka, *Disarmament Times*, June 6, 1978. It is interesting that there are different attributions and different versions of the proverb about the elephants and the grass. One publication attributes the proverb to African origin and gives a shorter version: "when two elephants fight it is the grass that suffers." See Cecil V. Crabb, Jr., *The Elephants and the Grass—A Study of Non-Alignment* (New York: Praeger Publishers, 1965), p. 9. This version fits the cold war's struggles of the superpowers. However, the more sophisticated version of 1978 by the Sri Lankan foreign minister expressed the growing resentment in the Third World not only for the competition between the superpowers but also for their love affairs (e.g. arms control agreements).

2. GAOR, A/S-10/PV.4, May 25, 1978, p. 7.

3. Leslie Wolf-Phillips et al., *Why 'Third World'?* Third World Foundation Monograph, no. 7 (London: Third World Foundation, 1980).

4. Michael Todaro, *Economics for a Developing World* (New York: Longman, 1977), pp. xix, 7. See also Irving Louis Horowitz, *Three Worlds of Development* (London: Oxford University Press, 1966); J.D.B. Miller, *The Politics of the Third World* (London: Oxford University Press, 1965); M. S. Rajan, "Non-Alignment: The Dichotomy Between Theory and Practice in Perspective," *Indian Quarterly* 36, no. 1 (January–March 1980): 44–45.

5. Peter Willetts, *The Non-Aligned Movement: The Origins of the Third World Alliance* (London: Frances Pinter, 1978), p. 12.

6. Robert A. Mortimer, *The Third World Coalition in International Politics* (New York: Praeger Publishers, 1980), pp. 10–12.

7. Ibid., p. 14.

8. U.S. Arms Control and Disarmament Agency, *Documents on Disarmament 1961* (Washington, D.C.: ACDA, 1962), p. 381.

9. Willetts, *The Non-Aligned*, p. 3. Willetts rejects the prevailing contention that Bandung was a forerunner of the non-aligned conferences.

10. David Kimche, *The Afro-Asian Movement Ideology and Foreign Policy of the Third World* (Jerusalem: Israel University Press, 1973), p. 97.

11. Presidents Sukarno and Keta went to the United States, and President Nkrumah and Prime Minister Nehru went to the Soviet Union. Ibid., p. 111 n.53.

12. Crabb, *The Elephants*, p. 101.

13. Ibid., p. 102.

14. See William Epstein, "Why a Special Session on Disarmament," *Transnational*

Perspectives (Geneva) 4, nos. 1–2 (1978); Homer A. Jack, "A UN General Assembly Special Session on Disarmament to Break the World Disarmament Conference Stalemate," *Bulletin of Peace Proposals* (Oslo) 8, no. 1 (1979): 56–59; Michael J. Sullivan III, "The Outlook for the UN Special Session on Disarmament," in *Negotiating Security— An Arms Control Reader*, ed. William H. Kincade and Jeffrey D. Porro (Washington, D.C.: Carnegie Endowment for International Peace, 1979), pp. 237–45 (appeared before an *Arms Control Today*, 1978).

15. GAOR, A/S-10/PV.27, July 6, 1978, P. 75.

16. Mortimer, *The Third World*, p. 116.

17. Jane Rosen, "How the Third World Runs the UN," *New York Times Magazine*, December 16, 1979, p. 39.

18. Kimche, *The Afro-Asian*, p. 115.

19. Crabb, *The Elephants*, p. 210.

20. Kimche, *The Afro-Asian*, pp. 115–16.

21. Willetts, *The Non-Aligned*, p. 14.

22. G. H. Jansen, *Afro-Asia and Non-Alignment* (London: Faber and Faber, 1966), chaps. 17–18.

23. Ashok Kapur, *International Nuclear Proliferation* (New York: Praeger Publishers, 1979), p. 308.

24. Hanspeter Neuhold, "Permament Neutrality and Non-Alignment: Similarities and Differences," *Indian Quarterly* 35, no. 3 (July 1979): 285–308.

25. Kimche, *The Afro-Asian*, p. 260.

26. Willetts, *The Non-Aligned*, pp. 31–36.

27. Neuhold, "Permament Neutrality," p. 290.

28. Epstein, *The Last Chance*, p. 118.

29. David A. Kay, ed., *The New Nations in the United Nations 1960–1967* (New York: Columbia University Press, 1970), p. 127.

30. Tucker, *The Inequality of Nations*, p. 45.

31. Mortimer, *The Third World*, p. 40.

32. Willetts, *The Non-Aligned*, p. 25.

33. Third Conference of Heads of State or Government of Non-Aligned Countries: Lusaka Declaration on Peace, Independence, Development, Co-operation and Democratization of International Relations, Lusaka, September 8–10, 1970, in *The Third World Without Superpowers: The Collected Documents of the Non-Aligned Countries*, ed. Odette Jankowitsch and Karl P. Sauvant, vol. 2 (New York: Oceana Publications, 1978), p. 83.

34. Rosen, "How the Third World Runs the UN," p. 70.

35. Jankowitsch and Sauvant, *The Third World*, p. xi.

36. For an analytical review of the pertinent literature, see Robert M. Cox, "Ideologies and the New International Economic Order: Reflection on Some Recent Literature," *International Organization* 33, no. 2 (Spring 1979).

37. Michael Manley, "Third World Under Challenge: The Politics of Affirmation," *Third World Quarterly* 2, no. 1 (January 1980):31.

38. Ervin Laszlo, Robert Baker, Jr., Elliott Eisenberg, and Venkata Raman, *The Objectives of the New International Economic Order* (New York: Pergamon Press, 1978), p. xix. Robert Mortimer pointed out that in fact it was OPEC that ushered in NIEO politics, providing a model and symbol of Third World assertion. See *The Third World*, p. 3. See also Statement by the Representative of Somalia at the UN Seventh Special

Session of the GA.A., GAOR, A/PV.234, p. 37, and Manley, "Third World Under Challenge."

39. Independent Commission on International Development Issues (Willy Brandt, Chairman), *North–South: A Programme for Survival* (London: Pan Books, 1980), p. 44.

40. *New York Times*, October 13, 1975.

41. Ali Mazrui, "The Barrel of the Gun and the Barrel of Oil in the North–South Equation," *World Order Models Projects* (New York: Institute for World Order), no. 5 (1978): 15–16, 24.

42. See the Charter of Economic Rights and Duties of States, GAOR, Res. 3281 (XXIX), December 12, 1974. For approaches in favor of the NIEO, see Khadija Hag, ed., *Dialogue for a New Order* (New York: Pergamon Press, 1980).

43. Neuhold, "Permament Neutrality," p. 291, John Conyers speaks about three stages of the non-aligned: (1) the pursuit of world peace in a cold war. At this stage the prevention of world conflagration through nuclear war was at the very heart of non-alignment; (2) the process of decolonization and the struggle for national liberation; and (3) the shift toward the preoccupation with the redistribution of world resources. See John Conyers, "Non-Alignment and the Afro-Asian People," in *The Non-aligned Movement in World Politics*, ed. A. W. Singham (Wesport, Conn.: Lawrance Hill, 1977), p. 24.

44. Karl P. Sauvant, "The New International Economic Order: Toward Structural Changes or a More Tolerable Status Quo," in *U.S. Policy in International Institutions, Defining Reasonable Options in an Unreasonable World*, ed. Seymour Maxwell Finger and Joseph R. Harbert (Boulder, Colo.: Westview Press, 1978), p. 125.

45. Ibid., p. 143 n.1.

46. This interpretation can be found in the articles already mentioned in note 4 and also in Louis B. Sohn, "Disarmament at the Crossroads," *International Security* 2, no. 4 (Spring 1978): 4–31; Homer A. Jack, "A Special Session of the UN General Assembly Devoted to Disarmament," *Review of International Affairs* (Belgrade) (June 20, 1976); the series of articles on the SSOD in the *Bulletin of the Atomic Scientists* (April 1978). Others have focused on the American approach to the SSOD without pointing out the changes that took place in the Third World position: Abraham Bargman, "Nuclear Arms Control: A New US Strategy at the United Nations," in *U.S. Policy in International Institutions*, ed. Seymour Maxwell Finger and Joseph R. Harbert (Boulder, Colo.: Westview Press, 1978), pp. 28–39; Bargman, "Nuclear Diplomacy," in *The Changing United Nations: Options for the United States*, ed. David A. Kay (New York: Academy of Political Science, 1977), pp. 159–69; Lincoln P. Bloomfield and Harlan Cleveland, "A Strategy for the United States," *International Security* 2, no. 4 (Spring 1978): 32–55.

47. William Sweet, "Delhi: A Third World Overture," *The Nation* (May 27, 1978): 629.

48. Tarig Osman Hyder, "Inchoate Aspirations for World Order Change," *International Security* 2, no. 4 (Spring 1978): 56–57. Hyder was a director in the Pakistan Ministry of Foreign Affairs.

49. M. A. Husain, "Third World and Disarmament: Shadow and Substance," *Third World Quarterly* 2, no. 1 (January 1980): 76. Husain has served as ambassador of India in various capitals.

50. From the Political Declaration (Chapter XVII), adopted at the Fifth Non-Aligned Summit Conference, Colombo, August 16–19, 1976. In GAOR, Tenth Special Session, Supplement No. 1 (A/S-10/1), Vol. III, 1978, A/AC.187.30, p. 51.

51. "Non-Aligned Working Documents," A/AC.187/55, p. 5, and add. 1, p. 3, in GAOR, Tenth Special Session, Vol. IV.

52. Ibid.

53. GAOR, SSOD Final Document, Tenth Special Session, Supplement No. 4, A/S-10/4, para. 109.

54. For a list of United Nations documents on the relationship between disarmament and development, see GAOR, "Report of the Ad Hoc Group on the Relationship Between Disarmament and Development" (Appendix II), A/S-10/9, April 5, 1978.

55. Report of the Secretary General, "Study on the Relationship Between Disarmament and Development," GAOR, A/36/356, October 5, 1981, para. 329.

56. GAOR, A/S-10/AC.1/PV.5, June 9, 1978, p. 7.

57. GAOR, SSOD Final Document, para. 95.

58. Ibid., para. 35.

59. "Study on the Relationship Between Disarmament and Development," para. 391.

60. GAOR, A/C.1/36/PV.5, October 20, 1981, p. 36.

61. "Reservations expressed by some experts on the study," GAOR, "Study on the Relationship Between Disarmament and Development," Apendix II, pp. 187–95.

62. Emile Benoit, *Defence and Economic Growth in Developing Countries* (Lexington, Mass.: Lexington Books, 1973), pp. 16–17, and the whole introduction, pp. 1–24. For comments and criticism on Benoit's study, see Nicole Ball and Milton Leitenberg, "Disarmament and Development: Their Interrelationship," *Bulletin of Peace Proposals* 10, no. 3 (1979): 251–52.

63. SIPRI, *World Armament and Disarmament, SIPRI Yearbook 1978* (London: Taylor & Francis, 1978), p. 310.

64. Gunnar Myrdal, quoted in Bert V. A. Roling, *Disarmament and Development: The Perspective of Security* (Memo) (Rotterdam: Foundation for Reshaping the International Order [RIO], 1979), p. 66.

65. *United Nations Bulletin*, May 1, 1951, p. 459.

66. The best sources for comparing social, economic, and military indicators are the annual publications by Ruth Leger Sivard, *World Military and Social Expenditures 1981* (Leesburg, Va.: World Priorities, 1981). See also Table 5 in Chapter 7.

67. Avi Beker, "The Oil–Arms Connection: Fueling the Arms Race," *Armed Forces and Society* 8, no. 3 (Spring 1982): 419–42.

68. See P. T. Bauer and B. S. Yamey, "East–West/North–South: Peace and Prosperity?" *Commentary* (September 1980); Bauer and Yamey, "Against the New Economic Order," *Commentary* (April 1977); Tucker, *The Inequality of Nations*; P. T. Bauer, *Poverty, Poor Countries and Perverted Economies* (Cambridge: Harvard University Press, 1981).

69. GAOR, A/C.1/36/PV.18, October 29, 1981. The representative of Cuba was even more explicit in his comments on the study: "The struggle for peace, detente, the cessation of the arms race and disarmament are inseparable parts of a New International Economic Order." A/C.1/36/PV.4, October 27, 1981.

70. Charles William Maynes, "A UN Policy for the Next Administration," *Foreign Affairs* 54 (Winter 1975–1976/July 1976): 807–8.

71. Mohammed Bedjaoui, *Toward a New International Economic Order*, A UNESCO Publication (New York: Holmes & Meier Publishers, 1979), p. 75. Bedjaoui was the Algerian ambassador to the United Nations and was elected in 1982 to serve in the International Court of Justice. According to Bedjaoui, already in 1973 the non-aligned

countries vigorously maintained that the East–West ideological rivalry is superposed by the "harsher and more obvious reality of the major contradiction between the South and the North." Ibid., p. 34.

72. Ibid., pp. 59–60, 97.

73. George C. Abott, "The NIEO: What Went Wrong," *Co-Existence* (April 1978): 11.

74. Manley, "Third World Under Challenge," p. 29.

75. Willetts, *The Non-Aligned*, p. 44.

76. *Department of State Bulletin* 69, no. 1790, October 15, 1973, p. 470.

77. On the institutionalization process, see Willetts, *The Non-Aligned*, pp. 36–43; Neuhold, "Permanent Neutrality," pp. 291–92; and Jankowitsch and Sauvant, *The Third World*, introduction.

78. Jankowitsch and Sauvant, *The Third World*, vol. 1, p. 1.

79. Mortimer, *The Third World*, p. 93.

80. Ibid., pp. 74–75.

81. Ibid., pp. 10–25. Peter Willetts in his comprehensive and quantitative study on non-aligned behavior says that from the beginning the denials by the non-aligned that they were forming a third bloc, though sincerely made at that time, were not valid. As a matter of fact, he argues, already in Belgrade in 1961, "They were setting up an informal, non-military alliance." All the more so is the case in the seventies, when the non-aligned developed the features of a formal institution. Since 1972 the members themselves have recognized the change by increasingly referring to the "Non-Aligned Movement." Willetts, *The Non-Aligned*, pp. 224, 44.

82. Indriss Jazairy, adviser to the president of the Republic of Algeria, in *Towards a New International Order* (Report on the Joint Meeting of the Club of Rome and the International Ocean Institute, Algiers, October 25–28, 1976).

83. GAOR, A/S-10/PV.4, May 25, 1978, p. 7.

84. "Disarmament, Development and a Just World Order," the International Workshop on Disarmament, New Delhi, March 27–31, 1978, sponsored by the Center for the Study of Developing Societies, Delhi. For the text, see *Bulletin of Peace Proposals* 3 (1978): 278–82.

85. El Sayed Yassin, "International Stratification as an Impediment to Disarmament," in *New Directions in Disarmament*, ed. William Epstein and Bernard T. Feld (New York: Praeger Publishers, 1981), p. 112.

86. Mazrui, "The Barrel of the Gun," p. 24.

87. Louis Wiznitzer, "Feeling of Pessimism Grips UN Disarmament Session," *Christian Science Monitor*, June 7, 1978.

5

The Challenge to Bipolarity, Deterrence, and SALT

The myth that some countries are more responsible than others and that so long as nuclear weapons remain in the hands of a few the safety of the world can be assured through a balance of terror has also to be categorically rejected.[1]

Representative of India, October 1980

The concept of balance of power... is a totally negative and counter-productive concept that also was against all concepts of the United Nations era.[2]

President Kyprianou of Cyprus

As soon as disarmament became an important element in the NIEO strategy, the Third World began to use disarmament debates at the United Nations as a major platform for challenging the existing world order. From the North–South vantage point, superpower management of international nuclear deterrence was taken as a barrier on the way to their new international order. In their opposition to existing hierarchies in the world and to the discriminatory distribution of power and the growing economic gap, they challenged the right and capability of the superpowers to manage international and regional security. At the United Nations, the Third World was questioning the notion, implied sometimes in the superpowers' actions and statements, that what is good for Soviet–American interests is good for world order. With that in mind, they started to tackle the rationale of superpowers' strategic deterrence.

United Nations deliberations on disarmament provide, as in the early days of the organization, an arena for "shadowboxing": the parties debate measures of disarmament, but in effect they mean to make statements on how they envisage international order. In the late 1940s and early 1950s, the debate was mainly between the superpowers and centered on issues of national sovereignty, control and inspection by an international authority, or even at times the idea of world government (Chapter 2). Since the 1970s disarmament has been viewed, mainly by the Third World, as an instrument for reforming the international order by means of a redistribution of world power. It remains questionable, however, whether the NIEO, even theoretically, means a transformation of the principles of power and order in the current nation-state system.

NUCLEAR DETERRENCE AND SALT

Third World spokesmen are often scathing in their criticism of nuclear deterrence theories and challenge the wisdom and responsibility of the practitioners—the superpowers. Since the end of World War II, nuclear deterrence between the superpowers has gradually become the mainstay of international peace and security. As the Stockholm International Peace Research Institute defines it, deterrence is a strategic policy that hinders or discourages other nations by means of credible threat.[3] This regime of deterrence is based on the status quo between the United States and the Soviet Union in the field of military power, primarily nuclear weapons. The heart of this regime, explains Michael Mandelbaum, is the strategic nuclear balance in a bipolar world in which "the superpowers act as distinct centers in the international system around which lesser states cluster." In this regime, "the two giants have common distinctive rights and privileges that they exercise competitively but they also collude with each other to maintain."[4] Criticism of superpowers' deterrence, in this respect, is directed mainly against the uneven, rank-ordered distribution of nuclear might creating hierarchy in international relations.

The developing countries criticize both aspects of nuclear deterrence: its premise of stability, and its exclusiveness, which justified the monopoly of nuclear weapons in the hands of a few. Critics raise doubts about the stability of nuclear deterrence in light of the stringent requirements to maintain it. A major target of the critics were the agreements negotiated in the Strategic Arms Limitations Talks (SALT), which became the central component of the equilibrium in the nuclear deterrence between the superpowers.[5]

SALT, more than anything else, epitomizes the basic strategic rationale of the superpowers "in the preservation of credible deterrence at a lower level of effort for both sides."[6] It has codified, as Mandelbaum explains, the three principal tenets of the equilibrium between the stategic nuclear forces of the United States and the Soviet Union.[7] The first element is the doctrine of mutual assured destruction (MAD), which exposes the civilian population in both countries to nuclear attacks. Second, by leaving each side with enormous strategic arsenals, SALT ratified another important element of the nuclear equilibrium: high force levels. Finally, the third characteristic of the nuclear deterrence between the superpowers is the principle of equality, which was a hallmark of the 1974 Vladivostok protocol. Later, in the course of the campaign launched by the administration of President Carter, there would be an official announcement on the "evolution from an earlier period of American strategic supremacy to an era of stable strategic equivalence."[8]

This is precisely why the framework of the SALT agreements and negotiations became central to the confrontation between the Third World and the superpowers. SALT has epitomized the approach* which "explicitly emphasizes the unique political status to be derived from nuclear weapons."[9] According to this view, the United States and the Soviet Union are, in effect, using their nuclear weapons capabilities to dominate the existing political hierarchy in the international system. This approach asserts that the two superpowers maintain their maximum reliance upon nuclear weapons in order to maintain their supreme status of great power.

It was agreed among observers that the non-aligned, in initiating the SSOD in 1979, were anxious to dramatize the relationship of the arms race to economic development. Their specific demand, in order to release resources for the NIEO, was that the superpowers should put a ceiling on their nuclear arsenals.[10] As pointed out by Louis Rene Beres, the objectives of SALT and the SSOD were, therefore, far from congruent. SALT was concerned mainly with the stabilization of mutual nuclear deterrence between the superpowers and therefore excluded general disarmament plans, which were aimed at a radical redistribution of global power. The non-aligned, the initiators of the session, were looking for disarmament measures far beyond SALT II, whereas the superpowers shared a commitment, albeit tacit, "to the extant distribution of global power—that is, to continuing their present bi-polar dominance of the planet."[11]

As reported by the *United Nations and Disarmament Yearbook*, SALT was among the issues to receive the greatest attention in the course of the SSOD. The statements made in that regard ranged from expressions of confidence in the rapid and successful conclusion of the ongoing negotiations to those of dissatisfaction and disappointment that the agreement had not yet been reached.[12] It was clear, however, that the United States and the Soviet Union would reject "any outside interference" in their bilateral talks and would continue to argue that since they have "global responsibilities" they alone would decide "how and when to limit the nuclear arms race."[13] The superpowers managed to fend off all phrases in the draft Final Document on SALT that they felt constituted outside pressure or intrusion. The outcome was another ambiguous compromise expressing the need for a SALT agreement without setting any specific conditions and deadlines.

CRITICIZING NUCLEAR DETERRENCE DOCTRINES

In numerous statements in the United Nations, representatives of the Third World have rejected the notion that nuclear weapons are stabilizing factors that

---

* This approach is often referred to as the "High Posture Doctrine," which is elaborated in the next chapter.

help to moderate international conflicts. In their working paper to the SSOD, the non-aligned countries stated that the arms race "is both the cause and result of great Power rivalry," and therefore it "impedes the realization of the objectives of the United Nations Charter." As shown in Chapter 2, this was not necessarily the view of the founding fathers of the United Nations on the relationship among the arms race, war, and the security system of the Charter.

For the non-aligned the link was clear and simple: the arms race is responsible for "jeopardizing the peace and security of all states" and by itself is a "stimulating factor for the persistence of international tension and conflicts in various regions of the world."[14] This was also at variance with the prevailing approach in the aftermath of World War II and in sharp contrast to the premise of the arms control process, in particular the SALT agreements, which envisaged competition between the superpowers as one aspect of their nuclear deterrence (see Appendix I). With their parliamentary power in the General Assembly the developing countries insisted upon including in the Final Document of the SSOD specific criticism of the premises of superpowers nuclear deterrence: "Enduring international peace and security cannot be built on the accumulation of weaponry by military alliances nor be sustained by a precarious balance of deterrence or doctrines of strategic superiority."[15]

The non-aligned were not satisfied with what they regarded as the limited reference to nuclear disarmament in the Final Document. Their spokesman, the representative of Sri Lanka, rejected the "theory of mutual nuclear deterrence," which provides for the security of the great powers and the rest of the nations of the world.[16] The prime minister of India, Morarji Desai, stated that nuclear deterrence failed to end the arms race and rather stimulated competition.[17]

The debate on the validity and stability of nuclear deterrence has intensified since the SSOD of 1978. Later, in 1980, it would take on official form as a United Nations study on nuclear strategy that would raise serious doubts about deterrence theories (see below in this chapter). At the United Nations General Assemblies, in the plenary and in the First Committee, or in the Disarmament Commission and in the Geneva Committee on Disarmament, similar points are raised time and again. In 1981, for the first time in the history of the disarmament negotiating forum in Geneva, the CD report to the United Nations General Assembly incorporated several paragraphs of forthright criticism of doctrines of nuclear deterrence made on behalf of the Group of 21 non-aligned states in the CD.[18]

Sometimes American allies speak on behalf of the concept of nuclear deterrence as a necessary evil in the global confrontation. Japan, for instance, explained that particularly in periods of increased international tension, such as after the Soviet invasion of Afghanistan, the "stabilized system" of nuclear deterrence is of ever-increasing importance as a factor to contain the further spreading of such tension.[19] Even a country like Ireland, not a member of a military alliance and a staunch proponent of disarmament at the United Nations, called for a realistic approach toward the issue of nuclear deterrence, including the notion of the use of nuclear weapons that is central to the logic of some strategic doctrines.[20]

It is interesting that although nuclear deterrence involves both superpowers, only the United States found it necessary to defend the concept. The Soviets could perhaps ignore the criticism since they enjoy a permanent advantage over the West in disarmament debates in the United Nations. As in the case of the North–South economic debate, the Soviets manage to remain on the sidelines, leaving the industrialized West alone against the Third World majority in the General Assembly and the CD (see below). Since the Soviets do not regard the attack on nuclear deterrence as implicating their role as the other superpower, the United States is alone in defending the system of global nuclear deterrence (other Western diplomats restrict their remarks to regional nuclear deterrence).

In the first major speech on arms control and disarmament of the Reagan administration, the U.S. representative to the CD, speaking in the summer of 1981, devoted most of his speech to many aspects of his country's strategic rivalry with the Soviet Union. However, in light of Third World criticism of the notion of nuclear deterrence, Ambassador Floweree felt it necessary to make a special comment, somewhat philosophically, in defense of deterrence. Floweree rejected the contention that deterrence is an "abhorrent doctrine" and pointed out that many nations and groups of nations, nuclear and non-nuclear alike, including even neutral countries, are practicing deterrence in one form or another. Deterrence, the U.S. representative concluded, is an integral part of the nation-state system that exists in the world today, and the adoption of a high moral tone in preaching about the evils of deterrence "may be satisfying to the psyche, but it doesn't get us anywhere."[21]

REJECTING THE SUPERPOWERS' BALANCE OF POWER

In various ways Third World countries challenge the assertion quite often implied by the superpowers in the 1960s and 1970s that they are "responsible managers of the affairs of international society as a whole."[22] According to this view, existing hierarchies in international relations are desirable and superpower hegemony vis-à-vis the rest of the world is necessary to maintain global stability. As Hedley Bull wrote, the concept of a great power has always had normative as well as positive connotations. A great power is therefore recognized in the front rank of military might but also is regarded, by itself and by other members of the international community, as having special rights and duties.

In their attack on the current regime, the Third World nations would dismiss everything that represents the international balance of power, its balance of terror, its structure of military blocs and alliances, and, above all, the right and re-sponsibility of the superpowers to manage international affairs. A resolution adopted by the non-aligned foreign ministers participating in the SSOD said the following: "peace, security and the relaxation of tensions cannot be based on the policy of the so-called balance of power, on the division into blocs and on the arms race."[23]

Third World delegates argue that the "balance of power" is "inherently unstable" and cannot provide security on a lasting basis; it also causes the diversion of resources from what they regard as more "productive and urgent" objectives.[24] Even moderate members of the non-aligned join the parade of criticism terming the existing balance of terror as a "false kind of peace and tranquility" and warning of the "tragic process of collective self-deception" that brought about the reliance on these arrangements.[25] Typical is the reaction of Cyprus, itself a victim of the collapse of a delicate balance of power that led to foreign invasion and partition of the island, which injects a new interpretation of the concept of balance of power in the United Nations Charter:

The concept of balance of power...is a totally negative and counter-productive concept that also runs against all concepts of the United Nations era, and to the principles and purposes of the Charter of the United Nations....The concept of balance of power has no place in our present day interdependent world of the United Nations and in a nuclear age.[26]

The intimate link between the process of disarmament, as envisaged by the Third World, and world order can be illustrated in their attitudes toward the idea of "superpower responsibility." For Third World theoreticians and delegates, the superpowers have no right and lack legitimacy for a responsible management of international affairs. In the words of the representative of India in 1978: "It would be unacceptable at least to my Government, to be told that nuclear weapons are safe only in the hands of the five present nuclear States, since we cannot accept the obvious implication that some States are more responsible than others."[27]

An interesting exchange took place during the 1978 SSOD between American Ambassador Andrew Young, who was considered to be a leading supporter of Third World nations, and the representative of Pakistan. The issue was, again, over the credentials of superpowers vis-à-vis Third World governments in responsible behavior. Addressing himself to the perils of nuclear proliferation, Ambassador Young, early in the debate in the SSOD Ad Hoc Committee, commented on the efforts of the U.S. administration to minimize the use of highly enriched uranium (HEU) in research reactors because of the fear that this material and sensitive technologies may come into the hands of "irresponsible Governments or terrorists."[28] Referring to Andrew Young as "our eminent friend and colleague," the representative of Pakistan replied in a way that underscored the gap between the nations on the issue of international responsibility:

Leaving aside this question of Governments and terrorists, who is to determine whether a government is responsible or not? At various moments in history, various Governments have committed actions which history has judged as irresponsible or worse. No individual State, however powerful, can set itself up as judge of the credentials of other sovereign states.[29]

THE CHARTER AND THE BALANCE OF POWER

The assault on the concepts of balance of power and balance of terror as well as on the superpowers' ability to manage international affairs cannot be dismissed as just another exercise of Third World rhetoric. This confrontation has immediate effects on the substance of disarmament debates at the United Nations, and, more important, its implication on world order amounts to an attempt to rewrite some fundamental provisions in the Charter of the United Nations. From the point of view of the Charter, disarmament matters cannot be dealt with within the framework of the NIEO. The Charter is to a very large extent a multilateral treaty dedicated to maintain the status quo of the postwar international order and balance of power. In providing special responsibilities and privileges to the great powers, the Charter exempts them from some of the restrictions upon sovereignty that ordinary states theoretically accepted in ratifying it. The politics of NIEO and its manifestations in disarmament debates mark a departure from the provisions of the Charter and should, therefore, be evaluated in terms of what the Charter was initially intended to be and not in terms of what the United Nations became under Third World stewardship.

From the beginning, the United Nations system that emerged in 1945 was based on a mixture of "collective security" (see also Chapter 2) and "balance of power."[30] Despite the affirmation of the "equal rights... of nations large and small" and the pledge to respect the "sovereign equality" of all member states, the Charter has practically conferred exclusive power and almost unlimited discretion upon the Security Council, which reflected the collective hegemony of the great powers in the postwar world. In this respect the Charter simply registered the world power relations. In the words of Robert Tucker, "The chief difference between the traditional balance-of-power system and the system of the charter is that the latter sought to make explicit and to legitimize what the former left rather obscure and never quite dared to legitimize."[31]

The Charter reflected the notion of the Big Five unity in which the great powers were intended to exercise their collective hegemony, a hegemony President Roosevelt insistently identified as "trusteeship" or the "Five Policemen." In light of the Charter provisions, Inis Claude concludes that there is an element of truth in the accusation that the Big Five unity is just a cynical device of an international oligarchy establishing the great powers as global dictators.[32] According to this interpretation, the veto right of the big powers is a "weighting device" that acknowledges the inequality of states by providing a special status to the most powerful and important states in the international organization. Inis Claude agrees therefore with other scholars who view Article 2, paragraph 1, of the Charter, speaking on "sovereign equality" of member states, as clearly "a myth."[33]

In addition to being deliberately weak and vague on disarmament, the United Nations Charter is, thus, a document aimed to preserve a particular structure of

balance of power in the international system. The U.S. secretary of state at the
time, Cordell Hull, explained that the notion of the Big Five unity was central
to the world order envisaged by the founding fathers of the United Nations.
Without it there would be a disaster, but, he added, "no machinery, as such,
can produce this essential harmony and unity."[34] For this reason, the right of
veto in the Security Council, which is so much criticized as unjust and unequal,
should be viewed not so much as a measure of great-power dictatorship over
the rest of the world "as a factor injected into the relationship of the great powers
among themselves."[35] This is exactly what balance of power is about: a device
to protect superpower interest and at the same time to secure the stability of the
system as a whole. It is understandable, therefore, why Claude distinguishes
between the collective security system of the Charter and the pure theory of
collective security. In the Charter the recognition of the interests of the great
powers is essential for its version of collective security.[36]

In essence the NIEO is not as much a call for a new system of international
order as it is a demand for a change in the balance of power. As Robert Tucker
elaborates in his essay on *The Inequality of Nations*, the NIEO does not envisage
a transformation of the international system. The system will remain unchanged
because the role and importance of the state will remain as central as it was in
the past and even will take on ever greater significance. The demand for a more
equitable international system, explains Tucker, is in no way found to contradict
an insistence upon the state's sovereign independence. To the contrary: "the
state's sovereign independence—the essence of its equality in both the old system
and the new—is largely identified with the right of self-help to defend the
collective's vital and, of course, legitimate interests."[37]

In this respect the North–South confrontation on disarmament is completely
different from the earlier debates in the United Nations between East and West.
As shown in Chapter 2, the Baruch Plan of 1946 was a sweeping proposal for
the dilution of national sovereignty for the sake of a supranational government.
The plan marked a major departure from the vision and arrangements of the
United Nations Charter. In order to achieve nuclear disarmament, the Americans
called for a revision in world order through the establishment of an international
authority at the expense of national sovereignty. The idea to abolish the veto
power was also a measure to allow the supranational organ to impose sanctions
on member states. Moreover, the control measures in the Baruch Plan meant
foreign inspection and interference within the territory of independent states, an
idea that the Soviets found "incompatible with state sovereignty."

In the North–South confrontation on disarmament in the 1970s, the focus was
on a completely different dimension of the international order. This time the
Third World proposed not a form of world government to implement disarmament
measures but rather a change in the international balance of power through the
disarmament of the powerful. As Robert Tucker points out, in the call for NIEO
Western observers may find a contradiction between the emphasis on interdependence, which requires a more internationalist system, and the growing in-

sistence upon the state's undiminished sovereignty: "Interdependence is not seen as a means for drawing the sharp teeth of sovereignty but as an opportunity for obtaining maximum concessions from those states that possess a disproportionate share of the world's wealth and power."[38]

The NIEO, as can be seen in various United Nations and non-aligned declarations, does not aim to develop an interdependent world system that would restrict the freedom of action by the member states. The NIEO is rather identified with increasing emphasis of the "full" and "permanent" sovereignty of the developing states. From its inception, the NIEO was meant to strengthen the sovereignty of Third World nations. The major document of the NIEO—the Charter of Economic Rights and Duties—adopted in December 1974, makes it clear that the principal of sovereignty will govern "economic as well as political and other relations among States."[39] In this respect the NIEO is a far cry from the notion of an international authority that would supervise a universal disarmament process. To the contrary, the NIEO is a demand made by states on behalf of the state system in order to challenge the global status quo as registered and legitimized by the United Nations' Charter. Disarmament as envisaged within the framework of the NIEO is a vehicle to alter the balance of power in the international system with a view to be rid of the "law of the great powers" (see Chapter 4).

UNITED NATIONS OFFICIAL DOCUMENTS ON SUPERPOWERS' DETERRENCE

Gradually, with their growing influence and determination, the Third World nations could inject their observations on disarmament and international order into official reports of the United Nations' secretary general. In a report entitled "Comprehensive Study on Nuclear Weapons," the secretary general, with the assistance of governmental experts, adopted the critical view of the Third World on the nuclear arms race and the deterrence doctrines.[40]

The study, made at the behest of the 1978 General Assembly, traces the development of nuclear weapons capability from its beginning. Typically, the General Assembly resolution requested the secretary general, with the assistance of qualified experts, to study the implications for international security of "the doctrines of deterrence and other theories concerning nuclear weapons."[41] It was the first time that the United Nations as such was ordered by an overwhelming majority of its members to take a stand on the central issue of superpowers' nuclear deterrence.

It is interesting that twelve years earlier the United Nations issued a study on nuclear weapons that, unlike its successor, did not take issue with the concept of nuclear deterrence. In 1968, the United Nations study on "Effects of the Possible Use of Nuclear Weapons and the Security and Economic Implications for States of the Acquisition and Further Development of These Weapons" was rather cautious, and as its cumbersome title suggests, it avoided value judgments on the strategic doctrines of the superpowers. The study said rather that the cause of the arms race, including nuclear weapons, is "the sense of insecurity on the part of nations." Typically, it gave priority to an agreement to prevent the spread of nuclear weapons as a "powerful step in the right direction."[42] It is another irony of United Nations disarmament politics that a decade later the idea of non-proliferation would not enjoy wide support at the United Nations and the Non-Proliferation Treaty (NPT) would be taboo in non-aligned meetings (see next chapter).

In 1980, the study had new focuses and different emphases, underscoring the profound changes in the United Nations' position on the question of the nuclear arms race. The fact that among the experts were representatives of countries that are protected under the nuclear umbrella of the United States[43] did not prevent a unanimous criticism of the superpowers' nuclear deterrence system. The report challenges the premises of deterrence and rejects its doctrines:

The danger of the annihilation of human civilization should not be made the subject of theoretical arguments....[44]

Doctrines, in a sense, are fictions built upon various hypothetical scenarios of nuclear war....It is therefore highly questionable whether the doctrines of deterrence would prove to be reliable instruments of control in a crisis.[45]

The report, reflecting the prevailing view in the United Nations of 1980, continues to cast doubts on the bipolar system of international order, and it questions the superpowers' ability and responsibility to manage international order and flatly rejects the concept of nuclear deterrence:

It is inadmissible that the prospect of the annihilation of human civilization is used by some States to promote their security. The future of mankind is then made hostage to the perceived security of a few nuclear-weapon States and most notably that of the two superpowers. It is furthermore not acceptable to establish, for the indefinite future, a world system of nuclear-weapon States and non-nuclear-weapon States. This very system carries within it the seed of nuclear-weapon proliferation. In the long run, therefore, it is a system that contains the origins of its own destruction.[46]

The concept of the maintenance of world peace, stability and balance through the process of deterrence is perhaps the most dangerous collective fallacy that exists....[47]

So long as reliance continues to be placed upon the concept of the balance of nuclear deterrence as a method for maintaining peace, the prospects for the future will always remain dark, menacing and as uncertain as the fragile assumptions upon which they are based.[48]

As expected, both superpowers opposed the United Nations study on nuclear weapons in the first place, questioning its wisdom and value. While the United States expressed reservations on the terms of reference of the study,[49] the Soviets were even more specific in criticizing the references to the doctrines of deterrence, present nuclear arsenals, and trends in the technological development of nuclear weapons. Such a study, in the view of the Soviets, "would not bring us any closer to the solution of the problem of the cessation of the nuclear arms race by a single step."[50] Two years later, after the submission of the report, the Soviets said that their reservations had been vindicated.[51] But superpower opposition in the United Nations is to no avail. Third World countries were eager to pass the resolution, which provided for a close scrutiny of the superpowers' deterrence doctrines. In 1978, at the Thirty-third General Assembly, the resolution authorizing the study was supported 117–0, with twenty-one abstentions. The twenty-one abstentions provided a telling proof of the superpowers' common interest in nuclear deterrence and maintaining the bipolar balance of power in the international system. The following countries from the West abstained: Belgium, France, Federal Republic of Germany, Greece, Italy, Luxembourg, Netherlands, United Kingdom, and United States of America. Israel joined these nine members of NATO. From the East: Angola, Bulgaria, Byelorussia, Cuba, Czechoslovakia, German Democratic Republic, Hungary, Mongolia, Poland, Ukraine, and the Soviet Union.[52]

The superpowers' cooperation is even more illustated by the defections from each camp. Several NATO countries and other allies of the United States joined the Third World and voted for the study: Australia, Canada, Denmark, Iceland, Japan, New Zealand, Norway, Turkey (Australia, Canada, and Japan even participated in the experts group). In the East, Romania, the *enfant terrible* of the Warsaw Pact, also voted for the study and sent an official from its Foreign Ministry, who joined the twelve experts to issue a critical report on the Soviet Union and the United States. In 1980, the United Nations Thirty-fifth General Assembly endorsed the report of the experts by 126–0, with nineteen abstentions,[53] and again, the joint forces of the superpowers were defeated by the United Nations' majority.

It seems that Secretary General Kurt Waldheim was aware of the discomfort shared by the superpowers over the report. In his foreword to the report issued as "Report of the Secretary General," he went out of his way to add these remarks:

It should be noted that the observations and recommendations contained in the report are those of the experts. In this connexion, the Secretary General would like to point out that in the complex field of disarmament matters, in many instances he is not in a position to pass judgement on all aspects of the work accomplished by experts.*[54]

BIPOLARISM AND COCHAIRMANSHIP

As mentioned in Chapter 3, both superpowers cooperated against the Third World initiative to "democratize" the machinery for multinational negotiations

---

*This disclaimer was understandable in light of the secretary general's campaign for reelection for a third term, which he started early in 1981 and finally lost to Perez de Cuellar from Peru.

on disarmament in Geneva. Observers regarded the CCD as the "illegitimate child of the unlawful USA–USSR amours."[55] The superpowers, however, realizing that they could not withstand the strong pressures of the United Nations majority on the matter, agreed reluctantly to the Third World initiative to eliminate their cochairmanship in the committee and to strengthen the links between the United Nations and the committee, which had been a virtually autonomous forum.[56] The demise of the cochairmanship of the CCD in Geneva was hailed by many and described as the most significant outcome of the special session.[57] The campaign for the democratization of the negotiating forum on disarmament should be viewed as part and parcel of the Third World attack on the bipolar system of the balance of power in the international system. The experience of the Committee on Disarmament (CD) since its inception in 1979 may serve as telling proof of the gap between United Nations' rhetoric and bureaucratic reforms and the reality of balance of power outside the United Nations.

The changes in the new organ in Geneva were aimed at securing Third World control over this forum of multinational disarmament negotiations. In addition to elimination of the cochairmanship, it was decided to enlarge the committee, to put it under rotating chairmanship, and to open its plenary meetings to the public. The secretary general appointed a secretary of the committee to act as his personal representative, and it was agreed that the CD would report annually to the General Assembly of the United Nations. There was a feeling that the arrangements to revamp the Geneva disarmament conference would at least stand as a concrete result of the SSOD, which failed to agree upon substantive issues.

But the superpowers were quick to demonstrate that the reforms in the machinery for multilateral negotiations of disarmament would not affect their own conduct of bilateral negotiations. In the General Assembly of 1979, the first after the establishment of the new CD in Geneva, both superpowers resisted virtually universal pressure to give the CD authority and power over disarmament negotiations. The resolution submitted to the General Assembly reflected Third World frustration in calling the CD "to proceed without any further delay" to negotiate on top-priority disarmament questions and asked the superpowers indirectly to conclude their negotiations outside the CD and to submit "a full report on the status of their separate negotiations and results achieved so far." The vote on the draft resolution provided a rare show of superpower unity. The United States joined the Warsaw Pact members in abstaining, while all the rest of its Western allies voted with the overwhelming majority of 130 to support the resolution. (The eleven abstentions were Afghanistan, Bulgaria, Byelorussia, the Soviet Union, Czechoslovakia, German Democratic Republic, Hungary, Mongolia, Poland, Ukraine, the United States. Romania voted *for* the resolution.)[58]

In their statements the superpowers underscored their shared interest in preserving the bipolar balance of power and the framework of bilateral negotiations on strategic arms control. The United States explained that the resolution "is often accusatory in its tone and unrealistic in its request." The Soviets, following suit, rejected the "extremely subjective approach" of the resolution. Similarly, the Soviets regarded as unacceptable the language on the link between the work of CD and the talks going on outside it. A disciplined Bulgaria added its rejection to the attempt to subordinate the efforts outside the CD to the authority of the CD, saying that it did not reflect the consensus on the constitution and status of the CD achieved during the Tenth Special Session of the General Assembly.[59]

Mrs. Thorson, the Swedish deputy minister for disarmament, blamed mainly the two superpowers, who "have not demonstrated readiness or even willingness to exploit the rich potential of the Committee on Disarmament, because of the way in which they interpret their own security needs and interests in the present international situation." Mrs. Thorson was speaking as a representative of the Group of 21 neutral and non-aligned countries in the CD, whose views and interests in regard to the international system were discussed in Chapter 4. She was more candid in her other remarks, which admit that the failure of the new, reformed machinery for multilateral negotiations on disarmament can be attributed to the international power structure.[60] What she did not say, however, was whether the United Nations can remain relevant to the realities of international power while pursuing bureaucratic reforms that ignore them.

Similar cooperation between the superpowers was exhibited in another debate, which touched upon the international balance of power and bipolarity. This time it was a French proposal submitted first in a memorandum to the SSOD in May 1978, calling for the establishment of an international satellite monitoring agency.[61] The idea was put forward by French President Valery Giscard d'Estaing when he addressed the SSOD, marking his country's return to the international disarmament arena after a sixteen-year absence.[62] The proposed agency would monitor and verify the implementation of disarmament agreements and would help, according to France, to strengthen international confidence and security.

The French proposal, following the Gaullist tradition of asserting its independence from superpowers' domination in world affairs, posed a major challenge to the Big Two powers, which enjoy a virtually complete monopoly in satellite surveillance. The proposal envisaged, in a gradual process, the ultimate removal of the superpowers' monopoly, when the international agency would have its own "observation satellites required for the performance of its tasks." In other words, the plan provided also for outside interference in superpowers' arms control through international supervision over the implementation of their bilateral agreements. According to Yugoslavia, which supported the French proposal, the new agency would be an "instrument of the whole international community" and would provide equal access to the information obtained by the monitoring and thus leading to "the widest possible democratizaton of decision-making and equal rights of all the members of the international community.[63]

Both the Soviet Union and the United States regarded the proposal as an attempt to undermine their bilateral framework of arms control and, perhaps, an infringement on the bipolarity of the international balance of power. The Soviets questioned whether a universal instrument for monitoring should be sought or was possible in view of the individual nature of disarmament agreements. The

Soviets explained that the formation of supervising and monitoring organs without practical disarmament measures might simply create the appearance of doing something or lead to a heightening of mutual suspicions.[64] The United States concluded that the project "is not feasible, necessary or desirable in the foreseeable future" and that the cost of developing such an agency would be enormous. Finally, the Americans raised the political considerations that might affect the agency, saying that "control over and access to its information could become highly controversial issues."[65]

The vote on the draft resolution on the subject was also interesting in the sense that it reflected the differences in the internal cohesion and discipline within the two camps, between an alliance whose members possess considerable latitude in their relations with each other and an alliance system whose members are bound by coercion. Thus, *all* the Western allies except the United States voted for it, whereas in the Communist camp only Romania could assert its independence on disarmament policies by supporting the French proposal and even by nominating its candidate for the expert group selected to study the subject. In 1979, the results were 124–0 with eleven abstentions: Bulgaria, Byelorussia, Czechoslovakia, German Democratic Republic, Hungary, Mongolia, Poland, Ukraine, the Soviet Union, the United States, Vietnam.[66] In this instance, the United States joined the Soviet Union and its allies, as if to demonstrate the special character of superpower common interest. Another telling indication of cohesion in the Soviet camp was provided by Cuba, which was the only country to join the two superpowers in expressing a negative view on the project. Cuba maintained that the proposed project might constitute interference in the internal affairs of states, and, therefore, "far from enhancing, it would impede the proper implementation of disarmament agreements."[67] It was quite symbolic that Cuba, which hosted that same year the sixth non-aligned summit and would serve as its chairman for the next three years, decided to align itself with the superpowers against the Third World and used a familiar Soviet argument in objecting to international inspection.

MILITARY BLOCS AND FOREIGN BASES

Another important aspect in the debate on the nature of the international balance of power is the issue of military blocs and foreign military bases. Indeed, from the beginning, the notion of military blocs and foreign military bases was alien to the non-aligned movement. This is one major issue, a leading component of the non-aligned credo on which no compromise is possible in the United Nations. This issue, as explained by Philip Towle, reflects also a philosophical debate on whether military alliances and foreign bases are a stabilizing or destabilizing factor in international relations.[68] Here, again, the debate amounted to a struggle between different political approaches on the nature of the international order itself.

In their working paper submitted to the SSOD, the non-aligned called for "the dissolution of military blocs, great power alliances and pacts rising thereof, the dismantling of foreign military bases and withdrawal of military forces from foreign territories.'' Similarly, the non-aligned demanded the ''prohibition of the creation of new foreign military bases and the stationing of troops and military equipment in foreign territories.''[69] But soon it became clear that on this issue there would be no concessions. The superpowers could swallow some vague criticism over nuclear deterrence, but in no way could they give in on essential ingredients of their structure of international power. The Western states immediately opposed these demands and put brackets around the non-aligned language on the matter.[70]

On this issue the official and declaratory policy of the Soviet Union is closer to that of the non-aligned than that of the West, since it was always a Soviet contention that the Warsaw Pact was established only as a reaction to NATO and that the Soviets are ready, on a reciprocal basis, to dissolve their military alliance.[71] Nevertheless, at the SSOD the Soviets and their satellites took a low-key stand during the debate, probably because it was viewed as another challenge by the Third World to the bipolar order. The working paper of the Warsaw Pact countries mentioned only ''the reaching of agreement at least not to expand the opposing military and political groupings and alliances in Europe by admitting new members.'' No reference was made to military blocs and foreign bases.[72] It is interesting to note that this debate provided Romania with yet another opportunity to assert its limited independence within the Soviet bloc by joining the non-aligned camp on the call for the dissolution of military blocs and the dismantling of foreign military bases and by adding something even more daring: ''the withdrawal behind national frontiers of foreign troops, their armaments and other combat equipment, and the demobilization of the troops withdrawn.''[73]

It is clear, however, that for the Western alliance the issue of foreign military bases is of paramount political and security importance, and, therefore, no compromise on the principle could be negotiated. For the West, declaratory policies cannot be twisted on such a principle even for propagandistic purposes at the United Nations. At the end of the SSOD, the non-aligned could only express regret for the failure to

incorporate the principle of the incompatibility between the maintenance of military bases and the presence of foreign troops in foreign territories, on the one hand, and international peace and security, on the other. Opposition to military blocs, their bases and the presence of foreign troops has been cardinal to the non-aligned movement from its inception.[74]

The confrontation between these contending approaches to international order and security would continue because of these irreconcilable positions. The non-aligned would continue to declare that the policy of balance of force, spheres of influence, and military alliances are inconsistent with international security. They would call again, in Havana in 1979, for dismantling foreign military bases and dissolving military blocs.[75]

In 1980, marking a departure from their low-key position at the SSOD, the Soviets would join the non-aligned camp on the issue of alliances and foreign military bases. As an integral part of their "peace offensive" against the West, the Soviets began to ignore their own interest as the other superpower.[76] The Soviets, thus, together with their allies in the non-aligned movement (Angola, Cuba, Laos, Vietnam, Benin, and Democratic Yemen),[77] revived the call for "the dissolution of existing military alliances" by referring to paragraph 125 of the Final Document, which listed the various proposals submitted to the SSOD but not agreed upon. In the vote, the Soviets and the majority of the Third World supported the resolution, while the NATO countries and a few other allies of the United States opposed it.[78]

The explanations that followed the vote lent further proof to the unbridgeable gap between the two opposing approaches. It was made clear that the essence of the debate was on the nature and character of world order, as well as on the correct interpretation of the provisions in the Charter of the United Nations on collective security. According to the representative of the Federal Republic of Germany, the call to dismantle military alliances is not in line with the Charter of the United Nations and it distorts the notion and the role of such alliances. He pointed out that, unlike what the sponsors tried to imply, military alliances do not pose a threat to international peace and security. Quite to the contrary, in Europe they have been successful in preserving peace and stability, and his country, as a member of NATO, has never been involved in any military conflict. At the same time, West Germany is actively involved in arms control efforts such as the Vienna talks on mutual and balanced force reductions.

The resolution, West Germany continued to explain, is in contradiction to the United Nations Charter provisions, which under Article 51 guarantee the inherent right of states to self-defense, individually and collectively. That right implies the possibility for states, whether or not organized in regional groups, to make arrangements for collective defense. In a clear allusion to the states of the Soviet bloc, which cosponsored the resolution, the delegate from West Germany referred to the Final Act of the Conference on Security and Co-operation in Europe (Helsinki agreements of 1975), which they signed and in which they recognized the right of the parties to belong to treaties of alliance.[79]

In conclusion, it is evident that since the debates on disarmament at the United Nations touch upon the foundations of the existing international order and hierarchy, the confrontation between the Third World and the superpowers can be sharp and diametrical. While the superpowers share sometimes an uncomfortable alliance, the Third World is united in its demands for a major change in the structure and organization of international affairs. As shown in Chapter 4, the Third World of the 1970s did not regard itself anymore as a "golden bridge" and mediator between the superpowers. In effect, its criticism of SALT and the attack on the notion of a superpower balance of power based on arms control amounts almost to a rejection of the process of detente. This attitude goes back to the early 1970s, when detente was interpreted by the non-aligned as, in the words of Algerian Foreign Minister Bouteflika, the "superpowers' pretension to reign over the world."[80]

It can be argued, therefore, that the real debate on disarmament at the United Nations is nothing but a political-diplomatic extension of the struggle to change the international order. As shown in this chapter, the contending parties disagree on the system of nuclear deterrence between the superpowers and their attempt to consolidate it in the SALT negotiations. SALT and superpower bipolarity are totally incompatible with the Third World's goals of a radical redistribution of global power and resources. Nuclear deterrence is rejected, as are the notions of great-power responsibility and balance of power. Moreover, the democratization of the Geneva organ for multilateral negotiations on disarmament secured Third World control over the process, which earlier had been conducted under the chairmanship of the superpowers. All these in effect challenge the premises of the United Nations Charter on collective security and balance of power and, consequently, its conception of world order.

The consensus documents adopted at the United Nations, such as the Final Document of the SSOD, are sometimes deceiving, pretending that there is some harmony among United Nations members on these fundamental problems. As the representative of Pakistan said in the closing debate of the SSOD:

Many of the differences have been reconciled in our final documents, but unfortunately only in a textual sense. Behind the differing texts put forward on various questions there are deep underlying differences of philosophy and approach among the various groups and Powers. There are those who, even while they are willing to make efforts to control the arms race and reduce its dangers, view the future essentially in terms of rationalizing the existing strategic balance.[81]

THE SOVIETS AND BIPOLARITY

The uncomfortable alliance between the superpowers on some disarmament issues at the United Nations should not conceal their broader relationship in this field, which continues to be highly competitive. In this competition the Soviet Union, despite its role and long record as one of the superpowers, enjoys a major advantage over the United States. The fact that there is an inherent asymmetry in United Nations' debates between open and closed societies is quite understandable and widely recognized. It is so much taken for granted that virtually no attention is paid to some practical consequences of this disparity. Conference diplomacy provides the Soviets with several advantages over the United States and its allies. United Nations forums offer the Soviets a setting in which they can demonstrate the monolithic unity of Communist states in contrast to the disunity and lack of resolve or common purpose of the West. The closed nature of the Soviet Union also seems to contribute most heavily to the Soviet penchant for sweeping but meaningless disarmament proposals at international conferences (already in 1927, the Soviets were the first to introduce a proposal for "General and Complete Disarmament" to the Preparatory Commission for the Disarmament Conference sponsored by the League of Nations).

First and foremost, the Soviets benefit from their absolute control over their satellites in the Warsaw Treaty Organization. As the late French scholar Raymond Aron has pointed out, in the Soviet bloc, unlike in the Western alliance, military policy toward the other camp is determined in a sovereign way by the Soviet Union. There is no general staff of the Warsaw Pact equivalent to the NATO general staff. The Soviets possess not only the monopoly of the thermonuclear system but also the quasi-monopoly of immediately utilizable conventional weapons by its own troops stationed in Central Europe. Similarly, diplomacy, says Aron, is determined by Moscow in almost as sovereign a way as strategy, and as a result the representatives of the Eastern bloc states at the United Nations "faithfully follow the line laid down by the Moscow leaders."[82]

A second Soviet advantage lies in the essence of the Soviet–Third World affinity, which is often manifested in United Nations forums. It has become a ritual in the West to say that the Soviet system offers no ideological attraction and that its weak economic system is not viewed as a model by Third World leaders. But as Henry Kissinger has noted, Marxism has proved attractive to many Third World countries, not because of its ideology but because it supplied an answer to the problem of political legitimacy and authority providing a justification and framework for centralizing political power.[83] Many of the developing countries, plagued by inherent instability and frequent upheavals, have been intrigued with the Soviet system, which succeeded in building the Communist party machinery in order to assert its absolute power and authority. Soviet aid to developing countries was never based on economic, technological, or agricultural transfers but instead on assistance in providing the necessary instrument of power (military might and training, police and intelligence, etc.).

Third, in the East–West struggle at the United Nations the Soviets are assisted by their proxies within the non-aligned camp (Cuba, the chair for 1979–1983, Vietnam, Laos, Afghanistan, Angola, Mozambique, South Yemen, Ethiopia, Syria, and others). These allies secure the support of the United Nations majority and at the same time block any pro-Western or anti-Communist initiative that may arise in various forums.

The fourth reason for the Soviet–Third World alliance on disarmament issues at the United Nations has to do with the centrality of the NIEO and development in the disarmament debate. From the early days of economic debates at the United Nations, Soviet delegates sought to place blame for the economic woes of the developing countries exclusively upon the capitalist states of the West and to deny any responsibility.[84] Veteran diplomats at the United Nations pointed out how conference diplomacy enables the Soviet Union to perpetuate and even institutionalize "the fiction of Western—and especially American—responsibility for the lack of development, poverty and every other ill that besets the Third World."[85] Though the Soviets belong, by almost every criterion, to the "North," they have managed to disassociate themselves from the industrialized West in the North–South confrontation. This fiction, enhanced also by the guilt feelings in the West, had immediate effects in the disarmament field. While disassociating themselves from the North, the Soviets exploited United Nations conferences devoted to the NIEO and "persistently sought to broaden the agenda to include discussions of their current favorite detente or disarmament proposals." As the non-aligned declared that "the arms race is inconsistent with efforts aimed at achieving the NIEO,"[86] the Soviets followed suit by announcing that "an important interdependence exists between the restructuring of international economic relations and problems of limiting the arms race, disarmament and consolidating security."[87]

This is precisely where the Soviets could mobilize Third World support for their sweeping and grandiloquent proposals for disarmament. Their proposals offer at least an illusion of a realistic framework for channeling huge resources from disarmament to development purposes in the Third World. This leaves the Western group in a minority, and in most cases their representatives make apologetic statements in order to explain their reservations to the grandiloquent approach to disarmament. For the Third World majority a call for "general and complete disarmament" seems more appealing than Western arguments for a gradual approach to disarmament with a special emphasis on inspection and verification.

In 1981, the Soviet "peace offensive" was building to a crescendo, reaching a record of fourteen initiatives, most of which were directed against NATO defense strategies. The proposals dealt with virtually every security aspect of the American–Soviet rivalry, ranging from a resolution criticizing the arms race in outer space (directed against the U.S. space shuttle program), through resolutions aiming to undermine NATO military preparedness in chemical warfare and the stationing of nuclear weapons, to proposals of sheer propaganda such as the "Obligation of States to contribute to effective disarmament negotiations." All these proposals were introduced by members of the Soviet bloc and after debates and votes in the First Committee were adopted by the majority in the General Assembly.[88]

Since debates in the United Nations are today closely related to the policy-making process of consolidating a consensus on strategic and military decisions within the Western alliance, the military and the diplomatic front are becoming interrelated.

The psychological-diplomatic pressure is understandable since the West in the United Nations is a minority of more or less 20 countries out of 157 member states. The non-aligned total 100, and together with other Third World countries they comprise a bloc of 120. The Soviets with their ten Communist votes are most often with the majority of these 120 Third World nations against the West European and other states who are always vacillating between opposition and abstention to the majority initiatives.

Western subgrouping makes the situation even worse. As the U.S. ambassador

Table 4

Soviet-Sponsored Resolution on Disarmament
(in the Thirty-Sixth Session of the General Assembly of the United Nations, September–December 1981)

Res. no.	Title	Sponsors	Highlights
36/89	Prohibition of the development and manufacture of new types of weapons of mass destruction and new systems of such weapons	Soviet bloc - allies.	Calls upon the great powers to declare their refusal "to create new types of weapons of mass destruction" etc.
36/91	World Disarmament Conference	Poland and others (Peru, Spain, Sri Lanka, Burundi)	An annual resolution (since 1971) calling for a world disarmament conference.
36-92-D	International cooperation for disarmament	Soviet bloc - allies (Cuba, Syria, Jordan, Ethiopia etc.)	Calls upon States not to hamper disarmament negotiations and, "in particular, not to hinder possible progress in negotiations on disarmament by the discussion of unrelated issues."
36/92-E	Nuclear weapons in all aspects	Soviet bloc - allies.	Criticism and expression of alarm on the "adoption of the new doctrine of limited or partial use of nuclear weapons gives rise to illusions of the admissibility and acceptability of a nuclear conflict." Calls for negotiation in the CD on nuclear disarmament.
36/92-H	Status of multilateral disarmaments agreements	Bulgaria	Updating the status of disarmament agreements.

Table 4 (continued)

Propagandistic objectives	Votes
Directed again R&D (research and development) of new weapon systems, in particular the neutron weapon. With the traditional Soviet oath: nothing on inspection and verification.	For - 116 Against - 0 Abstentions -27 (West)
An old Soviet idea, watered down to a wishy-washy text to allow adoption by consensus.	adopted without a vote.
Allusion to the 'linkage' concept of arms control which implies a broader perspective of the political relations between the parties to the negotiations.	For - 116 Against - 0 Abstentions -26 (West)
Against United States' official declarations of nuclear strategy, and its 'extended deterrence' in Europe.	For - 118 Against - 18 (Western allies) Abstentions - 5 (Greece)
Book-keeping. Directed also against countries such as China and France which are not parties to some major multilateral arms control treaties.	For - 115 (Japan, Ireland, Greece) Against - 0 Abstentions - 23 (West and few Third World countries, Argentina, Brazil, India)

Table 4 (continued)

Res. no.	Title	Sponsors	Highlights
36/92-J	World-wide action for collecting signatures in support of measures to prevent nuclear war, to cure the arms race and for disarmament	Bulgaria, Mongolia.	This action "would be an important manifestation of the will of the world public..."
	Obligation of States to contribute to effective disarmament negotiations	German Democratic Republic, Mongolia	calls for expanding negotiations.
36/92-K	Prohibition of the nuclear neutron weapon.	Soviet bloc - allies (Cuba, Vietnam)	The neutron weapon "significantly lowers the threshold to nuclear war" and has "inhumane effects" and poses a "grave threat to unprotected civilian population," and should be prohibited.
36/94	Conclusion of an International Convention on the strengthening of the Security of non-nuclear weapons States against the use or threat of use of nuclear weapons.	Soviet bloc - allies.	convention on "non use of nuclear weapons."
36/96-B	Chemical and Bacteriological weapons	Soviet bloc	calls upon States to negotiate agreement and to refrain from production and stationing chemical weapons "where there are no such weapons at present."
36/97-E	Non-Stationing of nuclear weapons on the territories of states where there are no such weapons at present	Soviet bloc countries - allies (Dem. Yemen, Ethiopia, Angola, Vietnam etc.)	Calls upon all NWS to refrain from further action involving the stationing of nuclear weapons on other territories.

Table 4 (continued)

Propagandistic objectives	Votes
How can one compare the collecting of signatures in Moscow and Prague with the disarmament movements in the West?	For - 78 Against - 3 (Brazil, Canada, United States) Abstentions -56 (West, Third World).
Sheer propaganda.	This draft resolution was dropped by its sponsors.
Against American plan to produce and deploy the weapon in Europe.	For -68 Against - 14 (Most members of NATO and other allies) Abstentions - 57 (Members of NATO, Denmark, Greece, Iceland, Netherlands, Norway and other Western and Third World countries).
Directed against NATO doctrines and policies of nuclear deterrence.	For -115 Against - 17 (American allies) Abstentions - 12 (Greece, Japan and other Western Countries).
Attempt to foil Western plans to produce and deploy chemical weapons.	For - 109 Against - 1 (United States) Abstentions - 33 (Western Countries).
Directed against American plans to deploy nuclear weapons overseas.	For - 84 Against - 18 (Allies) Abstentions -42 (Greece and other Western and Third World Countries).

Table 4 (continued)

Res. no.	Title	Sponsors	Highlights
36/99	Conclusion of a treaty on the prohibition of the stationing of weapons of any kind in outer space.	Soviet bloc - allies.	"Desiring not to all outer space to become an arena for the arms race and a source of strained relations between states."
36/100	Prevention of nuclear catastrophe	Soviet bloc - allies.	Outlaws the first use of nuclear weapons as the "gravest crime against humanity." Blasts these doctrines as "incompatible with human moral standards and the lofty ideals of the United Nations
36/104	Implementation of the declaration on the preparation of societies for life in peace	Poland, German Democratic Rep. and other Third World countries.	"Aware of the paramount value of positive moulding of human consciousness for the fulfilment of the purposes and principles of the Charter of the United Nations."

Table 4 (continued)

Propagandistic objectives	Votes
Against the American space-shuttle program. See for instance a statement by Ukrainian USSR, in discussing this resolution on the military dimensions of the space-shuttle program. (A/C.1/36/PV,14,27 Oct.1981)	For - 123 (including some Western countries) Against - 0 Abstentions - 21 (Western countries).
Directed against NATO's doctrine of nuclear deterrence and exploits the domestic opposition in some European allies to NATO's deployment programs.	For - 82 Against - 19 (American allies) Abstentions - 41 (Greece and other Western and Third World countries).
Sheer propaganda.	For - 143 Against - 0 Abstentions - 2 (The United States and Israel).

to the United Nations testified, it is hard today for the United States to rely upon its allies since they have developed a habit of voting together on almost all issues as members of an European bloc of the "Ten." Their positions, Mrs. Kirkpatrick said, usually represent the easiest possible "consensus" and are "often different from the United States position."[89]

When it comes to disarmament the situation is even more complicated. Among the European "Ten," there is Ireland, which is not a member of NATO, and proud of its neutral and pro-disarmament position. Another member of the "Ten" and NATO is Greece, which, under the new Socialist government of Papandreau, has already deserted the alliance's ranks in many votes on East–West questions on disarmament since the United Nations' Thirty-sixth General Assembly of 1981. Other members of NATO, such as Norway, Denmark, and Iceland, belong to the "Nordic" group of the Scandinavians, which often functions as a group on disarmament matters (non-proliferation, nuclear weapon–free zones, etc.) and therefore are exposed to the influence of Sweden and Finland. Sweden is a member of the Group of 21 of the non-aligned countries in the Committee of Disarmament in Geneva. Sometimes it is amazing to see how Sweden, which belongs to the industrialized West, maintains strong armed forces, has an advanced and diversified military industry, and is an active exporter of arms, succeeds in maintaining its positive image in the disarmament field.

There is nothing new in the East–West confrontation on disarmament at the United Nations. As shown earlier, during the cold-war period the General Assembly became a forum for cynical gamesmanship and propaganda warfare on disarmament. However in the late 1970s and the early 1980s the power equation in the General Assembly was different, and Soviet initiatives enjoyed a comfortable majority while the West remained in a minority. Soviet inherent advantages could now play a more profound role, and the West almost did not respond with initiatives of its own.

Since the Soviets need not worry about voters or demonstrators at home or among their satellites, they do not have to persuade their own public of the wisdom and sincerity of their statements and initiatives on disarmament. The juxtaposition of NIEO politics and the monolithic unity of the Communist bloc helps the Soviet Union to mobilize the majority of the United Nations. In contrast, the democracies of the West can only undertake policies that are broadly supported by populations and accepted by consensus in the alliance—which has become a difficult task to achieve. It would be inconceivable for the West to make modifications in its declarations on nuclear deterrence for the purpose of United Nations' debates. Western proposals and votes in the United Nations have to be accountable given the permanent scrutiny of their attentive publics. In the East–West confrontation over disarmament at the United Nations, the popular peace movement in Europe became a third party and its role has been significant. It prevents the West from professing more unity and assertiveness in the diplomatic-propagandistic struggles on critical issues of security.

The link between the struggle for the NIEO and disarmament underscores the complexities of the politics of disarmament at the United Nations. Though the Third World is trying to challenge the present bipolar dominance of the super-powers, the nature of contemporary conference diplomacy transforms the debate into a one-sided attack against the West and particularly the United States. Ever since disarmament deliberations at the United Nations have become part and parcel of the Third World campaign for NIEO, they have also become instru-mental for the Soviet Union. Again, as in the anti-colonialism days at the United Nations in the late 1950s and early 1960s, the Soviet Union can pretend to be the natural ally of the Third World.

NOTES

1. GAOR, A/C.1/35/PV.11, October 22, 1980, p. 48.
2. GAOR, A/S-10/PV.2, May 24, 1978.
3. "What is Deterrence?" in SIPRI, *World Armament and Disarmament, SIPRI Yearbook 1981* (London: Taylor & Francis, 1981), pp. 33–35.
4. David C. Gompert, Michael Mandelbaum, Richard L. Garwin, and John H. Barton, *Nuclear Weapons and World Politics*, 1980s Project Council on Foreign Relations (New York: McGraw-Hill, 1977), p. 17.
5. The criticism started before the North–South confrontation at the United Nations. For some of the leading critics of "nuclear deterrence" theories and strategy, see Anatol Rapport, ed., *Clausewitz, on War* (London: Penguin Books, 1968), in the lengthy intro-duction, pp. 1–83; Philip Green, *Deadly Logic: The Theory of Nuclear Deterrence* (Co-lumbus: Ohio State University Press, 1966). Other critics, in particular the revisionist historians, have singled out the United States' policies as responsible for the nuclear arms race (see Chapter 6 n.67).
6. William R. Kintner and Robert L. Pfaltzgraff, Jr., eds., *SALT—Implications for Arms Control in the 1970's* (Pittsburgh: University of Pittsburgh Press, 1973), p. 17.
7. Michael Mandelbaum, "International Stability and Nuclear Order: The First Nu-clear Regime," in Gompert et al., *Nuclear Weapons*, p. 31.
8. "Meeting the Challenges of a Changing World" (Speech by the Honorable Cyrus R. Vance, Secretary of State, before the American Association of Community and Junior Colleges, Illinois, May 1, 1979), *State Department*, No. 116.
9. SIPRI, *Postures for Non-Proliferation—Arms Limitation and Security Policies to Minimize Nuclear Proliferation* (London: Taylor & Francis, 1979), p. 37.
10. *Christian Science Monitor*, May 22, 1978.
11. Louis Rene Beres, *Apocalypse—Nuclear Catastrophe in World Politics* (Chicago: University of Chicago Press, 1980), p. 211.
12. United Nations, *The United Nations and Disarmament Yearbook, Vol. 3, 1978* (New York: United Nations, 1979), p. 188.
13. *Christian Science Monitor*, May 22, 1978.
14. GAOR, The Non-Aligned Working Document, Tenth Special Session, 1978, Sup-plement No. 1 (A/S-10/1), Vol. IV, A/AC.187/55/add.1, p. 2.
15. GAOR, SSOD Final Document, Tenth Special Session, Supplement No. 4, A/S-10/4, para. 13.
16. GAOR, A/S-10/PV.27, July 6, 1978, p. 77.
17. GAOR, A/S-10/PV.24, June 9, 1978, p. 7.

18. Report of the Committee on Disarmament, GAOR, Thirty-Sixth Session, Supplement No. 27 (A/36/27), para. 70; see also Chapter 3. With the lack of agreement in the committee on substance, the document has simply reported the views of different groups of states.

19. GAOR, A/C.1/35/PV.39, November 21, 1980, pp. 63–65.

20. Ibid., p. 62.

21. Documents of the Committee on Disarmament, CD/PV.146, August 13, 1981.

22. Hedley Bull, "The Great Irresponsibles? The United States, the Soviet Union, and World Order," *International Journal* 35, no. 3 (Summer 1980): 437.

23. GAOR, A/S-10/AC.1/6, May 30, 1978, p. 1.

24. Statement by Pakistan: GAOR, A/S-10/PV.7, May 29, 1978, p. 38.

25. Statement by Peru: GAOR, A/C.1/35/PV.10, October 22, 1980, p. 56.

26. Statement by Cyprus: GAOR, A/S-10/PV.2, May 24, 1978.

27. GAOR, A/C.1/33/PV.38, November 15, 1978, p. 7.

28. GAOR, A/S-10/AC.1/PV.5, June 9, 1978, p. 51.

29. GAOR, A/S-10/PV.27, July 6, 1978, p. 102.

30. Inis L. Claude, Jr., "The Management of Power in the Changing United Nations," *International Organization* 15, no. 2 (Spring 1961): 219–35.

31. Tucker, *The Inequality of Nations*, p. 34.

32. Claude, *Swords*, p. 72.

33. Ibid., p. 154.

34. Cordell Hull, *The Memoirs of Cordell Hull*, vol. 2 (New York: Macmillan, 1948), p. 1323.

35. Claude, *Swords*, p. 73.

36. Ibid., pp. 250–56.

37. Tucker, *The Inequality of Nations*, p. 179.

38. Ibid., p. 58.

39. GAOR, Res. 3281 (XXIX, Charter of Economic Rights and Duties), December 12, 1974.

40. "Comprehensive Study on Nuclear Weapons," Report of the Secretary General, GAOR, A/35/392, September 12, 1980.

41. GAOR, Res.33/91-D, December 16, 1978.

42. *Effects of the Possible Use of Nuclear Weapons and the Security and Economic Implications for States of the Acquisition and Further Development of These Weapons*, A/6858 (New York: United Nations, 1968).

43. The experts were selected by twelve governments under the usual UN practice of equitable geographical distribution. They represented the following countries: Algeria, Argentina, Australia, Canada, Ghana, India, Japan, Mexico, Pakistan, Romania, Sweden, Yugoslavia.

44. "Comprehensive Study," para. 494.

45. Ibid., para. 498.

46. Ibid., para. 497.

47. Ibid., para. 519.

48. Ibid., para. 520.

49. *UN and Disarmament Yearbook*, Vol. 3, 1978, p. 183.

50. GAOR, A/C.1/33/PV.57, November 30, 1978, pp. 8–10.

51. GAOR, A/C.1/35/PV.39, November 21, 1980.

52. *UN and Disarmament Yearbook 1978*, p. 530.

53. GAOR, A/35/PV.94, December 15, 1980, pp. 65–66, for the text of the resolution: Res.35/156-F.

54. GAOR, A/35/392, September 12, 1980, p. 2.

55. *Christian Science Monitor*, June 28, 1978.

56. See Epstein, "UN Special Session on Disarmament"; and *New York Times*, June 29, 1978.

57. See Ann Hallan Lakhdhir, "The UN Special Session: An Evaluation," in *Negotiating Security—An Arms Control Reader*, ed. William H. Kincade and Jeffrey D. Porro (Washington, D.C.: Carnegie Endowment for International Peace, 1979), p. 246; and *Disarmament Times*, June 29, 1978.

58. Res. 34/83-B. See *UN and Disarmament Yearbook, Vol. 4, 1979*, pp. 35–36.

59. GAOR, A/C.1/34/PV.38, November 21, 1979, pp. 61–67.

60. GAOR, A/C.1/36/PV.12, October 26, 1981, p. 22.

61. GAOR, A/S-10/AC.1/7, June 1, 1978.

62. GAOR, A/S-10/PV.3, May 25, 1978. For background on the international satellites agency, see Jozef Goldblat, "Monitoring Arms Control—Do We Need a Global Verification Institution?" in *Opportunities for Disarmament*, ed. Jane M. O. Sharp (New York: Carnegie Endowment for International Peace, 1978), pp. 69–78.

63. Report of the UN Secretary General on replies received from governments on "Monitoring of Disarmament Agreements and Strengthening of International Security," GAOR, A/34/374, August 27, 1979, pp. 29–30.

64. GAOR, A/C.1/33/PV.53, November 28, 1978, pp. 36–37.

65. Ibid., pp. 37–40.

66. *UN and Disarmament Yearbook, Vol. 4, 1979*, pp. 356–59, 471–72.

67. Replies received from governments, p. 9.

68. Philip Towle, "The UN Special Session of Disarmament—Retrospect," *World Today* 35, no. 5 (May 1979): 210.

69. GAOR, A/AC.187/55, May 18, 1977.

70. See GAOR, Draft Final Document, in Tenth Special Session, 1978, Supplement No. 1 (A/S-10/1). In order to identify who is bracketing who, one should consult the annotated version of the draft issued as an informal working paper (see Appendix II of this book).

71. The stationing of Soviet military troops in Eastern European countries does not depend exclusively on the Warsaw Pact. For the evolution of the Pact, see Malcolm Mackintosh, "The Evolution of the Warsaw Pact," *Adelphi Paper*, no. 58 (June 1969); and Thomas W. Wolfe, *Soviet Power and Europe* (Baltimore: Johns Hopkins Press, 1970).

72. GAOR, A/AC.187/98, February 2, 1978.

73. GAOR, A/AC.187/78, August 31, 1977.

74. Ambassador Fernando of Sri Lanka speaking on behalf of the non-aligned. GAOR, A/S-10/PV.27, June 30, 1978, p. 77.

75. Documents of the Sixth Conference of Heads of States or Governments of Non-Aligned Countries held in Havana, Cuba, September 30, 1979. GAOR, A/34/542, October 11, 1979, p. 67.

76. As Ashok Kapur points out, Moscow is not interested in seeing the emergence of the Third World or non-aligned nations as a third voice in international relations. It is an essential part of Soviet political psychology that they are one of the two superpowers in a bipolarized world. See Kapur, *International Nuclear Proliferation*, p. 359.

77. GAOR, A/35/665/add.1, December 9, 1980, p. 9.

78. GAOR, A/35/PV.94, December 15, 1980, pp. 47–50.

79. GAOR, A/C.1/35/PV.42, November 25, 1980, pp. 38–41.

80. Mortimer, *The Third World*, p. 39.

81. GAOR, A/S-10/PV.27, July 6, 1978, pp. 98–99.

82. Raymond Aron, *Peace and War—A Theory of International Relations* (New York: Anchor Books, 1973), p. 218.

83. Henry Kissinger, *White House Years* (Boston: Little, Brown, 1979), p. 69.

84. Robert H. Donalson, "The Second World, the Third World and the New International Economic Order," in *The Soviet Union in the Third World: Successes and Failures*, ed. Robert H. Donalson (Boulder, Colo.: Westview Press, 1981), pp. 367–68.

85. Arieh Eilan, "Conference Diplomacy," *The Washington Quarterly* (Autumn 1981).

86. The Fifth Non-Aligned Summit Conference, Colombo, August 16–19, 1976, The Political Declaration (Chapter XVII), in GAOR, Tenth Special Session, Supplement No. 1 (A/S-10/1), Vol. II, 1978, A/AC.187.30, p. 51.

87. Donalson, "The Second World," p. 364.

88. The list of resolutions and summaries of the debates can be found in the *UN and Disarmament Yearbook, Vol. 6, 1981*. For a detailed analysis and tables, see Avi Beker, "The Soviet Union and Disarmament in the United Nations," *Crossroads* (A Crane and Russak Journal on International Affairs), no. 12 (Spring 1984).

89. *Washington Post*, January 28, 1982.

6

Nuclear Proliferation: "Haves" and "Have-Nots"

> The Nonproliferation Treaty has in many ways been perceived as the most visibly discriminatory of the post-war arms limitation agreements.[1]

> The Nonproliferation Treaty did not simply reflect the hierarchical character of international politics informally: it was explicitly, and officially, an unequal treaty.[2]

From the narrow vantage point of NIEO politics, it is evident that the nuclear Non-Proliferation Treaty (NPT) must appear as a major obstacle to any future reform of the international system. More than any other treaty, the NPT symbolizes the attempt to institutionalize by law the inequalities of the post–World War II international order. The distribution of nuclear power in the international system as envisaged by the NPT provisions was a frustrating reminder for the Third World that its new, overwhelming power at the United Nations means very little in the real world outside. It is understandable, therefore, that the treaty became during the 1970s one of the major issues of confrontation between North and South in the United Nations. This chapter will examine how the struggle for a new international order has influenced the Third World attack on what they call the "discriminatory regime" of the NPT and to what extent this clash undermines the international consensus on nuclear non-proliferation.

At the beginning of the 1980s the international consensus on preventing the spread of nuclear weapons became dangerously strained. The Second Review Conference of the Non-Proliferation Treaty ended on September 7, 1980, in Geneva on a note of disappointment. Despite last-minute efforts after a two-day extension of the proceedings, the participants could not reach agreement on a final document outlining measures to strengthen the future operation of the treaty. The conference was held pursuant to Article VII(3) of the treaty, which called on the parties to hold review conferences at intervals of five years. The first review conference, in May 1975, adopted a compromise declaration. Albeit weak, it at least reaffirmed the conferees' support of the treaty's purpose. The second review conference was not able even to do that.[3]

A failure to produce an agreed document is probably unprecedented in United Nations conferences of this kind. The NPT second review conference was the fourth conference to review the operation of a multilateral arms control agreement. The others were the first review conference on the NPT (May 1975), the review conference on the Sea-Bed Treaty (June–July 1977; similarly the second review conference of the Sea-Bed Treaty on September 1983 adopted, by consensus a final document), and the review conference of the parties to the Convention on the Prohibition of Biological Weapons (March 1980). All three reached agreement on a final document that reviewed the operation of the treaty concerned and set out the parties' support for its provisions.[4] As one observer pointed out, the lack of agreement in the NPT second review conference reflected "the fundamental differences between the Third World and the developed countries over the interlocking problems of nuclear proliferation and nuclear disarmament."[5] At the same time the failure highlighted the increasing fragility of the Non-Proliferation Treaty.

RE-ENDORSING BIPOLARITY

The NPT, signed in July 1968, and entered into force in 1970, attempted to freeze the number of nuclear-weapon states. The terms of the treaty were directed at preventing the emergence of additional nuclear-weapon powers, there being five at that time, according to the treaty—the United States, the Soviet Union, the United Kingdom, France, and China. The NPT can be regarded as the major multilateral arms control agreement of the nuclear age. It was widely hailed as a remarkable and important achievement that could prove to be a turning point in human history. Characteristically, it was praised mainly by the superpowers. President Johnson addressed the General Assembly and called the treaty "the most important international agreement in the field of disarmament since the Nuclear Age began." Foreign Minister Gromyko said that "the conclusion of the treaty will be one of the most important steps ever undertaken to restrain the nuclear arms race in the name of the lasting peace."[6]

The key provisions of the NPT, Articles I and II, divide the international community into two classes of states: the nuclear-weapon states (NWS) and the non-nuclear weapon states (NNWS). The division was to be guaranteed by an undertaking on the part of the "haves" to keep nuclear armament as well as material relevant to its production out of the "have-nots" hands, and by a corresponding undertaking by the "have-nots" not to acquire this capability. Moreover, Article III stipulates that the "have-nots"—and they alone—would have to submit to periodic and systematic international safeguards to ensure that they were indeed fulfilling their obligations. In order words, the non-nuclear states make an important pledge that affects their foreign and military policy, while the nuclear states, in essence, take on no new obligation. None of the superpowers had any interest in the transfer of nuclear weapons to a non-nuclear country.[7]

This inequality and disproportion of rights and duties under the NPT were the cause of the loudest protests and criticism. Some observers claimed that the treaty sanctioned discrimination in law for the first time (a claim that ignores some discriminatory provisions in the United Nations Charter).[8] At the United Nations and in the Eighteen Nation Disarmament Conference in Geneva, delegates raised serious reservations and objections to the provisions of the treaty. India, for instance, regarded the treaty as an instrument of imbalance in international relations and demanded to eliminate it "by abolishing the special status of superiority that goes with the power and prestige these States enjoy through the possession of nuclear weapons."[9] Even a country such as the Federal Republic of Germany, which is protected by U.S. troops and nuclear forces, felt that the treaty institutionalized inequality to the detriment of non-nuclear powers. It is interesting that at the beginning Western countries such as West Germany, Italy, the Netherlands, Belgium, and Japan, which technologically were very advanced in nuclear technology, joined the non-aligned and other Third World nations in the effort to defend the interests of the non-nuclear states.[10] However, after lobbying efforts by the United States, these countries ratified the NPT only days before the 1975 review conference (Japan in 1976),[11] and since then they are among the stalwart guardians of the treaty in United Nations debates.

Switzerland, a country that professes neutrality in foreign policy, was also among the countries to raise reservations about the NPT provisions. Switzerland observed in 1967 that the treaty establishes "a lasting legal discrimination between States, according to whether or not they possess nuclear weapons."[12] Unlike the Western group of states, Switzerland would continue to air its reservations after its ratification of the treaty (March 1977). In a document submitted to the United Nations SSOD, Switzerland expressed its disappointment over the lack of the progress expected when the NPT was agreed upon. Still in the 1970s, the Swiss argued, the problem of nuclear weapons is basically a problem of inequality in international relations and, therefore, should not provide a model for other treaties on disarmament and arms control.[13]

There should be no doubt about it. As Michael Mandelbaum explains, the NPT was not merely an informal reflection of the hierarchical character of international politics. It was, rather, "explicitly and officially, an unequal treaty" that distinguishes between two different classes of signatories that incurred different responsibilities.[14] It was, in effect, an instrument to reassert the idea that the superpowers are, as termed by Hedley Bull, "responsible managers of international affairs," and therefore they deserve some special rights (see also Chapter 5). Naturally, explains Bull, "The idea of the special rights and duties of great powers embodies a principle of hierarchy that is at loggerheads with the principle of the equal sovereignty of states."[15]

It is clear, as pointed out by Mandelbaum, that there is a positive correlation between the strengthening of the principle of hierarchy in international relations and the prospects for curbing the spread of nuclear weapons. Soviet–American cooperation is important "since the two great powers tend to be either the main threat or the main source of reassurance" for the security of most members of the international system. "Nuclear hierarchy," concludes Mandelbaum, "will remain a glaring feature of international politics for the foreseeable future."[16] In this regard the NPT subscribed to the view shared by much of the literature on the spread of nuclear weapons that a world with more nuclear powers would be vastly more dangerous than a world with the existing few.[17]

Sometimes, in the heat of United Nations' debate on the NPT, people seem to forget that the discriminatory nature of the treaty parallels that of the Security Council. As shown in Chapter 2, President Roosevelt's ideas on the postwar international order were based upon the notion of "four policemen," which is basically a situation of inequality in terms of military power. These ideas had a direct bearing on the Charter of the United Nations, its treatment of international security, disarmament, and the role envisaged to the Security Council. Under the NPT, nuclear weapons are permitted to the five nuclear-weapon states, which are the permanent members of the Security Council with veto power, but not to other nations. Similarly, safeguards are imposed upon the nuclear facilities of the non-nuclear-weapon states but not upon those of the nuclear-weapon states. Therefore, to repeat, the Third World struggle against the NPT must be viewed against the broad background of their combat strategy on changing the world order.

In terms of balance of power, the NPT was just a reaffirmation of the special rights accorded to permanent members of the Security Council over matters of peace and security by updating it to the nuclear age. One can always argue that the United Nations Charter is simply a reflection in law of existing inequalities among the member states. Actually, with the entry of the NPT into force, the power distribution recognized by the United Nations Charter—namely, granting the veto power to the five permanent members of the Security Council—was now extended to include the exclusive right to have nuclear weapons. As one delegate from the Netherlands commented, a certain degree of discrimination is an inevitable element in a non-proliferation treaty, and "the different status of the two categories ought therefore to be accepted from the start as being the lesser evil under the actual circumstances."[18]

Moreover, as some authors point out, a measure that benefits one group of states should not be viewed as being necessarily harmful to another. The Non-Proliferation Treaty should not be judged by yardsticks of commercial agreements, which incorporate reciprocal obligations and concessions. It is, instead, an expression of the common interest of international society facing an urgent security problem and solving it in realistic terms.[19] This interest is based on the assumption that life in "a nuclear-armed crowd" would be dangerous, and the narrowing of the gap between the big and small powers will not increase stability.[20]

BIPOLARISM AND RATIONALIZATION OF THE
CAMPAIGN AGAINST THE NPT

As noted, it was only in theory that the NPT was negotiated under the auspices of the disarmament conference in Geneva. In fact, what happened was that "the United States and the Soviet Union worked out its terms between themselves, and then invited other nations to subscribe."[21] An analysis of the struggle over the NPT reveals that it became a viable option only when the superpowers decided to coordinate their activities in the field, and only under the terms that they both considered favorable. From the beginning, any attempt to extend the terms of the treaty beyond the framework of the existing bipolar international system was doomed to fail. This explains why only the Irish initiative at the United Nations on non-proliferation (1958) could survive, while all other counterproposals and amendments remained in the oblivion of United Nations protocols.[22] The basic difference between the Irish approach and all others was that Ireland wanted in effect to foreclose all options for additional countries to join the nuclear club. It was aimed at preventing the acquisition of independent control of nuclear weapons by non-nuclear power (weapons acquired from other states or manufactured by itself or with the assistance of others).

The Irish proposal could succeed because it had the required appeal to the superpowers, who were moving increasingly during the 1960s toward what was perceived as a responsible management of the affairs of international society as a whole (see Chapter 5). It was a proposal that represented, as Alva Myrdal explains, a political philosophy endorsing the concept that "nuclear weapons could be a national asset, but that they should be compulsorily abjured in the wider international interest, although only by newcomers."[23]

The superpowers favored the Irish proposal since it "allowed discriminatory distinctions to be established between nations possessing nuclear weapons and those without."[24] During the debate over the treaty in the ENDC (from 1966 on), it became evident that many other states did not view the proliferation problem in quite the same way as the superpowers did. Pointing out that there was a "spectrum of positions" on the matter, representatives of non-nuclear countries called for a package arrangement that would place more substantial responsibilities and obligations on the nuclear states.[25]

But both the United States and the Soviet Union were eager to have non-proliferation negotiated as a separate measure and not as one linked to other measures of arms control and disarmament. Adrian Fisher of the United States suggested that the negotiations over the NPT should not "link the entry into force of one measure with that of another for fear that we might not get either" and that it was a mistake to assume that a "non-proliferation treaty is advantageous to nuclear weapons States." Similarly, the Soviet delegate argued that "it would hardly be conducive to our purpose to tie up a series of measures in a single package. In our opinion this would complicate negotiations which are difficult enough already."[26]

Generally it can be argued that most nations of the Third World would agree that the probability of nuclear war will increase with the spread of nuclear weapons to more countries. Probably they would accept Bernard Feld's observation that the NPT was at least as desirable for the non-nuclear nations as for the nuclear powers. They would agree that under the circumstances it would be difficult to conceive something beyond the NPT, and the fact that it provides significant advantages to one of the parties is not necessarily disadvantageous to others.[27] It is not surprising that the campaign against the treaty in Geneva was conducted by a group of countries that regards the "nuclear option" as a potential element in their national security policies (Brazil, Egypt, India, and from 1969, also Argentina and Pakistan, which then joined the CCD).[28] Nevertheless, it is apparent that in their statements in international forums these countries have gradually rationalized their parochial national interests through proclaiming against discrimination in international relations. Later, with the domination of NIEO politics, the campaign against the NPT took the form of the united Third World front within the framework of the North–South confrontation.

In this respect the evolution of the Indian position is most illustrative. The approach of India to nuclear proliferation has undergone a similar transformation to its general approach to disarmament, as described in Chapter 4. India, which in December 1962, after the Chinese attack, had first discovered painfully the weakness of non-alignment, experienced another shock in October 1964, when China exploded its first atomic bomb. The military humiliation of 1962 was followed by intensive conventional rearmament by India. The Chinese nuclear test of 1964 further compounded India's security preoccupation and probably led it to reconsider its previous decision not to develop nuclear weapons under any circumstances.[29] Later, India would lead the Third World's emerging resentment of the efforts to conclude a non-proliferation agreement.

The change in the Indian position was quite significant if one considers its attitude before the Chinese explosion. During the test-ban negotiations in April 1963, neither India nor Sweden joined the other six non-aligned members of the ENDC in their memorandum on the test ban, presumably in order not "to embarrass the superpowers."[30] In those days, India, together with Ireland and Sweden, was in the forefront of those non-nuclear countries urging the non-dissemination and non-acquisition of nuclear weapons.[31] (The term *non-proliferation* of nuclear weapons came into general usage late in 1965. It was a broader term that included the concepts of dissemination [meaning the spread of nuclear weapons by existing nuclear powers] and acquistion [the production or obtaining of nuclear weapons by non-nuclear powers]).[32] Only six days before the Chinese nuclear test, the second summit conference of the non-aligned adopted a very favorable declaration containing all components of a non-proliferation treaty: non-dissemination, gradual liquidation of existing stockpiles of nuclear weapons, and commitment not to produce, acquire, or test any nuclear weapons.[33] It was only in the aftermath of the Chinese explosion that India, for the first time, argued that all non-nuclear countries needed nuclear guarantees by existing nuclear powers against nuclear attack.[34]

Thereafter, India led the camp that during the debates on the Non-Proliferation Treaty emphasized the need for security guarantees and a link between superpower disarmament and non-proliferation obligations.[35] On the issue of security guarantees by the nuclear powers, India introduced the most far-reaching measures to the United Nations Disarmament Commission[36] and demanded an agreement based on equitable measures consisting of a package or integrated approach that includes both elements: non-proliferation arrangements, and some other measures affecting directly the nuclear weapons capability of the nuclear powers.[37]

For its part, India consequently took some major steps to make crystal clear its position on the subject. On March 27, 1967, the foreign minister of India told his Parliament that India had a "special problem of security against nuclear attack and nuclear blackmail." Subsequently, at a press conference, he stated that if India was not to go nuclear, it must have a "credible guarantee" for its security.[38]

Most Western observers viewed the shift in India's position on both conventional and nuclear disarmament as a major setback. Many of them failed to understand that the Indian change was just a forerunner of that of many other non-aligned countries. People were accustomed to indulge in nostalgia and to long for the days of Gandhi and Nehru: "India is not capable of giving the world a scientific and military blueprint having the same importance and arousing the same keen interest as the blueprint for peace it offered world public opinion in the time of Gandhi and Nehru."[39] Particularly, people did not anticipate the change among the non-aligned and were wrong to expect that India's position on the NPT "is not likely to strengthen the links between her and other non-aligned States."[40] Experience has shown that just the opposite occurred: the non-aligned movement moved gradually to adopt India's policy on the NPT almost as its official blueprint. And when the Indians exploded their bomb in 1974, many Third World countries were simply encouraged and even inspired. As one observer put it in 1980:

Clearly, the political implications of the Indian explosion are of greater importance than their military significance because in the next fifteen years or more, India will not be in a position to match the nuclear strength of China, not to mention other nuclear powers. Nevertheless, Third World countries have in large part welcomed the Indian test as a technological achievement demonstrating that even a developing country could acquire the know-how to successfully accomplish the sophisticated task of exploding an underground nuclear device which had hitherto been the exclusive preserve of the five great powers. The pent-up disappointments and frustration of a number of NNWS may have found a psychological release in India's breach of the rules of the exclusive nuclear club.[41]

In 1974, Third World reactions to the Indian test were corollaries of the broader approach to the North–South conflict. In fact, reactions to the Indian nuclear explosion were divided, more or less, along rich–poor lines, in which Third World societies welcomed it as a blow to the discriminatory regime of the NPT.[42]

For the superpowers, the NPT was regarded as a major instrument to reassert the bipolar character of the international system. It is evident that, in the case of the United States, even some major national security interests such as relations with military allies were overtaken by the common goal of preventing nuclear proliferation in order to consolidate the nuclear status quo. The overriding interest in non-proliferation as a major national security issue was best illustrated in what was termed a "substantial revolution in thought"[43] that took place in Washington and led to a change of policy by the United States. After two years of deadlock over the proposed NATO multilateral nuclear force (MLF), which the Soviet Union viewed as being contrary to the principle of non-dissemination,[44] the United States decided that the NPT overrides alliance considerations.

In the course of the internal struggle over policy-making on the treaty, an unusual coalition was created between the Arms Control and Disarmament Agency (ACDA) and the Department of Defense against the State Department. Strangely enough, as observers pointed out, ACDA and the Pentagon were pushing for a formula that would achieve NPT agreement, while the State Department had little enthusiasm for any non-proliferation treaty that discriminated against West Germany and that would banish forever any kind of multilateral nuclear force in Europe.[45]

There is enough evidence to suggest, as Ashok Kapur does, that the concept of nuclear deterrence that prevailed in the West had a major impact on the development of the NPT regime. Proliferation was regarded by American scientists as a possible threat to an already complex relationship of deterrence between two superpowers.[46] Experts agree that deterrence and its mechanics were nurtured and developed within the intellectual context of the cold war as a means "of protecting vital security interests and upholding international order while simultaneously preventing war."[47] Naturally there was a widespread belief that in a multipolar nuclear world the operation of deterrence would be difficult if not impossible. Most arms control analysts inclined to the view that a world of many nuclear states would contain "a greater statistical probability of technical accident, unauthorized use, strategic miscalculation from a limited to a general war."[48] It is clear that the superpowers began to look favorably at ideas for a treaty of nuclear non-proliferation as soon as they "began to appreciate the problems of managing international relations in a world of multiple nuclear weapons powers."[49]

The NPT, as Elizabeth Young explains, offered the U.S. administration a major opportunity to pursue President Johnson's policy of bridge-building with the Soviet Union. The military considerations were less significant because the very magnitude of the U.S. and Soviet nuclear missile forces put them beyond the reach of competition. Since in this area the superpowers had political as well as military interests in common, the new bureaucatic alliance in Washington

(ACDA–Pentagon) revealed how "non-proliferation became a recognized arms control measure and an essential element in the prevailing strategic doctrine."[50]

In his study on the evolution of U.S. policy toward a non-proliferation treaty, William Bader underscored the effects of strategic doctrine and relations with allies. In the 1950s the United States had a "NATO first" policy and an emphasis on flexibility in the use of nuclear weapons that overrode its interest in elaborating international efforts to erect barriers to the acquisition of nuclear weapons. Gradually, in the 1960s, the United States became preoccupied (according to Raymond Aron, even obsessed) with the spread of nuclear weapons. With the NPT becoming "the centerpiece of United States nuclear policy," Bader concludes, the United States was ready to accept restrictions on the use of its nuclear resources and even to abandon a policy of flexible use of its nuclear weapons assets. The treaty was regarded, despite its shortcomings, as an "opportunity to work with the Soviet Union" and an "ideologically comfortable framework for East–West cooperation."[51]

On August 24, 1967, the United States and the Soviet Union submitted identical texts of a draft NPT to the ENDC.* With that, the way was paved for the approval of the treaty by the United Nations majority, but at the same time the seeds of an intensive and sharp confrontation with the Third World on disarmament issues had been planted. Soon it became apparent that the debate was no longer on disarmament goals but on the division of power among states and the nature of order. Third World countries would get more and more uncomfortable with the emerging framework of understandings providing for East–West cooperation. Later the debate on the NPT in the United Nations would center on issues such as international balance of power, hierarchy and order, and "nuclear sovereignty" for the Third World.

FROM YALTA TO THE NPT

For the superpowers the NPT was a major international security instrument that legitimized and institutionalized their pre-eminence in a bipolar regime. The treaty created two classes of states, and by disproportionate allocation of obligations it left the two leading NWS as the major custodians of world order. As SIPRI points out, it is a fact that the NWS, and particularly the United States and the Soviet Union, are the major "custodians" of world order since they currently occupy the dominant positions of power and status in the international security system. With the size and quality of their nuclear-weapon inventories, the two superpowers possess the pre-eminent military capabilities that enable them to construct and manage the international system in a world in which

---

*A similar procedure was followed for two other multilateral arms control treaties—the Sea-Bed Treaty and the Biological Convention—when the superpowers first submitted separate but identical drafts and later introduced a joint draft treaty.

military might constitutes the quintessential determinant of status in the international security system.[52]

For the Third World non-proliferation became a focal point in the emerging North–South confrontation on disarmament. The cleavages of North–South that were basically economic—development, allocation of food, commodities, natural resources, and exploration of the sea—were extended to the arena of international security between the "military haves" and the "military have-nots." In fact, a large part of the international debate on security and disarmament can be described in terms of two contending strategies for nuclear proliferation: the High Posture Doctrine and the Low Posture Doctrine. Originally these two alternative strategies were outlined by Hedley Bull in 1967, and after twelve years they were incorporated in a SIPRI study that used them as the essence of the confrontation between the NWS and the NNWS.[53]

In brief, the High Posture Doctrine aims at preserving and possibly even widening the gap between, on one hand, the superpowers, and, on the other, the small nuclear powers and non-nuclear states in order to preserve the essential bipolar structure of world power. In this view, there is an inverse correlation between the vertical and the horizontal proliferation of nuclear weapons. Thus, the larger the nuclear weapon inventories of the great NWS, the less likely it is that significant numbers of NNWS will acquire nuclear weapons since their strategic value of becoming NWS could remain insignificant relative to the might of the superpowers.[54]

The advocates of the Low Posture Doctrine assume just the opposite: there is a positive correlation between the vertical and the horizontal proliferation of nuclear weapons, namely, NWS disarmament will curtail proliferation among NNWS, and, conversely, by enlarging their nuclear inventories, the NWS will encourage nuclear weapons proliferation.[55] On the part of Third World countries the adoption of the Low Posture Doctrine had concrete objectives: to reduce the gap separating the NNWS from the NWS by demanding that the nuclear powers reduce the level of their nuclear armaments, restrict the qualitative development of their weapons, and diminish reliance on such weapons in diplomacy. It can be argued, therefore, that at the United Nations, Third World countries are pursuing a diplomacy of the Low Posture strategy by demanding "to stop the buildup of nuclear arsenals, to reduce stockpiles of nuclear weapons and to halt further development of nuclear armaments," specifying that "particularly the two leading nuclear-weapons States bear a special responsiblity for realization of these tasks."[56]

The superpowers, on the other hand, defend their High Posture policy and reject Third World demands for priority for nuclear disarmament (directed at them) and assertions of their responsibility. Instead, both suggested "parallel progress" in conventional disarmament, which was rejected by the non-aligned.[57] The NPT was for the superpowers a major component of their High Posture strategy, which reaffirmed their continuing bipolar dominance of the planet. The United States and the USSR worked to strengthen and consolidate the nuclear non-proliferation regime, "a call which was rejected outright by the Third World."[58] As Hedley Bull has written, Soviet–American cooperation in the arms control area has always been accompanied "by the attempt to legitimize very high ceilings of strategic arms, by political cooperation directed against third parties, and by enunciation of a principle of parity whose effect is to formalize the claims of these two states to a special position in the hierarchy of military power."[59]

Even before the entry of the treaty into force, experts had noted that one major condition requisite for its success is a "condominium between the United States and the Soviet Union."[60] Critics of the concept pointed out that this "condominium" was put into effect in the process of securing the passage of the NPT in the United Nations. Its passage at the United Nations is seen by Morton Kaplan as a "shameful chapter in recent history," accompanied as he argues by "threats, promises and pressures which were employed against reluctant nations in a way not seen since Stalin's ham-handed rule of the Soviet satellites—except for Moscow's attempt to halt the liberalization process in Czechoslovakia in 1968."[61] Morton Kaplan's assessment may be correct in terms of "equal sovereignty" of nations, but its premises are divorced from the balance-of-power realities, which, as shown, were recognized and even legitimized by the United Nations Charter.

Theoretically, at least, one can extend the concept of condominium to a possible collaboration between the superpowers against secondary nuclear powers. Indeed, as former Secretary of State Henry Kissinger testified, the Russians were begging the United States for license to humble China once and for all with a pre-emptive nuclear attack.[62] A similar account is provided by H. R. Haldeman, President Nixon's chief of staff in the White House, in his "Watergate" book on his days in the administration.[63] This sort of "condominium" operation was in the mind of French President Charles de Gaulle, who once envisioned a situation in which the United States and the Soviet Union actually join forces and collaborate in the establishment of a new pattern of global dominance.[64]

Against this background it should not come as a surprise to hear a Soviet delegate expressing the view that the NPT was the most important treaty since Yalta.[65] Similarly, when the penultimate draft of the NPT emerged early in 1967, West German ex-Chancellor Konrad Adenauer called it "a second Yalta" and referred back to the Morgenthau plan to raze German industry.[66] It was in Yalta, in the Russian Crimea, in February 1945, that Franklin D. Roosevelt and Joseph Stalin, the superpowers' leaders, divided the world into "spheres of influence."

It was also there that the Americans and the Soviets hammered out the controversial procedure in the Security Council and membership in the General Assembly, to pave the way for the United Nations San Francisco conference in April 1945 and the signing of the United Nations Charter. The Yalta Conference was among the most controversial events of World War II. Critics of the Roosevelt administration have repeatedly charged that Yalta was a sell-out of U.S.

interests. Some historians defended Roosevelt's wartime diplomacy but blamed the Soviet Union for misinterpreting and exploiting the Yalta agreements.[67] Both critics and defenders, however, agree that Yalta recognized the emerging new hierarchy of superpowers' domination of international affairs.

The NPT should be looked upon as a sort of a nuclear version of Yalta. The treaty defines and updates the missing provisions of the pre-atomic United Nations Charter on superpowers' relations and redraws the line between them and the NNWS for the future. The superpowers have a clear interest in preventing uncontrolled situations under which an entirely new structure of international relations could ensue. The impetus for their collaboration lies in their shared fear that the dual superpower club will be expanded or, conversely, dismantled. Unfair? Of course, this is the essence of international power politics. It is precisely under this code of conduct that such a treaty, in the words of its critics, proposes no balance and no mutuality of obligations and benefits between the NWS and the NNWS. Balance in international relations is balance of power, which has nothing to do with the concept of equality or mutuality of obligations. Indeed, what the superpowers meant was exactly what Alva Myrdal criticizes as an attempt to place the major responsibility on their shoulders amounting "to a clever design to get NPT to function as a seal on the superpowers' hegemonic world policy."[68] There should be no illusions about it: "there is a clash between the nuclear superpowers who stress the benefits of inequality, and the non-nuclear-weapon states, who seek to minimize the implications of hierarchy by stressing the benefits of equality."[69]

In other words, it should be understood that for both contending camps this diplomatic confrontation on disarmament and proliferation has less to do with disarmament measures as such and more to do with their contending approaches to hierarchy and order in the international system. In this regard, disarmament diplomacy at the United Nations is subordinated to national security interest as it is defined collectively by the two opposing camps. The Third World has committed itself under the NIEO platform to eliminate the sources of discrimination and inequality in the international system. The superpowers, on the other hand, share a common interest to maintain a "manageable" international system that can be endangered by the emergence of additional and smaller nuclear powers. A "manageable" system, from the superpowers' vantage point, means a High Posture Doctrine to preserve the gap among nations. This is the essence of the cleavage between the Third World and the superpowers on non-proliferation and disarmament.

INEVITABLE DEFICIENCIES IN THE NON-PROLIFERATION REGIME

It seems that as long as the NPT is examined in the United Nations with the yardsticks of "sovereign equality," "discrimination," or "equality" it will be difficult to consolidate a consensus within the organization on strengthening the non-proliferation regime. NIEO politics and Third World rhetoric on disarmament prevent any serious attempt in this direction. The debate over international order, justice, and equality blurs the real problems in the field of nuclear proliferation: What is the real economic significance of nuclear energy for developing countries? And what may be the consequences to their national security?

"Atoms for Peace" was a U.S. initiative enunciated by President Eisenhower in his speech to the United Nations in December 1953. His speech revived and inflated hopes for the world-wide benefits to be obtained from civilian nuclear energy. But already then people such as Robert Oppenheimer claimed that the plan has no firm connection with atomic disarmament and that its bearing on the prospect of nuclear war was "allusive and sentimental" rather than "substantive and functional."[70] A generation later many would question the desirability of the rapid development in atomic energy by the industrialized countries. More and more would warn that the easiest way to acquire nuclear weapons is through nuclear power programs, which are designed primarily, apparently, for civilian purposes.[71] But as seen from the Third World, the problem of proliferation was not the issue. There, the major problem with the NPT lay in the fact that it was "the first unequal multilateral treaty in the twentieth century international relations" and therefore dismissed as "a bad move and a lost opportunity."[72] Again, scholars and delegates tend to ignore the fundamental inequalities legitimized by the United Nations Charter.

The fact that the treaty was soon signed by over one hundred countries can be deceiving; indeed, some regard this achievement as hollow.[73] It should be noted that the bulk of the nations that joined the treaty did not have much of a chance, or intention, to produce nuclear arms. On the other hand, countries that contemplated going nuclear, because of their own perceptions of national interest, refused to adhere and kept their nuclear arms options open. It is there, between the adherents and the opponents of the treaty, that there is no ideological consensus, no real community of interest.[74] In this regard it is evident that the NIEO platform of the Third World has contributed to a large extent to the campaign against the NPT. As can be seen in resolutions of the non-aligned countries and even in the United Nations General Assembly, the Third World has adopted, in effect, the basic position of the anti-NPT lobby of the developing countries. (Further elaboration on the Third World's position is provided later in this chapter.)

The lack of concern in United Nations debates over the serious deficiencies in the international system of safeguards on nuclear activities may create the wrong impression that there exists an effective international system to prevent nuclear weapons proliferation. In recent years, however, one can note a growing concern among experts over the operation of the current international regime of non-proliferation. Some of the leading nuclear experts in the United States charge that the International Atomic Energy Agency (IAEA) is incapable of detecting diversions of nuclear materials to make nuclear weapons. Reports prepared for the United States Nuclear Regulatory Commission (NRC) have concluded that the IAEA safeguards system, which was designed to prevent diversion of uranium and plutonium from peaceful nuclear programs to atomic weapons, has gross deficiencies.[75]

The conclusion of a safeguards agreement with the IAEA, in accordance with Article II, paragraph 1 of the NPT, is the basic obligation of every NNWS party to the treaty. The system of safeguards consists of three main elements: material accountancy, containment, and surveillance. The purpose of these technical measures is to enable "timely" detection of diversion of "significant" quantities of nuclear material from peaceful activities to the manufacture of nuclear explosive devices, as well as deterrence of diversion by creating the risk of early detection. Experts agree, and the IAEA itself admits, that there are limits to the extent to which the agency is able to detect diversions and to guarantee an effective international response to a non-proliferation violation, even when it is detected.[76]

The problem with the safeguards system is not confined to the lack of sanctions or enforcement measures in case of noncompliance or violation of the treaty. The problem begins with the detection system since the NPT does not provide for the possibility of carrying out special inspections on the basis of accusations or suspicion, and the whole system of safeguards is dependent on the consent of the state involved.[77] These deficiencies are particularly alarming because of the "abrogation risk" inherent in the NPT system. According to Article X of the NPT, each party might at any time, if it chooses to do so, openly declare its withdrawal from the treaty on three months' notice in what it considered "exercising national sovereignty." In other words, the IAEA system, and particularly its promotional role, allows a state to proceed under the guise of the NPT as far as possible with all its plans for making nuclear weapons and, when ready, merely notify the IAEA and the United Nations Security Council that it is withdrawing from the treaty.

But apparently, as is reflected in United Nations debates, the Third World does not seem to be worried by the loopholes and weaknesses of the NPT and its safeguards. Instead, in its collective position as well as in statements by individual countries, the Third World challenges the whole notion of the treaty in its revolt against the "unequal" regime of non-proliferation. At the United Nations, representatives of the Third World like to emphasize the promotional role of the agency—i.e., promoting nuclear development programs, particularly in the Third World—and, at the same time, belittle its role as regulator—i.e., the function of preventing nuclear weapons proliferation, including the safeguards system.[78]

It is the logic of NIEO that leads Third World countries to assume that "the wider distribution of nuclear weapons is a requirement of distributional justice."[79] This logic dictates the preference for the promotional role of the IAEA at the expense of its safeguards system. A U.S. safety expert for the Nuclear Regulatory Commission pointed out that a large part of the deficiencies of the IAEA safeguard stem from the fact that the agency "combines both the function of a promotional agency and a regulator." From the point of view of nuclear proliferation, he said, the promotional role of the agency is unhealthy, and it creates a situation that "does not promote independent and even-handed regulation" and allows "a large potential for cheating and unauthorized diversion."[80]

A report published in October 1981 by the Ad Hoc Group on U.S. policy toward the United Nations—a group that included three former secretaries of state, Dean Rusk, Cyrus Vance, and Edmund Muskie—recommended that a Nuclear Security Planning Committee be attached to the Security Council, working with the IAEA to strengthen its enforcement capability and improve its information base.[81] However, as debates in the United Nations on the NPT demonstrate, this task is impossible as long as the problem of nuclear proliferation is measured by the yardsticks of NIEO distributional justice. In this context it may be expected that more experts will join the assessment that the existing system of safeguards cannot provide "timely warning" to avoid a sudden manufacture of nuclear bombs from "safeguarded" material.[82]

The anti-NPT lobby at the United Nations makes it impossible to inquire, even within the framework of the NPT review conference, why authorities such as Fred Ikle blame the IAEA for making it easier for the exporters of nuclear technology to pretend that their practices are safe.[83] Moreover, there was no reaction at United Nations General Assemblies or in the Second Special Session on Disarmament (SSD II) of June–July 1982 to the accusation of a nuclear safety analyst that statements by IAEA officials based on their accounting system was "dangerously misleading to the world."[84] It was not a surprise, therefore, when the growing disillusion with the safeguards system culminated, on November 27, 1981, in the first governmental warning ever, a document from the chairman of the Nuclear Regulatory Commission of the United States, on the ineffectiveness of IAEA safeguards. The letter by the chairman, Numzio J. Polladino, was approved unanimously by the five members of the independent commission and was sent to the chairmen of several congressional committees. The commission concluded that the IAEA is unable to detect diversions of nuclear material in some type of facilities and also declared that it could no longer be confident that the members of the agency "would be notified of a diversion in timely fashion."[85]

At the end of the 1970s two different reports by SIPRI, which is known for its general support for the United Nations system and the plight of the Third World, have blamed the developing countries for distorting the arms control aspects of non-proliferation (see below). This problem seems to be insoluble within the framework of multinational forums as long as there is no real political consensus on the premises of the non-proliferation regime. The North–South confrontation has overtaken the original security context of non-proliferation, and instead the debate has focused on systemic issues such as "discrimination" and "sovereign equality" in international affairs. Let us examine some highlights of this dialogue in the aftermath of the entry into force of the NPT.

REVOLT AGAINST THE NUCLEAR HAVES

Observers described the struggle of Third World countries at the first review conference of the NPT in Geneva (May 1975) as a revolt against the hegemony of the superpowers.[86] The conferees met in the aftermath of the 1974 underground test of a "peaceful nuclear device" by India, the first nation to cross the nuclear threshold after negotiation of the NPT. Also, on the heels of the conference came the unwelcome news that West Germany was about to conclude a multi-billion-dollar deal to provide all the elements of the nuclear fuel cycle (enrichment, reactors, and plutonium fuel separation facilities, adequate to make nuclear weapons if desired) to Brazil, a conspicuous non-party of the NPT.[87] Both events demonstrated the two sides of the fragile NPT coin: the Indian explosion demonstrated the failure to get nuclear threshold countries to join the treaty; and the German deal drew attention to the fact that its transaction was completey legal under the treaty. The conference was also a reflection of the new pattern of confrontation in international forums in the 1970s between the "have" and "have-not" countries. The NPT became just another source of frustration for the "have-nots" such as the other global problems that they tackled in United Nations conferences: development, environment, population, food, the law of the sea, energy, and raw materials.

The superpowers, on the other hand, did not intend to make any concessions. The three nuclear-weapon powers—the United States, the Soviet Union, and the United Kingdom (France and China did not sign the NPT)—held a private meeting in London just before the opening of the conference to secure its smooth running according to their wishes. Their basic policy was to avoid the so-called political issues and concentrate on the "technical" ones, seeking, in effect, only to rubber-stamp the performance of the NPT and to strengthen the international regime it envisaged. The superpowers succeeded in using the conference as a deadline before which important European signatory states (e.g., West Germany) would ratify the treaty and become full participants. During the conference itself, the superpowers spoke "in a singularly preharmonized manner" and rejected out of hand all proposals put forward by any Third World country.[88]

In the conference, the Third World sought in effect to amend the NPT, a motion that was procedurally flawed and went beyond the terms of reference of the review conference. They introduced (together with Romania) two additional protocols to the NPT specifically linking horizontal and vertical disarmament and specifying new ceilings for superpower nuclear capabilities (50 percent of the ceilings agreed under the Vladivostok accords of 1974). The Soviets rejected it flatly as "unacceptable interference" in U.S.–Soviet relations, and allied countries added that third parties should not dictate superpower bilateral negotiations.[89]

The conference also provided another illustration of the ill-conceived technique of "consensus" employed to draft final documents in United Nations forums. The review conference adopted a final document that was an attempt to conceal in ambiguous formulations the fundamental differences between the parties. At the same time, however, the non-aligned insisted on annexing the unacceptable protocols to the "consensus" document, annexes that served as clear testimony to the continuing gap between the two camps over the necessary disarmament measures and the kind of security regime appropriate to the NPT.[90]

As explained elsewhere, there is a strong correlation between the broader cleavage between the rich and the poor countries and nuclear proliferation. The evolution of the Third World into a "strong global bargaining power" may create nuclear incentives for those developing countries aspiring to leadership positions within the bloc. In this sense nuclear weapons capability is a "symbol of modernity and technological competence as well as a source of status and prestige."[91] In this process, the achievement of these economic and symbolic values is by no means an enchancement of security in the Third World. In fact, those developing countries that would probably seek to respond in kind to the increased power of the new nuclear state are likely to experience a decline in their security and independence from superpowers. The net result ironically would "reinforce or accelerate political hierarchical tendencies within the South."[92] Even from the point of view of NIEO politics, this process could seriously undercut the principal instrument of Third World strategy in the United Nations, that is, their solidarity or unity, by the divisions of the South into nuclear haves and have-nots.

Perhaps the most ominous implication of the North–South spillovers in the debate on non-proliferation lies in the fact that it depreciates the real dangers inherent in nuclear proliferation. By making proliferation just another element in a general pattern of challenge to an unjust status quo, the security consequences of the nuclear spread in the Third World are overlooked. NIEO makes the issue of nuclear proliferation a zero-sum game between the Third World and the superpowers; every measure to strengthen the regime of non-proliferation is looked upon by the Third World as infringing on their sovereignty and development programs. It is very likely, as David Gombert points out, that nuclear proliferation in the Third World would have splintering effects far beyond the nuclear security area. Third World solidarity in this regard is quite deceiving:

To believe that any increase in the prestige of particular Southern proliferation would somehow elevate their non-nuclear brethren in the South is to swallow the most indigestible of all self-serving national rationalization for acquiring nuclear weapons.[93]

As pointed out in a study by SIPRI, the serious rift between the Third World and the nuclear powers, which has developed along North–South lines, "presents a real threat to the NPT's survival."[94] The threat is particularly worrying since it is agreed that the NPT, because of its provisions for the transfer of nuclear technology for peaceful uses, "cannot deal with the potential for weapon proliferation inherent in the expansion of nuclear energy."[95] As we will see, United Nations debates on non-proliferation are doing just this: they undermine the non-proliferation provisions of the NPT while overemphasizing the nuclear transfer provisions under the guise of the peaceful uses of atomic energy.

IN THE SSOD: THE CULMINATION OF THE CONFRONTATION

Even before the convening of the First United Nations Special Session on disarmament, it became apparent that the debate on the non-proliferation regime would be a major source of controversy. In the working paper submitted by the non-aligned to the Preparatory Committee for the SSOD the NPT was taboo: nothing was said about the treaty, not a word on the IAEA safeguards, and not even lip service to the whole notion of non-proliferation. All this in a comprehensive document (ten pages) that enumerates a variety of disarmament measures, particularly concerning nuclear disarmament; they apparently found the idea of non-proliferation totally irrelevant to the disarmament process.[96]

It took more than eight months for the non-aligned movement to think the issue over and to introduce an addendum to their working paper that would include, only in passing, a vague reference (as the last item among eight) that calls for "prevention of proliferation of such [nuclear] weapons and system."[97] This is the utmost that a non-aligned consensus could achieve. Still no word on the NPT. Interestingly enough, the only allusion to international safeguards had a negative implication:

Measures of disarmament shall not be construed in such a way as to hamper the exercise of all States to develop or to acquire [nuclear technology] without any discrimination. Nuclear technology or nuclear materials should be subjected to universal, standardized and non-discriminatory safeguards agreed upon by supplier and recipient States.[98]

In contrast, the West and the East have collaborated in representing a united front of support for non-proliferation and the NPT. The working paper of the socialist countries listed as one of the major priorities in disarmament the "consolidation in every possible way of the regime of the non-proliferation of nuclear weapons," adding in this context the need to strengthen the NPT and IAEA safeguards. Similar points were made in the Western working paper. Almost identical expressions were used in both papers on the issue of the peaceful uses of nuclear energy. Both, while recognizing the right of all states to have peaceful nuclear energy programs, issued warnings on the perils of unsafeguarded nuclear activities.[99] In their statements to the SSOD both Vice President Mondale and Soviet Foreign Minister Gromyko paid tribute to the NPT as a major achievement in the field of arms limitation agreements.

The SSOD was an important crossroads for international efforts on nuclear non-proliferation and a major test for the viability and prestige of the NPT. Unlike the NPT review conference, which is restricted to the parties to the treaty, at the SSOD the leading opponents of the treaty could join the disillusioned majority of the parties in their struggle against the NWS. The verbatim of the debates at the SSOD reveal that the issue of nuclear non-proliferation was one of the key issues to which most delegations, each from its vantage point, attached great significance. It became clear that, despite superpower pressure supported by their allies, the member states of the United Nations could not reach agreement on language that would endorse the NPT. The degree of Third World opposition was reflected in a statement by Argentina, which viewed the NPT as "clearly discriminatory in nature" since "for the first time in history, it legitimizes a division of the world into two categories of countries: those who are to be given a completely free hand in the nuclear field and those who are to be subject to restrictions."[100] After a long diplomatic battle the compromise formula achieved in the Final Document was to omit specific recommendations and references to measures for non-proliferation and to refer to them in the vaguest of terms. What was left was only a general affirmation of the goal of non-proliferation. As SIPRI pointed out, the reference to non-proliferation of nuclear weapons in the Final Document was weaker than many United Nations resolutions adopted on the subject.[101]

As expected, the compromise did not satisfy either side. Several Western countries expressed dissatisfaction at the SSOD with the manner in which nuclear weapons non-proliferation was treated in the document.[102] The representative of the Netherlands expressed regret that the paragraphs on non-proliferation "lack a sense of urgency" and that they "reflect the absence of universally accepted principles in this field."[103] In a complete contrast, for the non-aligned countries even the Final Document's ambiguous phraseology was too much. Speaking on behalf of the non-aligned group, Sri Lanka criticized the nuclear-weapon states for coming out "strongest" on the subject of non-proliferation and putting restrictions on the peaceful uses of nuclear energy without committing themselves to nuclear disarmament.[104]

PEACEFUL ATOMIC ENERGY

With NIEO politics in the background, the gap between the two camps is unbridgeable and goes far beyond the differences over the text and interpretation of the NPT. The debate on peaceful nuclear energy created another arena for Third World grievances over "discrimination" and "monopoly." The debate here goes beyond the treaty: some of the industrialized countries (with Soviet support) regard the NPT safeguards provisions as inadequate to provide a foolproof barrier to nuclear proliferation. As shown, many experts in the field agree with this assessment on the inadequacy of the treaty. The Third World, on the other hand, views the already existing safeguards in the NPT and their application as discriminatory and harmful to the process of economic development.

The two camps advance views that reflect their different needs and interests on various aspects of peaceful nuclear energy. In sum, the clash is on two separate but related areas: on the terms of transfer of nuclear technology, its controls and safeguards, and over the evaluation of prospective dangers and benefits of the "plutonium economy," i.e., the use of plutonium in the nuclear fuel cycle. The latter issue involved also a disagreement between the United States and a number of developed countries—suppliers of nuclear know-how and material.[105] A study conducted by SIPRI concludes that neither the NPT nor the safeguards can prevent a country with a reprocessing plant from having access to fissile materials. Reprocessing involves the separation of plutonium from the other waste products, providing an access to fissile material directly usable for making nuclear weapons. There is no technological solution to this dilemma yet: "It has been impossible to find a proliferation-resistant process for plutonium separation."[106]

In the mid-1970s, the major nuclear suppliers began to pay increasing attention to the relationship between export policies and the implications on the proliferation of nuclear-weapon capabilities. There was a growing awareness of the dual nature of nuclear power and the recognition, to use the phrase of Ernest Bergmann, the former director of the Atomic Energy Commission in Israel, that "it is very important to understand that by developing atomic energy for peaceful uses, you reach the nuclear option: *There are no two atomic energies.*"[107] As soon as a NNWS acquires a nuclear power industry it proceeds along what George Quester has called the "innocent progress toward the bomb curve," where for some countries a very short time would be required to move from a peaceful nuclear program toward the production of at least a few crude nuclear weapons.[108]

In 1974, a number of suppliers reached an understanding on common safeguard requirements that was further expanded in a nuclear suppliers' conference in London (thus becoming known as the London Club). These countries defined, on what is known as the Trigger List, the materials and equipment whose transfers to an NNWS triggers the application of IAEA safeguards. In September 1977 the fifteen countries participating in those meetings adopted export policy guidelines and communicated them to the director general of IAEA. The fifteen members in the "Club" represent the group of countries that maintains the leverage over international transfer of nuclear technology: Belgium, Canada, Czechoslovakia, France, German Democratic Republic, Federal Republic of Germany, Italy, Japan, Netherlands, Poland, Sweden, Switzerland, the Soviet Union, the United Kingdom, and the United States.[109] The London Club meetings were held secretly and were followed by a series of bilateral talks between the United States and other suppliers. The results were announced in early 1978, and the agreement was sent to the IAEA. But the suppliers' consensus fell short of Washington's overall goals, and it failed, because of some divisions among Western suppliers, to insist that future transactions include "full-scope" safeguards, as the Americans wanted, and that recipient countries allow all their nuclear facilities to be inspected by international teams before they can order new equipment.[110]

Some suppliers (both Soviet bloc and Western countries) have adopted national export policies going beyond the requirements set out in London guidelines. The most comprehensive and far-reaching legislation on this matter was taken in the United States under the anti-proliferation strategy of the Carter administration. The Nuclear Non-Proliferation Act was passed in the U.S. Congress in March 1978, just two months before the opening of the SSOD.[111]

As their statements and working papers to the SSOD indicated, Third World countries widely criticized the restrictions over the transfer of nuclear technology. The secret meetings of the London Club aroused their fears of "a new suppliers cartel with the possible threat of price fixing."[112] The U.S. Non-Proliferation Act caused even a greater furor. In the Third World it was viewed as another attempt to perpetuate the supremacy of the industrialized countries over the developing ones. At the bilateral level, confidence in the United States as a dependable supplier of nuclear fuel has been shaken by unexpected cutoffs. Third World nations were not pacified by the U.S. initiative that led to the creation of the International Nuclear Fuel Cycle Evaluation (INFCE) in October 1977. The INFCE opened a dialogue at the technical level among developed and developing countries, suppliers and recipients of nuclear technologies, equipment, and material. From the point of view of the Third World, it seemed that while the NPT orientation was to discuss the *conditions* for receiving nuclear supplies, the post-NPT orientation was to discuss *restraints* on supply.[113] The measures taken by the suppliers (the guidelines and the "trigger list" of the London Club, and the Carter policies) were clearly directed toward curbing sensitive flows to Third World nations. In the view of Third World commentators, all this so-called post-NPT multilateral diplomacy on restraints on nuclear transfers has gone beyond NPT terms and therefore has overtaken and made the original bargain irrelevant.[114] Third World countries emphasized the importance of access to peaceful nuclear technology for the scientific, technological, and economic advancement of nations and criticized the suppliers for placing restrictions on such transfers under the guise of preventing the horizontal proliferation of nuclear weapons. According to their view, these imposed restrictions only served to consolidate the predominance of the few industrialized nations in science and technology and, on the other hand, to condemn the majority to a position of dependency.[115]

Algeria and Pakistan flatly rejected the idea that the "dissemination of nuclear technology would automatically hinder attainment of the goal of non-proliferation."[116] Pakistan was not satisfied even with the recognition of the inalienable right of states to acquire and develop nuclear technology for peaceful purposes incorporated in paragraph 36 of the Final Document. The language, according to Pakistan, was still "capable of being used to justify policies of restraint and restriction, deprivation and discrimination."[117] The net result of the debate on peaceful atomic energy in the SSOD was the further erosion of NPT provisions. Immediately after the vague reference to the NPT came the qualification: "Non-Proliferation measures should not jeopardize the full exercise of the inalienable rights of all States to apply and develop their programmes for the peaceful uses of nuclear energy."[118] This futile game between conflicting conceptions led SIPRI to conclude:

In terms of the NPT, some Third World states now tend to interpret Article IV as a promise of nuclear co-operation unrelated to the non-proliferation context. They were able to influence the discussion on proliferation at the 1978 United Nations General Assembly Special Session on Disarmament, to the extent that the Final Document focused little interest on the problem of nuclear weapon proliferation. In contrast, at the insistence of non-aligned countries, the document underlines the inalienable rights of all states to develop nuclear power programmes in conformity with their own priorities, interests and needs. Such excessive emphasis on peaceful uses of nuclear energy in the Final Document has distorted the arms control aspect of non-proliferation.[119]

The SSOD underscored the opposition in the Third World to any restriction on the export of nuclear technology. This opposition draws heavily from the philosophy and terminology of the struggle for NIEO. India, speaking as a leader of the non-aligned nations, blames the NPT for having perpetuated the technological monopoly of the nuclear weapon powers, using phrases such as "a bizarre new world of nuclear aristocracy ruling the non-nuclear serfdom."[120] Indian scholars are using NIEO parlance in discussing proliferation matters and speak about "India's adamant refusal to compromise its sovereignty on nuclear safeguards." They make no secret that at issue is "the present structure of power in the world," in which nuclear safeguards are essentially "a mask for the perpetuation of superpowers' hegemony."[121]

A leading nuclear physicist has claimed that the attempt to shift the emphasis in the NPT toward the transfer of nuclear technology represents a new danger to the integrity of the treaty. The priority given by the Third World to the peaceful uses of nuclear energy and the transfer of technology to developing countries amounts to a reinterpretation of the treaty and the overriding of its non-proliferation aspects. In this sense the NPT becomes a means toward achieving nuclear capability through the acquisition of nuclear technology. With this interpretation, which seems to prevail in the United Nations, J. Rotblat concludes: "The NPT will in effect become a treaty for the peaceful uses of nuclear energy, and as such may be instrumental in promoting the very spread of nuclear weapon capability that it was intended to inhibit."[122]

IN THE AFTERMATH OF THE SSOD

The gap between the great powers together with their allies and the Third World continued to widen after the SSOD. The debates in the CD, the United Nations Disarmament Commission, and in the General Assemblies followed the same patterns of growing resentment by the developing countries toward the NPT and non-proliferation policies of the great powers. At the sixth summit conference of the non-aligned in Havana in September 1979, there was no reference whatsoever to the NPT in the 310 paragraphs of the Political Declaration. Again, the only reference to non-proliferation as such was negative: "Concern for non-proliferation should not be used as a pretext to prevent States from exercising the right to acquire and develop peaceful nuclear technology."[123] After the SSOD the non-aligned established a Co-ordinating Bureau on peaceful uses of nuclear energy, which met in Belgrade in December 1978. This coordination, outside the United Nations, was in some ways a countermeasure to the nuclear suppliers' meetings, but even more important was the attempt to explore the possibilities offered by cooperation and mutual assistance among themselves in peaceful uses of nuclear energy.[124]

The issue reemerged in the annual deliberations in the plenary of the United Nations General Assembly on the IAEA report. A number of developing countries such as India, Nigeria, Pakistan, Romania, and Yugoslavia demanded an increase in the resources allocated to IAEA technical assistance activities. India expressed dissatisfaction at the "increasing stress being laid upon regulatory rather than promotional aspects of the Agency's functions."[125] In the General Assembly of 1980, India, while reaffirming its position on what it termed the narrow and illogical approach of the unworkable document of the NPT, complained in strong terms about the arrangements between the suppliers of nuclear technology. The Indian foreign minister referred to "discriminatory constraints" and "cartel-type arrangements" against the NNWS "aimed at perpetuating a kind of nuclear feudalism."[126]

As pointed out at the outset, the second review conference of the NPT of 1980 failed to agree even on a consensus document of the type achieved in previous United Nations conferences on similar matters. The differences were the same as earlier ones, and the contending approaches clashed again; only the circumstances became more complex. In a press conference the spokesman of the session told reporters that "in four weeks' of negotiations the participants had agreed on virtually nothing of significance."[127] It was agreed by diplomats and observers that the fact that the conference ended without a strong declaration of support for limiting the spread of nuclear arms "will undermine the treaty's credibility and extend North–South quarrels into the disarmament field"[128] (except that the essence of all disarmament quarrels at the United Nations was already for a long time a North–South confrontation).

Frank Barnaby, the director of the SIPRI, attributes the failure of the conference not only to the "intransigence of the superpowers" but also—though with less firmness—to the inflexibility of the non-aligned on some issues. As indicated by Barnaby, there was a "lack of overt hostility between the American and Soviet delegates" in the conference, despite the Soviet invasion of Afghanistan and the U.S. failure to ratify SALT II. In this regard superpower collaboration was highlighted by the disarray among the Western powers because of their differences over nuclear export policies.[129] It was expected that when non-proliferation is at stake—something similar in nature to their veto power in the Security Council—both superpowers would work together to ward off Third World attacks in order to pursue their High Posture approach.

Third World delegates criticized the High Posture policies of the superpowers and referred to the nuclear supplier group as "a secret conclave."[130] At one point in the review conference, the Peruvian ambassador said that his country might renounce its participation in the NPT out of dissatisfaction at the failure of the superpowers to meet their disarmament commitments. Some speculated that it was a warning of non-aligned restiveness, which might lead to a total collapse of the treaty since there was similar unrest among other Latin American, African, Arab, and Asian signatories to the NPT.[131] But it seemed that the NWS did not get excited by what they dismissed as "wild talk," an attempt by the Third World to use the threat of defection as a bargaining counter.[132] At the United Nations, it is agreed among diplomatic observers that there is a big dose of bluff in Third World periodic threats to pull out of the non-proliferation treaty.[133] It is a bluff since nuclear proliferation is not in the interest of most developing countries. However, it is apparent that the United Nations environment and the political culture of the NIEO are not conducive to the NPT or to the strengthening of the non-proliferation regime.

In the Thirty-fifth General Assembly, which followed the review conference, disappointment was expressed by almost everybody. In effect, only the superpowers (with some of their close allies) emphasized what they regarded as achievements of the conference. The U.S. secretary of state, Edmund Muskie, speaking on the NPT as a cornerstone of non-proliferation efforts, referred only to what he regarded as the "unanimous agreement at the conference on the fundamental soundness of the treaty and the desirability of *universal adherence to it*."[134] All Western countries expressed their disappointment in one way or another. Ireland, which recalls with pride its 1959 initiative as the origin of the treaty, while expressing profound regret and disappointment, warned that the unsuccessful outcome of the conference would make the task of preventing the nuclear spread more difficult.[135] Third World countries continued to criticize the treaty, using the failure of the conference as another vindication of their position. Sri Lanka, saying that the conference had ended "in disarray," blamed the superpowers for failing to negotiate nuclear disarmament as they had undertaken in Article VI of the treaty.[136] Nigeria took this opportunity to conclude that non-proliferation in the 1980s cannot be sustained by the same reliance as in the past on the Non-Proliferation Treaty. Instead, Nigeria said, an alternative multilateral instrument will have to be concluded urgently to prevent "both horizontal and vertical proliferation."[137]

Notwithstanding this campaign at the United Nations against the NPT, it would be too hasty to pronounce a death sentence on the treaty. It seems that, despite their blatant criticism, most Third World countries regard the non-proliferation regime created by the NPT as an important contribution to their national security. For the time being it seems that nuclear proliferation is slow "not because the NPT is necessarily working, but because the military and economic security perceptions of potential proliferators do not dictate a higher rate of proliferation."[138] Moreover, most Third World countries realize that in case of nuclear proliferation their own countries would be the first possible victims, not the superpowers. In effect they already recognized it by joining the NPT, which in its preamble gives an indication as to why it is preferable to limit nuclear weapons to the NWS since "the proliferation of nuclear weapons would seriously enhance the danger of nuclear war." To repeat, there is therefore a basic contradiction between the national interest of individual Third World countries and the platform of the group as a whole, a platform that might not exist except for the United Nations.

The spread of conventional conflicts and wars in the Third World (see next chapter) indicates that the military security risks of horizontal nuclear proliferation may run high. Richard Rosecrance has pointed out the risks of nuclear war in "minor power subgames," where primitive, vulnerable nuclear-weapon capabilities are deployed in various local or regional conflict situations.[139] Similarly, former U.S. Secretary of Defense James Schlesinger indicated what might be the reasoning of many Third World leaders who support the NPT:

If we are to dissuade others from aspiring to nuclear capabilities, what we should stress is that, if weapons spread, they are not likely to be employed against the superpower. The penalties for proliferation would be paid, not by the United States, or the Soviet Union, but by Third World countries. The likelihood that the first nuclear war, if it comes, will originate in and be confined to the underdeveloped world should play a prominent role in any assessment of proliferation's consequences. The tenor of the existing discussion of proliferation has led some people in the underdeveloped countries to conclude that the major powers would be the chief beneficiaries of curtailing the spread. If nuclear spread is to be effectively opposed, it should be made crystal clear just whose security is placed at risk and whose is not.[140]

There is always a possibility of deterioration in regional and international security, which may affect the strategic environment of potential proliferators. The increase of local, regional, self-contained conflicts among Third World nations, coupled with dizzying conventional arms races there, has ominous implications for horizontal nuclear proliferation. At the same time, growing international tension and a superpower military buildup may decrease their condominium coordination on nuclear proliferation. It should be noted that in the case of the Indian explosion of 1974, the superpowers were not capable, or at least were unwilling, to take joint concrete measures against India. At this particular juncture it is evident that the United Nations is not only unable to provide the necessary ideological consensus that is crucial for the viability of the nuclear non-proliferation regime, but may also be concealing emerging differences between the superpowers or conflicting ambitions in regional politics.

Eventually, under the banner of the new international order it is hard to expect a serious debate in the United Nations on issues relating to international security. As pointed out in Chapter 4, the United Nations has evolved from an organization primarily committed to maintaining the post–World War II international order into a world system intently devoted by its overwhelming majority to a radical change of world order and its power distribution. Disarmament issues, as a result, moved to a secondary spot on the Third World agenda, becoming, in effect, a bargaining chip in the larger context of the North–South dialogue. Within this new context the NPT symbolizes more than anything else the inequalities of the world system established by the great powers, inequalities that are also reflected in the United Nations Charter. The political culture of the NIEO does not allow the sorely needed exchange on the perils of the peaceful uses of nuclear technology. With the overriding considerations of "sovereign equality," non-discrimination, the right to development, etc., it is impossible to elaborate further non-proliferation measures.

The implications of the NIEO for non-proliferation are particularly ominous at a time when there is a growing recognition that the treaty is a fragile document with many loopholes and that advanced technologies in the nuclear field are challenging the basic premise of its safeguards system. As SIPRI writes in 1980, new technologies would make it impossible to rely on the International Atomic Energy Agency safeguards to detect the diversion of nuclear material to weapons production. In the case of plutonium or highly enriched uranium, it may require only a few days for diverted nuclear material to be transformed into an explosive, and then there is always the "abrogation risk"—the withdrawal from the treaty—which is inherent in the NPT system.[141] As Lewis Dunn points out, the world is entering a new and more perilous era in the nuclear age in which international cooperation is crucial to prevent the grave risks of a further spread of nuclear weapons.[142]

It is striking that when many in developed countries are having second thoughts about the economic desirability of nuclear power for commercial purposes the United Nations is prevented from serious examination of other alternatives to meet the energy needs of developing countries. Reality, as experts would agree, has "debunked the fantasy that enormous diversions of national resources for nuclear power would make deserts bloom, cities boom, and villages prosper."[143] Instead, North–South debates on nuclear proliferation divert attention from the security and economic aspects of nuclear programs and foster the illusion that nuclear power is central to national prestige and glamor in international forums. The attitudes reflected by Third World spokesmen create a psychological climate for promoting the nuclear option in developing countries. With the lack of community interest, the dictates of "consensus" politics at the United Nations tend to produce at best a document that completely distorts the arms control aspect of non-proliferation and ignores international safeguards, while reiterating excessive demands for the transfer of nuclear technology. In a sense, therefore, the proclamation in the nuclear field of NIEO philosophy, with its special emphasis on distributive justice and sovereign equality in international affairs, may make the United Nations instrumental in legitimizing nuclear weapons proliferation.

NOTES

1. SIPRI, *Postures for Non-Proliferation*, p. 8.
2. Mandelbaum, *The Nuclear Question*, pp. 193–94.

3. See *Second Review Conference on Nuclear Non-Proliferation Treaty Held in Geneva, 11 August-7 September*, Round-up of Session, United Nations Press Release, NPT/89, September 10, 1980 (New York: Department of Public Information, United Nations); Alessandro Corradini (Secretary General of the Conference), "The Second Review Conference of the Parties to the Treaty on the Non-Proliferation of Nuclear Weapons," *Disarmament 3*, no. 3 (November 1980): 5–27; Frank Barnaby, "The NPT Review Conference—Much Talk, Few Results," *Bulletin of the Atomic Scientists* (November 1980): 7–8; Philip Towle, "Nuclear Non-Proliferation: Deadlock at Geneva," *The World Today* (October 1980): 371–74; "Non-Proliferation Treaty Reviewed at Geneva but no Consensus Reached," *UN Chronicle* 17, no. 9 (November 1980): 15–17. For the results of the first review conference, see "Final Declaration of the Review Conference of the Parties to the Treaty on the Non-Proliferation of Nuclear Weapons," May 30, 1975, NPT/Conf./53/1, Geneva, 1975, Annex: Final Declaration.

4. See the relevant *UN and Disarmament Yearbooks*.

5. Towle, "Nuclear Non-Proliferation," p. 371.

6. Epstein, *The Last Chance*, p. 85.

7. George Fischer, *The Non-Proliferation of Nuclear Weapons* (New York: St. Martin's Press, 1970), p. 67.

8. Elizabeth Young, "The Nonproliferation Treaty: An Acceptable Balance," *Bulletin of the Atomic Scientists* (November 1967): 37–38.

9. Eighteen Nations Disarmament Conference, ENDC/PV.370.

10. Fischer, *Non-Proliferation*, pp. 70–78, 217–18.

11. Epstein, *The Last Chance*, p. 245.

12. ENDC/204, p. 3.

13. GAOR, "Views of the Swiss Government on Problems to Be Discussed at the Tenth Special Session of the General Assembly," A/S-10/AC.1/2. Since Switzerland is not a member of the UN, its letter was transmitted by a group of member states, which together with Switzerland are the "non-aligned" or the neutral states of Europe: Austria, Finland, Sweden, Yugoslavia. Switzerland provided an interesting observation on the complex issues of world order, sovereignty, and discrimination:

These weapons not only have given mankind the means of annihilating itself but also—by virtue of the Non-Proliferation Treaty—have divided States into two categories: on one hand, a minority of States which are granted the right to possess nuclear weapons and which sometimes derive important political and military advantages therefrom and, on the other hand, all the remaining States, which have renounced that right. In other words, differences in the realm of military power show a tendency to grow rather than diminish.

In ratifying the Non-Proliferation Treaty, like nearly 100 other States, Switzerland has shown its willingness unilaterally to limit its sovereignty in order to diminish the dangers caused by the proliferation of nuclear weapons.

However, the Federal Council wishes to point out that such discriminatory measures are contrary to the principle of the equality of all States. In that regard, the Treaty on the Non-Proliferation of Nuclear Weapons cannot under any circumstances constitute a model for other disarmament measures.

14. Mandelbaum, *The Nuclear Question*, p. 194.

15. Bull, "The Great Irresponsibles?" p. 438.

16. Michael Mandelbaum, "International Stability and Nuclear Order: The First Nuclear Regime," in *Nuclear Weapons and World Politics*, ed. David C. Gompert,

Michael Mandelbaum, Richard L. Garwin, and John H. Barton, 1980s Project Council on Foreign Relations (New York: McGraw-Hill, 1977), p. 71.

17. See Albert Wohlstetter et al., *Swords from Plowshares* (Chicago: University of Chicago Press, 1977), p. 128. This research project sponsored by the U.S. Arms Control and Disarmament Agency became immediately influential for changing government policy ushering in a major departure in U.S. policy against nuclear proliferation (see the foreword by Fred Charles Ikel).

18. Fischer, *Non-Proliferation*, p. 69.

19. Ibid., p. 219; and B. T. Feld, replying to comments by Elizabeth Young, in *Bulletin of the Atomic Scientists* (November 1967): 38.

20. Wohlstetter et al., *Swords*, p. 141.

21. Mandelbaum, *The Nuclear Question*, p. 139.

22. *The United Nations and Disarmament 1945–1970* (New York: United Nations, 1970), pp. 258–63.

23. Myrdal, *The Game of Disarmament*, p. 166.

24. Ibid., p. 168.

25. John Barton and Lawrence D. Weiler, eds., *International Arms Control* (Stanford, Calif.: Stanford University Press, 1976), p. 297.

26. Ibid., pp. 297–98.

27. Bernard Feld, replying to Elizabeth Young, p. 38; see also Louis Rene Beres, who lists various perils for international security in nuclear proliferation to the Third World, in *Apocalypse*, pp. 14–15. On proliferation to unstable regimes and the threat of nuclear terrorism, see Yeheskel Dror, *Crazy States—A Counterconventional Strategic Problem* (Lexington, Mass.: Heath Lexington Books, 1971); Robert H. Kupperman, *Facing Tomorrow's Terrorist Incident Today* (Washington, D.C.: Law Enforcement Assistance Administration, October 1977); David Rosenbaum, "Nuclear Terror," *International Security* 1, no. 2 (Winter 1977).

28. On the security interests of nuclear threshold countries, see George Quester, *The Politics of Nuclear Proliferation* (Baltimore: Johns Hopkins Press, 1973).

29. D. E. Kennedy, *The Security of Southern Asia* (London: Chatto & Windus, 1965), p. 61. Studies in International Security, No. 8, Institute for Strategic Studies series. For an extensive analysis of India's nuclear decision-making, see Ashok Kapur, *India's Nuclear Option: Atomic Diplomacy and Decision Making* (New York: Praeger Publishers, 1976).

30. Arthur S. Lall, *Negotiating Disarmament: The Eighteen Nation Disarmament Conference: The First Two Years 1962–64*, Cornell Research Papers in International Studies, No. 2 (Ithaca, N.Y.: Center for International Studies, Cornell University, 1964), pp. 24–25.

31. Epstein, *The Last Chance*, pp. 64–65.

32. Ibid., p. 65.

33. "Second Conference of Heads of State or Government of Non-Aligned Countries: Cairo, 1964," in *The Third World Without Superpowers: The Collected Documents of the Non-Aligned Countries*, ed. Odette Jankowitsch and Karl P. Sauvant (New York: Oceana Publications, 1978), p. 53.

34. U.S. ACDA, *Documents on Disarmament 1964*, pp. 444–45.

35. Epstein, *The Last Chance*, pp. 65–66.

36. GAOR, DC/PV.75, May 4, 1965.

37. *UN and Disarmament 1945–1970*, p. 269.

38. U.S. ACDA, *Documents on Disarmament 1967*, pp. 176–206.

39. Fischer, *Non-Proliferation*, p. 157.

40. Ibid.

41. Husain, "Third World and Disarmament," p. 76.

42. Kapur, *International Nuclear Proliferation*, pp. 182–83.

43. Young, *A Farewell to Arms Control*, p. 96.

44. See U.S. ACDA, *Documents on Disarmament 1964*, pp. 444–45; also in Epstein, *The Last Chance*, pp. 64–70; and Barton and Weiler, *International Arms Control*, pp. 294–99.

45. Barton and Weiler, *International Arms Control*, p. 296; and Young, *Farewell to Arms Control*, p. 96.

46. Ashok Kapur, "Nuclear Proliferation in the 1980's," *International Journal* 36, no. 3 (Summer 1981): 540.

47. Phil Williams, "Deterrence," in *Contemporary Strategy: Theories and Policies*, ed. John Baylis, Ken Booth, John Garnett, and Phil Williams (New York: Holmes & Meier Publishers, 1975), p. 68.

48. James E. Dougherty and Robert L. Pfaltzgraff, Jr., *Contending Theories of International Relations* (New York: J. B. Lippincott, 1971), p. 273. Dougherty and Pfaltzgraff provide a long list of authors who regard proliferation of nuclear weapons as a major source of instability. For a broader elaboration of the case for bipolarity, see Kenneth N. Waltz, "International Structure, National Force, and the Balance of World Power," *Journal of International Affairs* 21, no. 2 (1967). Waltz argues that a bipolar international system with its inherent disparity between the superpowers and the lesser states provides more stability than a multipolar system. Other writers emphasize the threat of nuclear proliferation to states with extremely militant ideologies that are profoundly dissatisfied with the status quo or to leaders of unstable regimes with a "give me victory or give me death" philosophy. In these cases deterrence may be completely useless. See Dror, *Crazy States*.

49. Philip Gummett, "From NPT to INFCE: Developments in Thinking About Nuclear Non-Proliferation," *International Affairs* 57, no. 4 (Autumn 1981): 550.

50. Young, *Farewell to Arms Control*, p. 96.

51. William B. Bader, *The United States and the Spread of Nuclear Weapons* (New York: Pegasus, 1968), pp. 40, 129.

52. SIPRI, *Postures for Non-Proliferation*, pp. 8–9, 25.

53. Hedley Bull, "The Role of the Nuclear Powers in the Management of Nuclear Proliferation," in *Arms Control for the Late Sixties*, ed. J. E. Dougherty and J. T. Lehman (Princeton, N.J.: D. Van Nostrand, 1967).

54. As the SIPRI study mentions, the High Posture Doctrine has been advocated as an anti-proliferation strategy by such analysts as Walter Hahn, Malcolm Hoag, Uri Ra'ana, James Schlesinger, and Alton Frye. SIPRI, *Postures for Non-Proliferation*, pp. 27–39. A more recent and modified version of this approach can be found in Michael Mandelbaum, "International Stability and Nuclear Order: The First Nuclear Regime," in *Nuclear Weapons and World Politics*, ed. David C. Gompert, Michael Mandelbaum, Richard L. Garwin, and John M. Barton (New York: McGraw-Hill, 1977); and Mandelbaum, *The Nuclear Question*.

55. Proponents of the Low Posture Doctrine are, for instance, Richard Falk, Hedley Bull in his more recent writings, Leonard Beaton, John Maddox, Max Singer, and Ian

Smart. See SIPRI, *Postures for Non-Proliferation*, pp. 39–66. Another new publication can be added to the above: Beres, *Apocalypse*.

56. GAOR, Non-Aligned Working Documents: A/AC.184/55. These demands were bracketed by the Eastern bloc as indicated in the annotated version of the draft final document (see Appendix II).

57. See Appendix II.

58. Ibid. The gap was apparent in the working group on the program of action that met during the SSOD. The final outcome demonstrates that the superpowers agreed to water down the references to the NPT in the document.

59. Bull, "Arms Control," p. 5.

60. Yuter, *Orbis* (Winter 1969).

61. Morton A. Kaplan, "The Nuclear Non-Proliferation Treaty: Its Rationale, Prospects and Possible Impact on International Law," in *Great Issues of International Politics*, ed. Morton A. Kaplan (Chicago: Aldine, 1974), pp. 193–94.

62. Henry A. Kissinger, *Years of Upheaval* (Boston: Little, Brown, 1982), p. 233.

63. H. R. Haldeman, *The Ends of Power* (New York: Times Books, 1978), pp. 90–94.

64. See Herman Kahn, *On Thermonuclear War* (Princeton, N.J.: Princeton University Press, 1960), pp. 30–31. See also Hedley Bull, "Arms Control and World Order," *International Security* 1, no. 1 (Summer 1976): 12.

65. Epstein, *The Last Chance*, p. 104.

66. Karl Winnacker and Karl Wirtz, *Nuclear Energy in Germany* (La Grange Park, Ill.: American Nuclear Society, 1979), p. 201.

67. Gaddis, *The United States*; and Diane Shaver Clemens, *Yalta* (New York: Oxford University Press, 1970). For the critics, see Gerald Kurland, ed., *The Failure of Diplomacy—The Origins of the Cold War* (New York: Simon and Schuster, 1975), p. 13. See also Averell W. Harriman, *America and Russia in a Changing World* (London: George Allen & Unwin, 1971), pp. 34–42.

68. Myrdal, *The Game of Disarmament*, p. 168.

69. Kapur, *International Nuclear Proliferation*, p. 137.

70. Quoted in Wohlstetter et al., *Swords*, p. 63.

71. Ibid. *Swords from Plowshares* analyzes in an extraordinary range the relations between civil nuclear technology and the proliferation of nuclear weapons. See also a more recent book, Peter Pringle and James Spigelman, *The Nuclear Barons* (New York: Holt, Rinehart and Winston, 1981).

72. Kapur, "Nuclear Proliferation," p. 553.

73. See Myrdal, *The Game of Disarmament*, p. 172.

74. Kapur, *International Nuclear Proliferation*, p. 81.

75. See the following series of articles in *Bulletin of the Atomic Scientists* (October 1981): Sidney Moglewer, "IAEA Safeguards and Non-Proliferation"; Roger Richter, "Testimony from a Former Safeguards Inspector"; Singuard Eklund, "The IAEA on Safeguards" (statement by the IAEA director-general in defense of the system of safeguards). See also the following reports in the *New York Times*: "Report on Bomb Safeguards: Gross Deficiencies," November 16, 1981; "Nuclear Cheating: Why the Experts Are Worried Over Safeguards," December 22, 1981.

76. William Epstein, "Measures Necessary to Curb Nuclear Proliferation," in *U.S. Policy in International Institutions, Defining Reasonable Options in an Unreasonable World*, ed. Seymour Maxwell Finger and Joseph R. Harbert (Boulder, Colo.: Westview

Press, 1978), p. 20; *A Short History of Non-Proliferation* (Vienna: IAEA, February 1976), p. 22. The new IAEA director, Hans Blix, has gone on record saying, "You can't stop proliferation by safeguards." In addition he disclosed that the agency had made no progress in persuading Pakistan to allow additional monitoring facilities in its Karachi reactor, where "anomalies and irregularities" have been detected. "UN Aide Sees Little to Curb Spread of Atom Arms," *New York Times*, February 18, 1982.

77. Paul Szasz, *The Law and Practices of the International Atomic Energy Agency* (Vienna: IAEA, September 1970), pp. 549, 564.

78. SIPRI, *The NPT: The Main Political Barrier to Nuclear Weapons Proliferation* (London: Taylor & Francis, 1980), p. 28.

79. Wohlstetter et al., *Swords*, p. 126.

80. Moglewer, "IAEA Safeguards," p. 28. For further elaboration on the inadequacies of existing systems of safeguards, see Wohlstetter et al., *Swords*, chap. 2; Ted Greenwood; Harold A. Feiveson; and Theodore B. Taylor, *Nuclear Proliferation: Motivations, Capabilities and Strategies for Control*, 1980s Project Council on Foreign Relations (New York: McGraw-Hill, 1977), pp. 125–54; A.R.W. Wilson, "Multinational and International Controls," in SIPRI, *Nuclear Energy and Nuclear Weapon Proliferation* (London: Taylor & Francis, 1978), pp. 251–52; J. Rotblat, "Nuclear Proliferation: Arrangements for International Control," in ibid., pp. 272–82.

81. Ad Hoc Group on United States Policy Toward the United Nations, *The United States and the United Nations. . .A Policy for Today* (Memo), New York, October 1981. The group was chaired by Morris B. Abram, and the working draft was prepared by Seymour M. Finger. Originally the idea of the Nuclear Security Planning Committee of the Security Council was introduced by Abraham Bargman, himself a member of the Ad Hoc Group. See Abraham Bargman, "The United Nations, the Superpowers and Proliferation," *Annals of the American Academy of Political and Social Science* 430 (March 1977). Nuclear Proliferation: Prospects, Problems and Proposals issue.

82. A. B. Lovins, L. Hunter Lovins, and L. Ross, "Nuclear Power and Nuclear Bombs," *Foreign Affairs* (Summer 1980): 1140.

83. In the introduction to Wohlstetter et al., *Swords*, p. xii; see also in p. 3.

84. Moglewer, "IAEA Safeguards," p. 28.

85. "Nuclear Safeguards, Deemed Weak by U.S. Regulatory Commission," *New York Times*, December 1, 1981. In a later report the Nuclear Regulatory Commission went beyond previous expressions of concern and determined that IAEA safeguards alone could not "reliably" warn on diversions of weapon-grade materials.

86. Epstein, *The Last Chance*, p. 249.

87. Thomas A. Halster, "NPT: Report from Geneva," in *Negotiating Security*, ed. William M. Kincade and Jeffrey D. Porro (Washington, D.C.: Carnegie Endowment for International Peace, 1979), pp. 146–47.

88. See Myrdal, *The Game of Disarmament*, p. 174; Epstein, *The Last Chance*, pp. 146–47, 245–53; SIPRI, *NPT*, p. 11; SIPRI, *Postures for Non-Proliferation*, p. 131.

89. See NPT Review Conference Document: NPT NPT/Conf./17/Add, 1–4; and Halster, "NPT: Report," p. 148; SIPRI, *Posture for Non-Proliferation*, pp. 136–37.

90. SIPRI, *Posture for Non-Proliferation*, pp. 138, 144.

91. Greenwood, Feiveson, and Taylor, *Nuclear Proliferation*, pp. 50–51.

92. Ibid., pp. 16–17 (introduction by David C. Gompert).

93. Ibid., pp. 17–18.

94. SIPRI, *Internationalization to Prevent the Spread of Nuclear Weapons* (London: Taylor & Francis, 1980), p. 6.

95. Ibid.

96. GAOR, A/AC.187/55.

97. GAOR, A/AC.187/55/Add.1.

98. Ibid.

99. East: GAOR, A/AC.187/82, September 7, 1977; West: GAOR, A/AC.187/87, December 13, 1977.

100. GAOR, A/S-10/PV.5, May 26, 1978, p. 56. See also Algeria: A/S-10/PV.12, June 1978, p. 11, and Prime Minister Desai of India, A/S-10/PV.24, June 9, 1978, p. 8.

101. SIPRI, *World Armament and Disarmament, SIPRI Yearbook 1979* (London: Taylor & Francis, 1979), annex p. 18. See also Jay Axelbank, "Clean Final Document," *Disarmament Times*, June 30, 1978, p. 1; and Epstein, "UN Special Session on Disarmament," p. 250.

102. *UN and Disarmament Yearbook, Vol. 3, 1978*, p. 239.

103. GAOR, A/C.133/PV.16, October 26, 1978, p. 35.

104. GAOR, A/S-10/PV.27, July 6, 1978, p. 78.

105. The analysis is based on *UN and Disarmament Yearbooks 1970–1979*.

106. SIPRI, *Internationalization*, p. 6.

107. *New York Times*, May 14, 1966.

108. George Quester, "Some Conceptual Problems in Nuclear Proliferation," *American Political Science Review* 66, no. 2 (June 1972): 491.

109. See the following *UN and Disarmament Yearbooks*: 1976, pp. 123–24; 1977, pp. 132–39; 1978, chap. 13; 1979, chap. 13; and Rotblat, "Nuclear Proliferation," pp. 275–78.

110. *New York Times*, January 12, 16, 1978.

111. *UN and Disarmament Yearbook, Vol. 3, 1978*, p. 251; and Robert Brennis, "Carter Anti-Proliferation Strategy," in *Negotiating Security*, ed. William M. Kincade and Jeffrey D. Porro (Washington, D.C.: Carnegie Endowment for International Peace, 1979), pp. 163–66; and W. H. Donnely, "Applications of U.S. Non-proliferation Legislation for Technical Aspects of the Control of Fissionable Materials in Non-Military Applications," in SIPRI, *Nuclear Energy*, pp. 190–240.

112. SIPRI, *The NPT*, p. 28.

113. Kapur, *International Nuclear Proliferation*, p. 67. For further discussion of the INFCE, see Gummett, "From NPT to INCFE."

114. Ashok Kapur, "The Nuclear Spread: A Third World View," *Third World Quarterly* 2, no. 1 (January 1980): 62.

115. *UN and Disarmament Yearbook, Vol. 3, 1978*, p. 257.

116. GAOR, A/S-10/PV.12, June 1, 1978, p. 12; and A/S-10/PV.7, May 29, 1978, pp. 28–30.

117. GAOR, A/S-10/PV.27, July 6, 1978, p. 102.

118. GAOR, SSOD Final Document, Tenth Special Session Supplement, No. 4, A/S-10/4, para. 67.

119. SIPRI, *The NPT*, p. 28.

120. Benjamin Sanders, "Nuclear Exporting Policies," in SIPRI, *Nuclear Energy*, p. 243. In opening the twenty-third annual meeting of the IAEA in New Delhi, Prime Minister of India Charan Singh stated, "Nonproliferation is a much-abused word which

prevents developing countries from peaceful uses of nuclear energy." "India Calls Effort to Curb Nuclear Arms a Hindrance to Development," *New York Times*, December 5, 1979.

121. Baldew Raj. Moyar, "India Wants Nuclear Sovereignty," *Christian Science Monitor*, May 17, 1979. For further discussion on Indian attitudes, see T. T. Poulsode, ed., *Perspectives of India's Nuclear Policy* (New Delhi: Young Asia Publication, 1977), esp. pp. 136–60.

122. Rotblat, "Nuclear Proliferation," p. 273.

123. Sixth Conference of Heads of State or Government of Non-Aligned Countries, GAOR, A/34/542, October 11, 1979, para. 232.

124. *UN and Disarmament Yearbook, Vol. 3, 1978*, pp. 253, 274; also in the Programme of Action for Economic Cooperation adopted by the non-aligned in their sixth summit, ibid., pp. 163–64.

125. GAOR, A/34/PV.35, November 5, 1979, p. 21.

126. GAOR, A/35/PV.23, October 3, 1980, p. 68.

127. *New York Times*, September 6, 1980.

128. Ibid.

129. Barnaby, "NPT Review Conference," p. 8.

130. UN Press Release, Department of Public Information, UN, New York, NPT/78, August 27, 1980, p. 4.

131. *New York Times*, September 6, 1980; and UN Press Release, NPT/54, August 13, 1980, p. 3.

132. *Washington Post*, August 13, 1980, p. 3.

133. "Short Fuses at the Nuclear Treaty Review," *New York Times*, August 17, 1980. It was confirmed also in private talks at the UN.

134. GAOR, A/35/PV.4, September 22, 1980.

135. GAOR, A/35/PV.17, September 30, 1980, p. 77.

136. GAOR, A/AC.l/35/PV.27, November 4, 1980, p. 18.

137. GAOR, A/AC.1/35/PV.15, October 27, 1980, p. 27.

138. Kapur, *International Nuclear Proliferation*, p. 160.

139. Richard Rosecrance, ed., *The Future of the International Strategic System* (San Francisco: Chandler Publishing, 1972), pp. 1–9 (introduction), 175–84.

140. James Schlesinger, "The Strategic Consequences of Nuclear Proliferation," in *Arms Control for the Late Sixties*, ed. J. E. Dougherty and J. T. Lehman (Princeton, N.J.: D. Van Nostrand, 1967), pp. 174–84.

141. SIPRI, *The NPT*, pp. 8, 21.

142. Lewis A. Dunn, *Controlling the Bomb—Nuclear Proliferation in the 1980s* (New Haven: Yale University Press, 1982). See in particular Chapter 4, where Dunn explains why the nuclearization of conflict-prone regions in the Third World may have costly and dangerous consequences.

143. Lovins, Lovins, and Ross, "Nuclear Power and Nuclear Bombs," p. 1170.

7

The Conventional Arms Race: The Third World's Double Standard

The Third World's share of global military expenditure has been on the increase.... The Third World's contribution to the cause of arms control and disarmament should not be confined to delivering moral sermons to the super-powers and to the other nuclear-weapon States.... We must not allow this special session of disarmament to become yet another United Nations exercise in propaganda and collective hypocrisy.[1]

Ambassador T. T. Koh of Singapore, June 1978

We cannot really hope to achieve such peace simply by measures limiting transfers of arms to countries of the Third World.... Such an initiative not only would be misguided but would do serious damage to the rights of States to ensure and organise their own national defence in a sovereign manner.[2]

Representative of Algeria, November 1980

While the Third World insists upon nuclear disarmament as the key to international peace and security, it is conspicuously ambiguous about and even reluctant to discuss the issue of conventional disarmament in United Nations forums. It is again the NIEO environment, in addition to the traditional national security considerations, that shapes the Third World position on conventional disarmament, making it another arena for North–South confrontation. Though there is more than a grain of truth in the Third World argument that sometimes the issue is exploited to divert attention from the nuclear arms race, it is also a fact that the world's conventional weapons situation is evolving at a rate that is dizzying compared with that in the nuclear area. At a time when the race for conventional weapons becomes a major striking characteristic of contemporary world politics, the issue becomes a prerequisite in any discussion on international security and disarmament. Since proportionally the largest increase in conventional weaponry has been in the Third World, the attitudes and policies of these countries are crucial for international efforts to curtail the conventional arms race. This chapter will scrutinize the role of the Third World in the conventional arms race and its position on this matter at the United Nations.

THE CONVENTIONAL ARMS RACE

Indeed, in terms of destructive potential, even a fraction of existing nuclear weapons may cause a catastrophe of unimaginable proportions. In 1980, the nuclear arsenals of the world contained more than 60,000 nuclear weapons—the equivalent of about four tons of explosives for every man, woman, and child on the earth.[3] Nonetheless, the fact is that since 1945 mankind has been mercifully spared the horrors of nuclear war. Instead, however, the world has witnessed about 150 wars, mostly in the Third World, all with conventional weapons resulting in the killing of 25 million people. Since 80 percent of global military expenditures goes to conventional purposes, any serious proposal with a view to major reductions in armed forces or military budgets (particulrly for the purposes of reallocation and conversion of resources) would have to include conventional arms. In short, the conventional arms race cannot be dismissed and ignored just because of the potential horrors of the nuclear buildup.

SIPRI data have indicated the relatively sharper rise—from very much lower absolute levels—of the *rate* of increase of military expenditures in the Third World. In 1957, the two major alliances, NATO and WTO, accounted for 85 percent of total military expenditures; the Third World share was about 5 percent. In the late 1970s the figure of the alliances had fallen below 70 percent, and the Third World share rose to more than 23 percent (without China, which accounts for 9.9 percent). Over these two decades, military spending in the Third World increased at an average annual rate of nearly 10 percent, compared with a world increase of about 3 percent. While per capita military expenditures remained level during the 1970s in the industrialized countries, they rose—at a time of great population expansion—in the developing world by one-third.[4] The increase was not restricted to the Middle East, where the largest accumulation of arms has occurred, but also occurred in Africa, where arms sales increased twentyfold, and tripled in Latin America from 1969 to 1978.[5]

The figures of the international trade in arms are even more illustrative than military expenditures in the Third World. In 1979, the value of global arms exports was five times greater than it was in 1960, and twelve times what it was in 1959. In the 1970s—which was declared by the United Nations the "Decade of Disarmament"—the total value of major arms imports to the Third World was about three and a half times more than in the previous decade and seven times greater than in the 1950s. The growth is not only in the volume of the arms trade but also in the number of importing countries and in the demand for more sophisticated weapon systems. According to SIPRI, "Two-thirds of the global arms trade involves transfer of weapons to the Third World, a good part of which suffers from under-development, starvation and disease."[6] According to official U.S. estimates in 1978, 81 percent of global arms imports were by developing countries.[7]

There are, of course, many reasons for this staggering demand for arms. The most important is the breakup of colonial empires and the multiplication of new and independent states—the same process that has changed the character of United Nations debates. In many of these countries the creation of national military establishment was a top priority, and its existence under the command of the head of state is generally perceived as an important attribute of sovereignty. The quantity and quality of arms acquired by a state, explains Andrew J. Pierre, became "a symbol of both its strength and its status."[8] Again, the concept of sovereignty and the drive for status became factors in Third World arms races, adding to inherent conditions of instability in many of these regions. Some observers criticized this process of creating a New International Military Order as an undesirable side effect of the yet-to-be-established NIEO.[9] Perhaps the growing militarization of the Third World can be viewed as a spillover of the interrelationships between the NIEO, world order, and disarmament (see Chapter 4).

DISREGARD FOR CONVENTIONAL DISARMAMENT

Against this background it is even more telling that conventional disarmament has been constantly and deliberately neglected by the United Nations. In the Final Document of the SSOD, the reference to conventional weapons and arms transfers was weak and in fact meaningless. It was drafted in tortuous and cumbersome language amounting to a justification of arms buildup in the name of just causes such as national security, independence, the inherent right of self-defense, and the principle of equal right of self-determination of peoples.[10] The non-aligned approach, which attaches absolute priority to nuclear disarmament (and even ignores conventional disarmament), has survived the painstaking consensus process of the SSOD. The nuclear dimension overshadows everything else in the Final Document in quantitative and qualitative terms. Nuclear disarmament gets special priority in the various sections of the document, and there are many more paragraphs, and stronger language, devoted to it. It is clear that the non-aligned do not consider conventional disarmament a matter of urgency, particularly when it is directed to their own military power.

After gradually downplaying their official references to conventional disarmament, Third World countries adopted a policy that not only ignores the worldwide conventional arms race but also foils all attempts to discuss it in multilateral forums on disarmament. In 1961, at the first non-aligned summit conference in Belgrade, there was no distinction whatsoever made between nuclear and conventional disarmament. Disarmament was perceived as an imperative need "in the present states of armament," and more specifically it meant

the elimination of armed forces, armaments, foreign bases, manufacture of arms as well as elimination of institutions and installations for military training, except for purposes

Chart 1
Trends in Military Expenditures

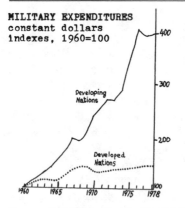

MILITARY EXPENDITURES
constant dollars
indexes, 1960=100

Developing Nations

Developed Nations

400
300
200
100

1960 1965 1970 1975 1978

Since 1960, expenditures of developing nations have risen four-fold (estimated in constant prices), while those in developed countries have gone up a more modest 44 per cent.

Source: Ruth Leger Sivard, *World Military and Social Expenditures—1979* (Leesburg, Va.: World Priorities, 1979), p. 7.

Chart 2
Relative Resource Distribution in Developed States for Military, Education, Health—1977

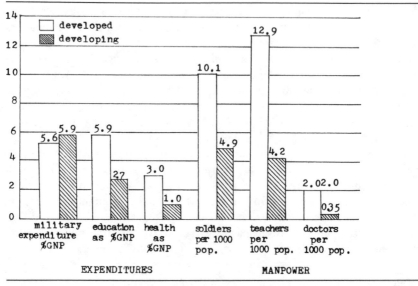

□ developed
▨ developing

military expenditure %GNP — 5.6 / 5.9
education as %GNP — 5.9 / 2.7
health as %GNP — 3.0 / 1.0
soldiers per 1000 pop. — 10.1 / 4.9
teachers per 1000 pop. — 12.9 / 4.2
doctors per 1000 pop. — 2.0 2.0 / 0.35

EXPENDITURES   MANPOWER

Source: U.S. ACDA, *World Military Expenditures and Arms Transfers, 1968-1977* (Washington, D.C.: GPO, 1978), p. 7.

of internal security; and total prohibition of the production, possession and utilization of nuclear and thermo-nuclear arms, bacteriological and chemical weapons as well as the elimination of equipment and installations for the delivery and placement and optional use of weapons of mass destruction on national territories.[11]

Such an order of disarmament measures, even in a random list of measures, would be inconceivable for the non-aligned in the 1970s.

The second conference, in Cairo in 1964, already marked the shift toward some sort of priority list under which the emphasis was placed upon nuclear disarmament, a nuclear ban, and non-dissemination of nuclear weapons. There is a relatively vague reference to reductions in the military budgets of the great powers but, surprisingly, nothing else specific on conventional disarmament (in the sixteen paragraphs of the chapter on disarmament).[12] In the 1970s, at the third non-aligned summit conference in Lusaka, conventional disarmament was already a taboo. Here, the participants were very precise and specific in listing a "general order of priorities"—all of them nonconventional: various specific measures of nuclear disarmament, prohibitions of chemical and biological weapons, and even "non-armament or confidence-building measures" dealt particularly with nuclear weapons and demilitarization of the sea bed.[13] In Algiers in 1973, there was just a brief expression of concern "with the flow of conventional weapons to non-nuclear states," a concern that would disappear three years later.

Since 1973, the non-aligned countries have not found it necessary even to pay lip service to the regulation of the conventional arms race and international arms transfers. Neither in Colombo in 1976 nor Havana in 1979, at the fifth and sixth summit conferences,[14] was there any reference whatsoever to these important aspects of international security. Again, the overwhelming concern was nuclear disarmament by the nuclear-weapons states. The only place where the term *conventional weapons* is used is in regard to the conference on the "prohibition of certain conventional weapons of an indiscriminate or cruel nature particularly the prohibition of the use of napalm and other incendiary weapons." The prohibition of these particular types of weapons should not be considered as a measure to curtail the conventional arms race; instead it belongs to the so-called principles and practice of humanitarian law. The question of the prohibition of such weapons has been considered over the years by a variety of international bodies, such as the Diplomatic Conference on the Reaffirmation and Development of International Humanitarian Law Applicable in Armed Conflict and the International Committee of the Red Cross (ICRC).[15]

Already from the work of the Preparatory Committee of the SSOD it became apparent that conventional disarmament, which was strongly supported by some Western countries, would not get sufficient consideration even in the limited and ambiguous fashion of United Nations formulations. The working paper of the non-aligned revealed their attitude toward the problem. Conventional disarmament was dealt with as an issue of secondary importance (sometimes giving the impression of being "face-saving" formulas). The document focuses almost entirely on nuclear disarmament. There is no mention of actual conventional wars and their consequences, but just of the dangers of the nuclear arms race. The non-aligned made it clear in their order of priorities that conventional arms and reduction of armed forces are the last items in their program of action on disarmament.[16] Interestingly enough, the only concrete proposal on conventional disarmament by the non-aligned is directed toward a region outside the Third World—Central Europe. Only there the non-aligned paper refers to conventional disarmament, which "would constitute a significant step for the attainment of the goal" of the limitation and gradual reduction of conventional weapons on a global basis.[17] One may infer from this that the situation in Europe is to be blamed for the military buildup in the Persian Gulf region, Africa, or Southeast Asia.

FAILURE TO DISCUSS ARMS TRANSFERS

Attempts to have the arms trade discussed in the United Nations General Assembly and the CCD met with the negative or even hostile reaction of most non-aligned countries.[18] Some of these proposals favored the revival of the League of Nations concept of an international register of arms. These proposals were initiated or supported by the major suppliers of weapons in the West but were always rejected by the recipient countries and their allies.

In 1965, at the twentieth session of the General Assembly, Malta proposed that the ENDC consider the question of transfers of arms between states, but the Assembly failed to take up this matter.[19] In 1966, the president of the United States sent a message to the ENDC on regional disarmament,[20] and again, in 1967, as one of President Johnson's five principles for peace in the Middle East, the United States proposed the reporting to the United Nations of all arms shipments to the Middle East. This initiative encountered strong opposition from the Soviet Union, the Arab states, and some Western nations. It was not put to a vote. Some similar ideas on United Nations registration and publishing of all exports and imports of conventional arms were introduced again in 1968 by a group of Western states, but a number of developing countries (particularly Argentina, India, the United Arab Republic, Syria, with the support of the Soviet bloc) strongly opposed it, and the sponsors decided not to put it to a vote.[21]

Thus, quite a while before "rich–poor" issues began to dominate international forums, a North–South confrontation between the Third World (then supported by the Soviet Union) and the arms producers/suppliers started to emerge. As a matter of fact, the arguments were borrowed from the debate over the NPT (see Chapter 6) and applied to the conventional field with the same terminology of the NIEO. Third World countries argued that registration of arms transfers is discriminatory in the sense that it would reveal the arms acquisition activities of the recipients but not of the producers. The proponents of arms registration argued that the secrecy surrounding the acquisition of armaments creates uncertainty, which increases insecurity among neighboring states, which may over-react by an excessive military buildup.

For the next seven years the whole issue of the conventional arms race virtually disappeared from the United Nations agenda (except for some marginal and general references in the framework of the perennial grandiloquent resolutions on "general and complete disarmament"). The issue was revived in 1976 at the CCD by the United Kingdom and the United States, who urged restraint by exporters and importers in the arms trade. Nigeria, representing Third World opposition, held that the suppliers were primarily responsible for the arms trade and that it "could not accept attempts to shift emphasis in the CCD from nuclear and general and complete disarmament to such questions as the arms trade."[22]

In the same year, a Japanese initiative supported by the West was submitted to the United Nations Thirty-first Session proposing a United Nations study on the subject with the assistance of qualified governmental experts. This time the initiative was defeated by means of procedural tricks in which a vote was taken for adjournment of the debate in the First Committee.[23] The issue reemerged in 1977 in the CCD and the General Assembly. This time several Third World countries (Colombia, Nepal, Singapore, Tanzania) joined the camp that took the position that the priority attached to nuclear disarmament should not distract attention from the conventional arms race. Japan and Singapore held that the continuing technological sophistication of conventional weapons tended to blur the difference between conventional and nuclear arms. Nepal and Tanzania pointed out that since the end of World War II no nuclear weapons had been used in war, whereas millions of people had suffered as casualties of conventional warfare. But still the opposition led by India reemphasized the position that nuclear and conventional weapons could not be weighed equally. India explained that conventional weapons must take lower priority since they do not threaten mankind's total annihilation and were the only weapons available to the developing countries for their defense and to national liberation movements. Japan expressed concern over the danger that the influx of sophisticated weapons in large quantities into troubled areas might escalate military conflicts into a nuclear holocaust.[24] Nevertheless, despite this growing awareness of the perils of the conventional arms race in 1977, no draft resolution was submitted on the subject to the United Nations General Assembly. Attempts to reintroduce the issue of the international arms trade to the United Nations agenda have provoked vociferous protests from the Third World.

A debate over conventional weapons did take place at the SSOD, again mainly because of the comprehensive nature of the Final Document, which was designed to cover all aspects of disarmament measures. It seems also that the conventional arms issue was used by Western countries as a bargaining chip against the Third World attack on nuclear weapons. In a sharp contrast to the non-aligned disregard for conventional disarmament, the Western working paper to the SSOD said the following:

Most of the world's military expenditure is being devoted to the acquisition and maintenance of conventional military power. This absorbs essential material and human resources. All States should make all *possible efforts parallel to* those in the field of nuclear disarmament to halt this diversion of resources and to achieve concrete measures for their reallocation from military to civilian purposes. To this end it will be necessary to intensify research on how best to achieve this goal.

The increasing build-up of conventional arms in many parts of the world involves a potential risk of heightening military tension and endangering international peace and security. The unabated international transfer of conventional arms should be brought under control.[25]

The SSOD has also witnessed some modifications in the Soviet position in this regard, which appeared to have moved closer to the Western approach on the need for conventional disarmament, thus extending the non-aligned–superpowers confrontation, though to a lesser extent, to the conventional field. The working paper of the socialist countries said:

Limitation and reduction of armed forces and conventional weapons. Military conflicts involving the use of conventional weapons lead to the tragic and often mass destruction of human lives and of the material values created by man. Accordingly, practical steps should be taken to limit and reduce aircraft, artillery, tank forces and other modern types of conventional weapons as well as armed forces equipped with them. Foreign military bases in foreign territories should be dismantled; foreign troops should be withdrawn from such territories.[26]

However, in the course of the general debate, Soviet bloc countries tried to impress the non-aligned countries by using the same anti-imperialist arguments against restrictions on conventional arms that may "prejudice the rights of countries and peoples waging a struggle for freedom and independence."[27] But at the same time the Soviets raised similar arguments to those of the West pointing out the record world-wide expenditures on conventional arms and the fact that, unlike nuclear weapons, since the end of World War II they had killed millions of persons in warfare.[28]

The apparent coordination on conventional weapons between the superpowers at the United Nations was closely related to their new bilateral preliminary exchange of views on the international arms trade, which started in December 1977 in Washington, D.C.[29] The meetings resumed in Helsinki, on the eve of the SSOD, in May and again in July 1978.[30] These meetings followed the announcement of a new "policy of arms restraint" by the Carter administration (May 1977), which focused on the shipment of advanced weapons to the Third World and called for multilateral cooperation among arms suppliers, including the USSR. Along with high-level consultations with the French, British, and West German governments, the United States and the Soviets established their intergovernmental working group on arms transfers.[31]

However, these preliminary attempts (which would soon become another futile exercise) were not encouraged by the majority of Third World countries. The debates in the SSOD and in the preceding General Assemblies revealed two different philosophical approaches in the field. These approaches differ on the importance and urgency of conventional disarmament as well as on its scope (Who should disarm? Who should get arms deliveries?). One group, mainly Western states, proposes that nuclear and conventional disarmament should be considered simultaneously and with equal attention. They maintain that conventional conflicts may escalate to nuclear confrontations, and therefore developing countries bear the same responsibilities as the industrialized countries in the field of conventional arms limitation. The other group—mostly non-aligned and developing countries—emphasize that such equal treatment of nuclear and conventional arms matters would detract from the urgency and priority of nuclear disarmament. These countries also add that efforts in that direction should not serve to deny legitimate arms acquisitions ''necessary for the security of nations, peoples or liberation movements fighting against colonialism and apartheid in the exercise of their right to self-determination and independence.''[32] In addition, the arms-purchasing countries of the Third World treat the question of arms transfer together with the question of production, and since the superpowers are responsible for most of the weapons production (for their own economic and political benefit), they should be the first to initiate meaningful reduction of their own conventional armaments. In this debate the Soviet Union and its satellites played a low-key role, and while expressing an inclination to support the Western argument on the perils of the conventional arms race, the Soviets supported, at the same time, the Third World position on the right of states to legitimate defense and of peoples under colonial and racist domination to use the means available to them, including arms, to achieve and secure their freedom and independence.

DISCORDANT NOTES IN THE THIRD WORLD

It should be noted that among the non-aligned there were some notes of discord on the tendency to belittle the gravity of the conventional arms race, particularly its manifestations among Third World countries. The statement of the representative of Singapore, Ambassador T. T. Koh, in the general debate of the SSOD was quite revealing and, no doubt, irritated some of the militant members in the non-aligned. Singapore told the Third World to put its own house in order first and to stop delivering so many ''moral sermons'' to the superpowers. Ambassador Koh pointed out that the arms race is not confined to the superpowers and their allies but is a universal phenomenon. He described the sharp rise in the Third World's military expenditures at the expense of their expenditures for food and development. Koh made it clear that the Third World should concentrate on regional agreements on conventional weapons and admitted:

Unfortunately, conditions of mutual trust and confidence do not exist in many parts of the Third World today. The Third World is riven by conflicts and disputes based upon conflicting territorial claims and racial, tribal, religious, linguistic and ideological differences.[33]

Singapore was joined by Papua New Guinea, which focused on the situation in the field of international arms trade where the Thrid World share reached a staggering 75 percent of the total. Military expenditures, explained the representative of Papua New Guinea, are made at the expense of economic, health, and social programs.[34] In a moment of truth, a rare admission could be recorded when the representative of Nigeria, a leading actor in the non-aligned group, stated: "It must be said in all candour that the developing countries themselves were not immune from the increase in military expenditures. That is most unfortunate."[35]

Western countries, on the other hand, have persistently demanded discussion of the conventional arms race and disarmament as a high-priority item. The prime minister of Canada, Pierre Elliot Trudeau, gave expression to this concern in his statement to the SSOD. Trudeau pointed out that conventional weapons comprised 80 percent of the world's military expenditures and, particularly among developing countries, assumes massive proportions of public spending. Therefore, he rejected in plain words the attempt by the Third World to concentrate almost exclusively on nuclear disarmament:

There can be no first and second priorities, therefore, as between the nuclear and a whole series of conventional arms races. Both are relevant to the maintenance of world security; both are absorbing resources better devoted to other purposes; both are the legitimate business of an Organization whose purpose it is to harmonize the actions of nations.[36]

The Western countries have, of course, some more parochial considerations in their persistence to focus on conventional disarmament. The issue is raised by the West not merely as an opposition to the Third World's exclusiveness approach to nuclear disarmament but also because of its special connotations for East–West relations. It is well known that the NATO deterrent in Europe is based upon the tactical nuclear option and the strategic umbrella of the United States in order to compensate for the disparity in conventional weapons between NATO and Warsaw Pact forces. Unlike most Third World countries, Western allies, by definition of their security system, view nuclear weapons as the only stabilizing element to offset their relative weakness in conventional weapons. Having that in mind, their tendency at the United Nations is, thus, to give special consideration to conventional disarmament in the framework of the debate on nuclear disarmament. In a typical statement by the United Kingdom, its representative explained that the situation in Europe must be recognized as unique since their nuclear weapons are an integral part of the East–West security system and without it there would be a dangerous disparity in conventional forces: "It is illusory to believe that just because nuclear weapons are unique in their destructive power they can be treated in isolation for arms control purposes. We therefore consider that this Committee should give greater attention to conventional arms control."[37]

But most Third World countries remain unwilling even to discuss the issue. For them the idea of conventional disarmament is a ploy of the nuclear-weapon states to brush aside accusations on the lack of progress in nuclear disarmament and an attempt "to reverse the legal as well as strategic disarmament priorities."[38]

India reaffirmed this position reiterating, in 1980, the three familiar principles: (1) rejecting the concept of "a conventional arms race in which all or a majority of countries are engaged"; (2) pointing out that the discussion on the conventional arms race diverts the focus from the main issue: nuclear disarmament; and (3) demanding "a modicum of conventional capabiltiy" as essential to newly independent nations to safeguard their "hard-won independence from the aggressive interpositions of great-power ambitions which straddle the globe and from other threats to their security."[39]

FOREIGN AND COLONIAL INTERVENTION

One of the arguments invoked by the Third World to reject discussions on the conventional arms race is that the superpowers, or, as in most cases, imperialism and colonialism, should be blamed for military conflicts in the Third World. At the SSOD, Foreign Minister of Algeria Abdelaziz Bouteflika elaborated on a radical interpretation of war in the Third World. Bouteflika accused the former colonial powers of using the Third World as a "testing ground for new techniques of mass destruction." These powers invent "imaginary ideological conflicts" in order to justify their foreign intervention. This, concluded Bouteflika, is similar to the colonial conquest, which "was rooted in the so-called civilizing mission of the West."[40]

The great powers, mainly the Western, are blamed for everything: for the creation of the conflict and for its exploitation for their arms sales. According to Niger, the industrialized countries deliberately spread "hot beds of conflict" in Africa in order "to maintain a psychosis of insecurity," which leads the Africans to buy arms from them. These arms sales "constitute a tremendous drain on our meagre resources which are thus unjustly used to swell the bank accounts of the arms merchants of the industrialized countries."[41] Third World countries complain that they become pawns in the big powers' rivalry for spheres of influence and, thus, are forced against their will to increase their military expenditures.[42]

In 1980, there were a few outbursts of intra–Third World conflict in the United Nations deliberations on disarmament. In addition to exchanges between Iraq and Iran over their military conflict and some statements concerning the occupation of Cambodia by Vietnam, there were indirect allusions to Libya's adventurist policies in Africa. It took a painstaking effort for Tunisia, a staunch

member of the non-aligned movement and the seat of the Arab League, to deliver
harsh words directed at Libya, although without referring to it by name. Tunisia,
itself a victim of one of Qaddafi's military adventures, delivered an unusual
statement for a non-aligned and Arab state on the sources of conflict and tension
in the Third World. Tunisia made it clear that a new phenomenon of polarization
is emerging in the Third World that is "neither the prolongation nor the reflection
of the East–West confrontation." It is a phenomenon in which

some developing countries, through their own choice, consider themselves possessors of
a hegemonistic mandate over their neighbours and, in this one-term adventure, squander
enormous financial, human and technical resources in order to accumulate enormous
quantities of luxury weapons, greatly out of proportion to their populations, and then to
engage in a policy of annexation, intervention and intimidation as a prelude to overtly
military operations. The appearance of such pockets in the Third World is accompanied
by a new surge of rearmament, and soon by a real initiation of armament programmes,
which are planned and diversified in relation to the disturbances occurring around them.[43]

Libya is of course the model state for a rearmament process greatly out of
proportion to its population, manifesting hegemonistic policies over its neighbors
by engaging in intimidation, annexation, and intervention.[44] In an allusion to
Libya's vast amounts of oil reserves, the representative of Tunisia pointed out
that for such developing countries rearmament is an easy task since they can
"without much difficulty by simply transferring natural resources" continue to
acquire weapons. Continuing in this Aesopian language, Tunisia denounced the
phenomenon, which brings with it foreign influence, since the developing nation
is unable to absorb the massive flows of armament and needs, therefore, foreign
assistance. Finally, Tunisia appealed to experts and negotiators in the field of
disarmament not to concentrate exclusively on the nuclear arms race and the
threat of the macro-military arsenals, but to give special consideration as well
to the neglected phenomenon of regional military buildup by developing countries.

REJECTING NEW EFFORTS ON ARMS TRADE

Within non-aligned forums it is impossible to find any reflection whatsoever
of the problem of international arms trade, as if it does not exist (although three-
quarters of it goes to the Third World). The problem is even more significant
since many of these Third World countries are purchasing their weapons with
scarce resources, which as they claim should be used for urgent economic and
social needs. Some of these developing nations are unable to ensure an adequate
food supply for their growing populations. In 1978, the year of the SSOD, of
the ninety-four developing nations that imported arms, more than one-third were
among the poorest nations on earth, with average annual per capita income of
under $500.[45]

Against this background it is striking that the Havana summit of the non-aligned (1979) did not mention the problem at all, nor did the Final Document of their foreign ministers' summit in New Delhi (1981). However, on some occasions the non-aligned are forced to make a reference to the problem of the arms trade. In the Disarmament Commission, for instance, the non-aligned had to pay lip service to the issue of the arms trade since it was raised by other countries within the framework fo the so-called Comprehensive Programme of Disarmament, which encompasses all aspects of disarmament. The non-aligned working paper tried, of course, to belittle the significance of the issue of world trade in armaments since it "constitutes a fraction of the total production of conventional weapons." Again it was asserted by the non-aligned that the major problem is the arms trade "between members of the two major alliance systems" and therefore it "should be restrained through their bilateral and regional negotiations."[46]

Usually the Third World countries oppose limitations on the international transfer of conventional weapons because it "may adversely affect the interests of the smaller powers." They say that an arbitrary policy of arms denial to one state would affect the regional balance of forces, bring deterioration of stability, and provoke armed conflicts.[47] A restraint on the transfer of conventional weapons, a non-aligned spokesman argued, may force small nations to seek their requirements from arms dealers at exorbitant financial cost, thus worsening their economic situation.[48]

Again, the same Third World countries that dared to stand up on the issue of Third World conflicts continued to speak out on weapons transfers. In addition to Singapore, both Fiji and its neighbor in Oceana, Papua New Guinea, pointed out that some Third World countries are even profiting from the arms trade and are heightening the competition.[49] It was reported, in 1981, that over the last decade the number of developing countries capable of building or assembling military equipment, and not just small arms, has more than doubled. Leaders of the Third World, such as Yugoslavia and Brazil (both members of the group of non-aligned in the Geneva Committee on Disarmament), are selling arms to their fellow developing countries.[50] Fiji was one Third World country, though not a member of the non-aligned movement, that was ready to expose some of the double standards in the arguments of developing countries:

The last decade has further seen the emergence of third-world arms producers—supplementing the deplorable efforts of the industrialized countries of both East and West in the export of their domestically produced arms and military equipment to the rest of the world. For these developing countries, now secondary producers of arms, the diversion of their scarce resources to armaments is in turn adversely reflected in their social and economic development needs not being fully met.[51]

Few Third World countries will admit that there is at least a need for some cooperation on their part in the field of conventional disarmament. Sierra Leone, for example, advocated cooperation between producers and exporters of con-

ventional weapons and recipient states in order to realize effective measures to
regulate the development, production, transfer, and acquisition of conventional
armament.[52]

However, the Third World as a bloc and particulary the non-aligned continue
to represent the radical interpretation of the arms trade. Algeria, which, of course,
does not recognize any military conflict between Third World countries and
blames everything on great-power intervention, flatly rejects international agreements aimed to put restraints on arms transfers. In a statement delivered in the
end of 1980 at the First Committee of the General Assembly, Algeria provided
the radical interpretation of the issue that explains why the non-aligned could
not agree upon any formula that would allow multilateral discussions on limiting
international arms transfers:

we cannot really hope to achieve such peace simply by measures limiting transfers of
arms to countries of the Third World—as if it were a case of exorcizing their warlike
frenzy in this way; as if war had suddenly become the prerogative of the poor. Such an
initiative not only would be misguided but would do serious damage to the rights of
States to ensure and organize their own national defence in a sovereign manner and it
would also affect the right of peoples fighting for their self-determination and independence.[53]

THE SOVIET DOUBLE GAME

As in other instances of the North–South confrontation (see Chapter 5), the
Soviets have managed to disassociate themselves from the Western countries in
the debate over conventional arms transfers. Initiatives on the conventional arms
race are supported by Western countries, while the Soviets—sometimes by expressing general reservations to the financial costs of new initiatives—join the
non-aligned countries in opposing these proposals.[54] Similarly, for several years
the Soviet Union has abstained on a Swedish proposal on the reduction of military
budgets that would establish a reporting instrument that will take into consideration the problem of comparing military expenditures among different states
and the problems of verifications. The Soviets regard the question of compar-
ability and verification as pretexts for military budgets to continue to increase.[55]

Soviet attitudes on the conventional arms race are particularly illustrative in
light of their growing role in recent years in the international transfer of arms
to the Third World. According to SIPRI estimates, during the period 1979–1981
the Soviet Union became the world's largest supplier of major weapon systems.[56]
Although there is no doubt that Western arms exports are often guided by political
motives, the Soviet approach is more politically oriented than that of other
exporters, including the United States. A large part of Western exports of arms
during the 1970s were characterized by a lack of any political strings, being
mainly commercial. Particularly in their arms sales to the oil-rich countries,
Western allies plunged into wild competition for a share of the petromarket even

at the expense of political and strategic interests.[57] The Soviets, on the other hand, since their first arms deal negotiated with Egypt in 1955–1956, regarded arms agreements as points of departure for their advances and penetrations in the Third World. In most cases Soviet weapons were offered on better terms, i.e., low prices and favorable credit terms. In Soviet policy, arms transfer play a far greater role than economic aid or trade to the developing world. Unlike the transfer of technology or agriculture assistance, arms transfers have become the only area in which the Soviets have successfully rivaled the West.[58] The Soviets are managing therefore to enjoy both worlds: they are rarely blamed for their lack of economic aid to the Third World, and their role in spreading the arms race to developing countries is overlooked in the United Nations. As shown earlier, the juxtaposition of disarmament and NIEO by the Third World helps to enhance inherent Soviet advantages over the West in United Nations debates.

UNITED NATIONS' STUDY ON CONVENTIONAL DISARMAMENT

At the disarmament *negotiating* forum of the United Nations—the CD in Geneva—there is no item on the agenda dedicated to conventional disarmament or to the international trade in arms. While there are more references to the subject in the debates at the United Nations and the CD, no concrete resolution or even negotiations has emerged from these organs.

In 1980, for the first time in the history of the United Nations, a resolution specifically on the subject of conventional disarmament was adopted by the Thirty-fifth General Assembly (Res. 35.156). The vote on the issue revealed that the non-aligned countries could not develop a unified position on this matter and instead were split on a major issue of disarmament. The resolution was introduced by the West (Denmark) and may serve as an example of a hollow document that, in order to get some qualified support by part of the Third World countries, had undergone further cosmetic changes, reiterating the "disarmament priorities established in the SSOD" (nuclear disarmament first).

In addition, because of the strong opposition from non-aligned countries, the sponsors agreed to send the issue to the Disarmament Commission of the United Nations to work out the general approach to the study, its structure, and its scope. In other words, even though the resolution dealt just with a study without offering any concrete measures in the field of conventional disarmament, it fell victim to further procedural delaying tactics. Still the results were telling; among the fourteen votes against the study (in addition to the Soviets) were the two leading opponents of the NPT in the Third World, India and Brazil, and another twenty-seven non-aligned countries abstained (among them, Algeria, Cuba, Egypt, Ghana, Iraq, and Yugoslavia). The Soviet bloc countries objected to the study because of their consistent opposition to the financial costs of various United Nations studies. The Soviets said that the essential task was to begin concrete negotiations toward curbing conventional arms instead of undertaking "an absolutely fruitless study."[59] It is interesting that both India and Brazil, the only Third World countries that voted against the study, have a remarkable role in the growing militarization of the Third World. SIPRI indicates in its 1982 year-book the sharp rise in military expenditures in India (together with Pakistan) since 1979. Both Brazil and India are among the leading producers of arms in the Third World, and Brazil in particular has a booming arms industry.[60]

If somebody had hoped that the Disarmament Commission of the United Nations would make some progress on conventional disarmament, the session of 1981 dashed all such hopes. The commission, designed as a deliberative body of all United Nations members, was unable to agree even on the general approach to a study on all aspects of the conventional arms race. Last-ditch efforts of the chairman, which produced a compromise in a working paper on the subject, were rejected. The commission reported back to the General Assembly:

The intensive discussions and consultations revealed a significant divergence of views on the matters before the Commission on this item, and it became clear that it was not possible at this stage for the Commission to discharge the responsibility assigned to it by the General Assembly in resolution 35/156-A.

Still, the commission found it worthwhile to point out that the above conclusions were "adopted by consensus."[61]

THIRD WORLD GLASS HOUSES

Since there are fundamental differences in the vantage points of the parties, it is hard to find acceptable criteria by which to determine the scope and seri-ousness of the problems giving rise to demands for conventional disarmament. What is clear, however, is that United Nations rhetoric appears to be obfuscating reality. The motives of many developing countries in these debates are disturbing, particularly at a time when commentators speak with increasing frequency about militarization in the Third World. Outside the United Nations it is a time of major military conflicts between non-aligned countries (Iraq–Iran) and of the emergence of non-aligned expansionism and occupation (Vietnam and Libya). In this context three major problems are worth further elaboration:

First, how can one determine whether the Third World is caught up in sig-nificant arms procurement? This question should be addressed since there is a tendency to belittle Third World military expenditures as a small fraction, com-pared to the great powers, of world military spending.

Second, is it true, as non-aligned countries argue, that this military buildup always enhances self-defense and provides national security for Third World nations?

And third, who is to be blamed?

Scholars as well as official delegates often use in their publications and state-ments various measurements and indices of a nation's military burden of expenditures as important components of their evidence of criticized tendencies of weapons buildup. The problem with some of the arguments concerning the conventional arms race is that they are derived from premises that were established at a time when the race was confined to the industrialized world and most of the Third World countries were still under colonial domination. With the dramatic decolonization process and the rise in the intra–Third World conflict, there seems to be a need to reconsider these premises. It seems that at this stage it is hard to blame the "North," and particularly the West, as the source for all evils in the "South," including their internal military conflicts. What should be, therefore, the right yardstick to measure the arms buildup in Third World countries?

The problem is, thus, first and foremost about the right research methods and agreed tools of measurement. At the United Nations, the most popular yardstick is the comparison of the nominal value of military expenditures between nonaligned and industrialized countries. Such an approach will always point its finger at the five or six most heavily armed states that have the largest and increasingly sophisticated and growing arsenals of conventional weapons. Another very popular yardstick to measure the "militaristic" tendencies of governments is that of comparing its military budget with the amounts it allocates for foreign aid and development projects in the Third World.[62] This should be viewed against the background of the attempt to establish the so-called link between disarmament and development.

The problem with these links and correlations is that they were not investigated in an impartial manner, free of parochial political consideration. The fact that the United Nations SSOD has accepted "the close relationship between disarmament and development" in which "progress in the former would help greatly the realization of the latter"[63] does not make it yet the iron law of international disarmament. This indicator, thus, should be viewed as a moral judgment (which can be challenged also on moral grounds; see Chapter 4), but not as a scientific tool of measurement.

There are several major indicators of a nation's military expenditures, such as percentage of GNP, expenditures per capita, soldiers per capita, and expenditures per soldier.[64] The most frequently and widely used indicator outside the United Nations is the indicator of military expenditure as percentage of GNP. This at least gives a fair picture of military expenditures in a particular country in relation to the rest of its economic activities. Nevertheless, even this indicator is receiving more and more criticism since it obscures changes in nations with sizable GNPs and does not tell about the priorities of national policymakers.[65]

As a result, some researchers view as the most useful the indicator that measures military expenditures as a percentage of the country's national budget. This indicator, more than any other, focuses primarily on the priorities and choices of a particular nation in its budgetary allocations. Using this measurement, the picture of the rearmament in the Third World is rather bleak and ominous. The data aggregated on military expenditures as a proportion of state budget on ninety-three developing countries already in 1974 revealed the following conclusions: (1) nearly 25 percent of Third World countries spent over 25 percent of their budget on military expenditures; (2) nearly thirty percent spent over 20 percent of their budget on military expenditures; and (3) 57 percent spent over 10 percent of their budget on military expenditures.[66] These findings mean that nearly 30 percent of Third World countries allocate more money percentagewise, out of their national budget than does the United States, for instance.

Does rearmament enhance the security of Third World countries?

As the following pages suggest, rearmament of Third World countries in the Middle East, the Persian Gulf region, Southeast Asia, and Africa has brought deterioration in the security of the Third World countries involved. These military conflicts demonstrate how developing countries are dependent on supply from exporting countries not only for the main instruments of war but also for spare parts. The growing sophistication of conventional weapons demands a highly developed technological infrastructure for their constant maintenance, which most Third World countries lack.

Mary Kaldor, writing on "Arms and Dependence," challenges the conventional wisdom that rearmament in the Third World helps to reduce their military inequality and increases their political power. By means of this process, she says, Third World countries are accepting a dependent ideology and limiting their development potential. For most underdeveloped countries, armaments represent a very high proportion of their total capital. In addition, they experience difficulties in absorbing this new technology:

The increased vulnerability of all weapon platforms—ships, tanks, aircraft—calls into question the utility of equipment which is difficult to hide and expensive to replace. In addition, modern equipment entails considerable logistical problems. A squadron of F-4 Phantoms, for example, requires an inventory of 70,000 spare parts to be kept operational under wartime conditions.[67]

In the First Committee's debate in the Thirty-fifth General Assembly (1980), the representative of Israel commented on this phenomenon in the same vein:

It can therefore be said that hand in hand with the growing sophistication of conventional weapons goes their transfer to an ever increasing number of recipient countries which are not always in a position to provide for their adequate deployment or use in case of war without continued aid from supplier countries. The proliferation of sophisticated weapons all over the globe serves, therefore, to create an illusion of military power which itself endangers world peace. This illusion promotes States party to a regional conflict to opt for military solutions instead of seeking pacific means of negotiations and settlement.[68]

Another study on the "Economics of Third World Military Expenditure" concludes that, on balance, military spending represents a burden on the economy and that, given the limited resources of Third World countries and the ambiguous nature of the concept of deterrence that justifies most military spending, it does not, on the whole, contribute to national security.[69] More and more countries in the Third World with sharply rising external debt continue to invest to import arms. In these countries military budgets are at the expense of their spending for public health, housing, or education.[70] Under such circumstances the link between disarmament of the great powers and development cannot but be regarded with skepticism (see also Chapter 4). In 1981 there were fifty-four military-dominated governments in the Third World, the bulk of them with records of violating the rights of their own citizens to safety under law and security forces that employ oppressive policies, including torture and summary executions.[71] With such trends of militarization of regimes and arms races among developing countries, there is no guarantee that transfer of resources from the developed world would be wisely used for common good by dictators or authoritarian regimes in the Third World.[72]

A THIRD WORLD ARMS RACE

Events in a certain group of nations in the Third World over the last decade make even the improved and refined indicators on military expenditures inadequate. The 1980 yearbook of the Stockholm International Peace Research Institute (SIPRI) has identified for the first time a new group of nations in its charts and tables on world military expenditures—all of them Third World countries—belonging to the oil cartel OPEC (Organization of Petrolum Exporting Countries).

In their review of the prevailing trends of the 1970s, the editors of the SIPRI yearbook concluded: "OPEC states have spent a considerable part of their vastly increased income on expanding their military sector—with a growth rate of 15 percent."[73] Figures on the growing volume of arms transfers in the 1970s reveal an undeniable fact: the greatest single boost to arms sales in the last decade came with the 1973 Arab oil cutoff, the subsequent crisis, and the immediately resulting quadrupling of oil prices. The billions of dollars that flowed first into the coffers of the oil-producing countries, and then into the pockets of the arms merchants, were spent primarily by these same Middle Eastern Oil Producing (MEOP)* countries, the world's largest exporters of energy resources. The shift was quick and dramatic: "The explosive rise in crude oil prices has brought new and quick 'wealth' to some Middle Eastern countries, which has been used for· expensive purchases of modern arms and military equipment as well as for investments in respective infrastructure projects."[74]

In this particular case of the MEOP countries, the conventional indicators on defense expenditure may mislead. These "nouveaux riches" have sometimes

---

*It is important and analytically appropriate to distinguish the MEOP countries (Saudi Arabia, Iran, Iraq, Kuwait, United Arab Emirates, Libya, Algeria, Oman, and Qatar) from the rest of OPEC, since they alone account for more than 90 percent of the total military expenditures by all OPEC countries.

apparently no limits on their expenditures, and have been able simultaneously to increase their allocations for both economic development and military expenditures dramatically. In this case, there is no question of priorities in a nation's federal budget, and therefore the indicator of military expenditures as percentage of national spending may deceive and even completely conceal the spiraling increase in military spending.

The quantitative dollar figures alone suggest that a large portion of the dizzying escalation of the world's arms race is literally fueled by fuel. MEOP countries have reached record heights, up to tenfold and even up to thirtyfold increases in defense budgets within four years. In 1979 Iraq received more arms than any other Third World country. Saudi Arabia, which in addition to arms imports is engaged in major military construction and training programs, in 1980 exceeded the defense expenditure of France.[75]

This new "arms–oil connection" put heavy responsibility on the Third World majority in the United Nations. Worn-out cliches about the imperialist powers that create tensions and conflicts in the Third World fail to convince even the staunchest supporters of the non-aligned. The long war between Iraq and Iran and Libya's military interventions and occupations in Africa have become a source of irritation and grave concern for the Third World. It becomes apparent that the new trends in international arms transfers, precisely because of the new role of Third World nations, brought about revolutionary changes in the world weapons market. The role and policies of these nations proved to be more effective and powerful than attempts at restraint in sales by some major producers: they created wild competition among allies that indeed even thwarted nuclear non-proliferation attempts.

During the 1970s there was a dramatic shift toward government-to-government foreign military purchases for cash and credit, and in most cases the terms of the trade, as well as the order, were dictated by Third World countries. No longer is the political leverage held by the supplier over the recipients by the controlling framework of military aid programs. In the case of MEOP countries, the "oil weapon" is used to apply pressure on the suppliers and to impose the new pattern of arms-for-oil deals. This kind of package deal between governments (notably pursued by Iraq) indexed the volume and price of oil exports to reciprocal commitments of arms deliveries. As oil-rich countries sought arms, supplying governments soon lost all control over arms transfers and plunged into a wild competition to grab their share of the petromarket. The oil-exporting countries have demonstrated their twofold power in this inflationary race: they can draw on staggering amounts of money, and they can dispense that money however they please. In the West, this race to please the Arabs has been rationalized as an attempt to *recycle* the petrodollars: "to bring those dollars back home." Arms sales were justified as a necessary evil to meet the economic crisis posed by stagflation (the simultaneous inflation of prices and growing unemployment). It helped to recover the huge deficits in the national balance of payments and provided new jobs in the new flourishing arms exports industries. Typically,

Chart 3
Military Expenditures by Third World Oil-Producing Countries

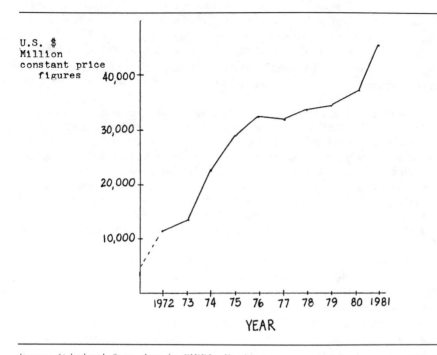

Source: Calculated from data in SIPRI, World Armament and Disarmament, SIPRI Yearbook 1982 (London: Taylor & Francis, 1982), p. 140, on world military expenditures.

even a neutral state such as Austria has joined the competition for the arms market in the Middle East, justifying it "partly on the need to keep down unemployment at home and partly to aid its balance of payments."[76]

Alva Myrdal, former minister of disarmament of Sweden and leading spokesman for the non-aligned in the Committee on Disarmament in Geneva, drew a direct link between oil revenues and arms:

With the monopolistic rise in oil prices, some underdeveloped countries have suddenly become very rich and these countries have become major importers of highly sophisticated and expensive weapons. Besides the superpowers' continued deliveries to them, almost all the developed Western countries (in the wake of the 1973 Middle East war and the Arab oil boycott) have been racing to please the Arabs and simultaneously reap profits. There has been a resultant strong upsurge in trade according to a new pattern of arms-for-oil deals. When contracted orders are filled, Kuwait, for instance, with only around a million inhabitants, will have one of the world's most modern air defense systems, and all the Gulf sheikdoms are acquiring sophisticated counterinsurgency weaponry.[77]

A pattern common to all MEOP countries' arms imports policies is the consistent attempt to diversify their sources of imports. This approach only enhances the already competitive nature of the market and provides the MEOP countries with a range of arms sources while freeing them from exclusive dependence on East or West or any single supplier. In this case, Third World countries are not just rearming themselves in a dizzying pace but also playing a major and active role in the international arms race. Ironically, in this game the supplier countries represent the weaker partner in the game of arms transfers.

Some of the ramifications of the emerging arms–oil connection are reflected in the role of some MEOP countries as re-exporters of weapons (mainly Libya) and financies of other rearmament programs (mainly Saudi Arabia). This oil–arms mechanism has also crossed the nuclear threshold, and heavy-handed, oil-smeared tactics have been exerted to extract nuclear deals.[78] All indications show that MEOP countries will continue to order arms. They will continue to have the liquid financial assets, coupled with growing fear for security and/or increasing drive for prestige and regional power. The situation in this region ensures that arms supplies will begin an upward ratchet mechanism destroying any possible stability. Since the operational lifetime of weapons tends to become increasingly shorter, the value and volume of their order will increase. The war in the Persian Gulf will be perhaps a major boost for future orders by the combatants to replace their loss in the battlefields.

Military conflicts in Southeast Asia (Vietnam and its neighbors) and in the Persian Gulf (the Iraq–Iran war) and the Libyan military adventures in Africa may well be the bellwether of the growing militarization of intra–Third World relations. Under these circumstances it will be more difficult to organize the same Third World front in the United Nations on issues of conventional disarmament. In the case of Third World MEOP countries, it has become apparent that with their new oil power they can dictate the terms of trade to the arms suppliers. By virtue of the oil–arms connection, MEOP countries were able to manipulate the West in both markets—as sellers in the seller's market of oil, and as buyers in the buyer's market of arms.[79] At this point it is hard to focus on initiatives of restraint from the suppliers' side—as most experts suggest[80]—without addressing these dramatic changes in the international market of arms. What remains clear, however, is that these Third World arms races raise further doubts about the credentials of the non-aligned movement as a proponent of global disarmament at the United Nations.

NOTES

1. GAOR, A/S-10/PV.20, June 7, 1978, p. 46.

2. GAOR, A/C.1/35/PV.27, November 4, 1980, p. 27.

3. SIPRI, *World Armaments and Disarmament, SIPRI Yearbook 1980* (London: Taylor & Francis, 1980), introduction.

4. Ibid.; and in U.S. Arms Control and Disarmament Agency, *World Military Expenditures and Arms Transfers 1969–1978* (Washington, D.C.: ACDA, 1980), pp. 33, 75.

5. Ibid., pp. 117–19.

6. SIPRI, *Armaments or Disarmament?* (London: Taylor & Francis, 1980), p. 10.

7. ACDA, *World Military Expenditures*, p. 117.

8. Andrew J. Pierre, *The Global Politics of Arms Sales*, A Council on Foreign Relations Book (Princeton, N.J.: Princeton University Press, 1982), p. 131.

9. See Andre Gunder Frank, "Arms Economy and Warfare in the Third World," *Third World Quarterly* 2, no. 2 (April 1980): 228–50; and Mary Kaldor, "International Military Order," *New Statesman* (May 25, 1979).

10. GAOR, SSOD Final Document, Tenth Special Session 1978, Supplement No. 4, A/S-10/4, para. 83.

11. "First Conference of Heads of State or Government of Non-Aligned Countries: Belgrade, September 1–6, 1961," in *The Third World Without Superpowers: The Collected Documents of the Non-Aligned Countries*, ed. Odette Jankowitsch and Karl P. Sauvant (New York: Oceana Publications, 1978), p. 3.

12. Ibid., p. 54.

13. Ibid., p. 132.

14. Ibid.; and for Havana 1979: *Documents of the Sixth Conference of Heads of State or Governments of Non-Aligned Countries*, held in Havana, Cuba, September 3–9, 1979, GAOR, A/34/542, October 11, 1979, p. 72, para. 224.

15. *UN and Disarmament Yearbook, Vol. 4, 1979*, p. 256.

16. "Non-Aligned Working Documents," GAOR, Tenth Special Session 1978, Supplement No. 1 (A/S-10/1), Vol. IV, A/AC.187/55.

17. Ibid., pp. 6–7.

18. Edward C. Luck, "The Arms Trade," in *The Changing United Nations: Options for the United States*, ed. David A. Kay (New York: Academy of Political Science, 1977), p. 177.

19. *UN and Disarmament 1945–1970*, p. 152.

20. Ibid.; and Barton and Weiler, *International Arms Control*, p. 283.

21. Barton and Weiler, *International Arms Control*, p. 283; and also *UN and Disarmament 1945–1970*, p. 152.

22. *UN and Disarmament Yearbook, Vol. 2, 1977*, p. 264.

23. Ibid.

24. Ibid., pp. 266–67.

25. GAOR, Tenth Special Session 1978, Vol. IV, A/AC.187/87, p. 5.

26. Ibid., A/AC.187/82, p. 2.

27. *UN and Disarmament Yearbook, Vol. 2, 1978*, p. 415.

28. Ibid., p. 411.

29. *Disarmament* 1, no. 1 (May 1978); 71.

30. *Disarmament* 1, no. 2 (October 1978): 103.

31. Luck, "The Arms Trade," p. 181.

32. For a round-up of the arguments, see *UN and Disarmament Yearbook, Vol. 3, 1979*, chap. 19; *UN and Disarmament Yearbook, Vol. 2, 1978*, chap. 22.

33. GAOR, A/S-10/PV.20, June 7, 1978, pp. 46, 56.

34. GAOR, A/S-10/PV.15, June 2, 1978, pp. 63–65.

35. GAOR, A/C.1/34/PV.18, October 26, 1979, p. 36.

36. GAOR, A/S-10/PV.6, May 26, 1978, p. 17.

37. GAOR, A/C.1/35/PV.16, October 27, 1980, pp. 13–14.

38. Husain, "Third World and Disarmament," p. 85.

39. See GAOR, A/C.1/35/PV.46, November 28, 1980, p. 31; and GAOR, A/C.1/35/PV.14, October 24, 1980, p. 45.

40. GAOR, A/S-10/PV.12, June 1, 1978, p. 11.

41. GAOR, A/C.1/33/PV.44, November 20, 1978, pp. 2–7.

42. GAOR, Malaysia, A/C.1/35/PV.20, October 27, 1980, and Tunisia, A/C.1/34/PV.29, November 5, 1979, p. 15.

43. GAOR, A/C.1/35/PV.27, November 4, 1980, pp. 48–51.

44. Claire Sterling, "Qaddafi Spells Chaos," *The New Republic* (March 7, 1981).

45. Pierre, *The Global Politics*, p. 36.

46. GAOR, A/CN.10/20, May 29, 1980, p. 4.

47. Pakistan in GAOR, A/S-10/PV.7, May 29, 1978, p. 32.

48. GAOR, A/C.1/33/PV.12, October 23, 1978, p. 44 (Sudan).

49. Papua New Guinea, GAOR, A/C.1/35/PV.21, October 1980, p. 37.

50. "Third World Lands Join Hands of Arms Exporters," *New York Times*, December 13, 1981. See also SIPRI yearbooks, and Pierre, the chapter on "New Third World Suppliers," in *Global Politics*, pp. 123–27.

51. GAOR, A/C.1/35/PV.12, October 23, 1980, p. 54.

52. GAOR, A/C.1/35/PV.10, October 22, 1980, p. 50.

53. GAOR, A/C.1/35/PV.27, November 4, 1980, p. 27.

54. *UN and Disarmament Yearbook, Vol. 5, 1980*, p. 351.

55. Ibid., p. 379; and see previous yearbooks.

56. *SIPRI Yearbook 1982*, p. 185.

57. Beker, "The Oil–Arms Connection," pp. 419–42.

58. *SIPRI Yearbook 1982*, pp. 185–87; and Pierre, *The Global Politics*, pp. 78–80. The industrialized countries of the West are far more vulnerable than the Soviets to being deprived of resources. Sometimes their arms sales are motivated by this fear, as arms sales are seen as a way to buy the friendship of raw material–exporting countries. See Peter M. Dawkins, "Conventional Arms Transfers and Control: Producer Restraints," in *Controlling Future Arms Trade*, ed. Anne Hessing Cahn, Joseph J. Kruzel, Peter M.

Dawkins, and Jacques Huntzinger, 1980s Project Council on Foreign Relations (New York: McGraw-Hill, 1977), pp. 123.

59. *UN and Disarmament Yearbook, Vol. 5, 1980*, pp. 350–52.

60. *SIPRI Yearbook 1982*, pp. 123, 187.

61. GAOR, Report of the Disarmament Commission, July 2, 1981. Thirty-Sixth Session, Supplement No. 42 (A/36/42), pp. 13–14, para. 21.

62. See GAOR, Nigeria in the SSOD or India, A/C.1/33/PV.38, November 15, 1978, p. 15.

63. Final Document of the SSOD, paras. 35, 94, 95.

64. See Milton Leitenberg and Nicole Ball, "The Military Expenditures of Less Developed Nations as a Proportion of Their State Budgets," *Bulletin of Peace Proposals*, no. 4 (1977): 310–15; R. L. Sivard, *World Military and Social Expenditures—1980* (New York: Institute for World Order, 1980).

65. Leitenberg and Ball, "Military Expenditures," p. 310.

66. Ibid., pp. 310–11.

67. Mary Kaldor, "Arms and Dependence," in *Opportunities for Disarmament*, ed. Jane M. O. Sharp (New York: Carnegie Endowment for International Peace, 1978), pp. 62–63.

68. GAOR, A/C.1/35/PV.20, October 29, 1980, p. 21.

69. David K. Whynes, *The Economics of Third World Military Expenditures* (London: Macmillan, 1979).

70. Pierre, *The Global Politics*, pp. 36–37.

71. Sivard, *World Military and Social Expenditures—1981*, p. 7.

72. An interesting illustration of links between armament and development was manifested by India. A few days after the International Monetary Fund (IMF) approved a loan of $5.8 billion to India, Prime Minister Indira Gandhi showed up in Paris and ordered a $3.3 billion fleet of Mirage 2000 fighter planes. The arms deal explained also, as the *Wall Street Journal* editors suggest, why France "was plumping so strongly" for the IMF credit package to India. As a result the IMF, supposedly assigned to helping nations with short-term cash-flow problems, is financing, at least indirectly, major arms transactions. *Wall Street Journal*, November 28, 1981.

73. *SIPRI Yearbook 1980*, p. 15.

74. Ibid., p. 95.

75. For an extensive discussion on the role of oil in the international transfer of arms, see Beker, "The Oil–Arms Connection."

76. *Washington Post*, September 2, 1980.

77. Myrdal, *The Game of Disarmament*, p. 162.

78. Beker, "The Oil–Arms Connection," pp. 425–27.

79. Ibid., p. 439. In this article the writer suggests that the glut in the oil market since 1981 provides the West with a golden opportunity to reassess its arms transfer policies and decouple the oil–arms connection.

80. Pierre, *The Global Politics*, p. 42, and the final chapter. Similarly the conclusions of other studies such as Anne Hessing Cahn et al., *Controlling Future Arms Trade*.

8

Conclusion: Disarmament and Order

When the United Nations Charter was signed in June 1945, "to save succeeding generations from the scourge of war," the world had a few more days to learn about the potential scourge of a nuclear war. Soon the United Nations made disarmament a top priority in its first resolution. But after thirty-seven years of deliberations it seems that the world is no nearer that much-desired goal of nuclear disarmament than it was at the beginning. In criticizing the role of the United Nations in the field of arms control and in exposing the futility of its deliberations on disarmament, this work did not mean to underestimate the challenges of the nuclear age. If one takes the doomsday clock that has appeared on the cover of the *Bulletin of the Atomic Scientists* since 1974 as a reliable indicator, mankind stood in June 1982 at four minutes before midnight. Even those who cast doubts on the accuracy and premises of such a method—particularly after more than thirty-seven years of workable nuclear deterrence—cannot absolve themselves from this awesome responsibility simply by relying solely on the delicate presumptions of rational calculations and behavior that underlie nuclear deterrence.

The question, thus, that guided our inquiry was rather whether the United Nations, with its polemical debates on disarmament, is capable of promoting achievable disarmament and arms control policies. As in 1946, United Nations deliberations continue to ignore the advice of Salvador De Madariaga, the top official in the League of Nations dealing with disarmament, who said some time before the nuclear age that disarmament can be achieved only in a well-organized world community. Otherwise, warned Madariaga, the profound mistrust among nations guarantees that "all disarmament conferences are bound to degenerate into armament conferences."[1] Indeed, when the United Nations began to confront the endless minefield of controlling nuclear weapons, the idea of a supranational authority for nuclear activities was discussed for the first time. But, as shown at the outset, the world of 1946 was not ripe yet for sweeping changes at the expense of national sovereignty in the nation-state system on which the United Nations was erected.

In 1982, with the outburst of public interest on nuclear policy issues in the Western world,[2] attention had been drawn again to the same "indissoluble connection between sovereignty and war." Jonathan Schell, who writes dramatically on this connection in *The Fate of the Earth*, succeeded in publishing the most compelling thesis on the consequences of a nuclear catastrophe. In his third and final essay, "The Choice," Schell blames the concept of sovereignty as the original sin: "It was into the sovereignty system that nuclear bombs were born, as 'weapons' for 'war.'...The system of sovereignty is now to the earth and mankind what a polluting factory is to its local environment."[3] As Schell explains it, the world has chosen "to refashion the system of sovereignty to accommodate nuclear weapons."[4] Since the bomb cannot be disinvented, Schell suggests disinventing the nation-state and thus getting rid of the cause of major war.

But as the debates in the wake of the Baruch Plan in 1946 have demonstrated, diplomats at the United Nations found it easier to continue their clinging to the understandings arrived at in the United Nations' pre-atomic Charter. In the mid-1980s, it is apparent that members of the United Nations are still not ready to engage in a reexamination of the system based on sovereignty in order to promote disarmament.

In the United Nations of the 1980s, more than ever before, the concept of sovereignty has been elevated into a sacred principle of the organization. During the decolonization process the United Nations enhanced and multiplied the claims of statehood as the key to identity for peoples. The concept of one nation–one vote has come to be considered a kind of natural right, like the civil rights of the individual. This voting system, which is disproportionately weighted in favor of the weaker members, has made the Third World the master of decisions in the General Assembly. With this, the organization placed the NIEO at the top of its agenda, calling for a more egalitarian international system while at the same time insisting upon the state's undiminished sovereignty. There is an inherent contradiction between the Third World demand for international justice backed by special machinery for its implementation and the reluctance to accept supervision of internal redistribution and realization of human rights. As seen clearly in NIEO resolutions that emphasize the state's sovereign rights, the call for redistribution of power and resources has no bearing on the nation-state system and its security mechanism of self-help. In this international order the state would remain the basic unit, which protects its people and its interests with the military at its disposal. The philosophy of the NIEO thus runs counter to the idea of a new centralized security system that would limit states in the exercise of traditional freedom and sovereign rights.

The NIEO has changed dramatically the political culture and the climate in which security, disarmament, and world order issues are examined. Even in studies sponsored by the United Nations, the view is that there is a change in the role and functioning of the organization established upon the notion of collective security guaranteed by the privileged great powers. As a result of the NIEO revolution, the United Nations has changed its character and emphasis: "An organization primarily committed to political and security issues above all, the United Nations has now evolved into a world system intently devoted to assuring the equitable development of the world's peoples."[5]

This change in the United Nations system had immediate implications for the notions of international security and order. Within the framework of the NIEO, disarmament is different in character and purpose than in both the League Covenant and the United Nations Charter. Both in the Covenant and the Charter, disarmament, despite differences in role and relative significance, is closely related to the relevant approach to world order and the system of security. Within the NIEO system, however, disarmament is not a security concept but rather a vehicle to reallocate resources in order to get rid of the "law of the great powers" and create a more equal world order. Sovereignty, rather "sovereign equality," has replaced security as the guiding principle for the pursuit of disarmament.

With the NIEO becoming a top-priority item on the international agenda, disarmament has come to be regarded as an important instrument for the redistribution of world resources. Nuclear non-proliferation is not tackled as a security issue but rather as another source of "discrimination" between the "haves" and "have-nots." The Third World emphasizes its "sovereign rights" to nuclear know-how and dismisses non-proliferation concerns as "unworkable" and "non-democratic." The net result is that United Nations debates undermine the status of the Non-Proliferation Treaty (NPT) and become instrumental in legitimizing nuclear weapons proliferation. In a similar fashion, Third World countries reject initiatives on the conventional arms race and attempts to restrain international arms trade since they infringe on their sovereign rights. This does not mean that individual Third World countries do not have national security concerns. It could well be that some of them might consider arms control efforts on a bilateral or regional level, but they have no choice at the United Nations but to maintain their bloc solidarity on disarmament as part of the NIEO.

Shifting majorities at the United Nations have created innovative concepts— such as the NIEO—that were undreamed of by the founding fathers of the United Nations. The United Nations Charter does not only express certain values, principles and objectives that still need to be promoted; it also envisages a certain structure of international order and balance of power. As shown in this book, there was a sense of realism in the Charter's approach to collective security in its recognition of the necessity for great-power unity. The Third World in its call for NIEO rejects the notion of balance of power and the hierarchical international order legitimized by the Charter. Instead they invoke the weak and vague provisions on disarmament to direct them against the big powers. On the other hand, the major document of the NIEO, the Charter of Economic Rights and Duties of States (Res. 3281—XXIX, December 12, 1974), fails to recognize, perhaps deliberately so, that the use of sovereign rights can be limited by international law and does not acknowledge that functional sovereignty on specific subjects may have to be transferred to an international organization. In the light of this attitude, it is unlikely that under the NIEO the role of force in international politics would be reformed to a meaningful extent.

It is almost taken for granted in the literature that a comprehensive approach to disarmament would require some revisions in the United Nations Charter. These revisions are always at variance with the conceptual framework of the NIEO. Such, for instance, is the work of Grenville Clark and Louis B. Sohn, who collaborated in developing the most impressive scheme for disarmament as part and parcel of their plan for world government. In this process sovereign nations would give up their sovereign rights for the sake of an international federal system in which all individuals are citizens of a global state.[6] Even modest plans for disarmament and order require a discriminatory approach to sovereign rights of states. So is the plan by Leonard Beaton, which provides also for the security of many small nations. Beaton, who rejects the notion of world government as impossible and even undesirable, still provides for international forces. He emphasizes that any attempt to build a permanent structure of world order "must be a great power system" in which supranational forces—including nuclear forces—are provided and controlled by the five nuclear powers.[7] In sum, it is evident that both the all-encompassing concept of world government or the limited and restricted system of supranational great-power forces are necessarily alien to the NIEO philosophy and mentality.

The Soviet Union, which has managed to disassociate itself from the North–South confrontation,[8] is a major beneficiary of the new United Nations disarmament approach. The Soviets were smart enough to develop the link between the NIEO and the control of the superpowers' arms race.[9] The Soviets have introduced the idea that superpowers' political detente and cooperation in arms limitation "constitutes an indispensable condition for the establishment of a new international order."[10] At this particular juncture, the Soviets imply more than they are prepared to explicate that the notion of world government or any limitation on the sovereign approach to security is foreign to their ideology.

With the deterioration in East–West relations, United Nations debates on disarmament in the late 1970s and the early 1980s were reminiscent of the cold war era. But this time the power equation in the General Assembly was completely different, adding significanty to Soviet inherent advantages. The Soviets can be confident that their "peace offensive" will enjoy a comfortable majority in United Nations forums. The West, which remains in a minority and sometimes in disarray, realizes that there is limited utility if any in relying on the United Nations as a means for pursuing disarmament and arms control policies. If there is any hope for some progress in arms control, it is likely to be taken bilaterally, outside the United Nations.

This juxtaposition of North–South and East–West confrontations tends to foster the tendency to introduce grandiloquent and sweeping but hollow plans of General and Complete Disarmament (GCD) or Comprehensive Program of Disarmament (CPD). These proposals do not provide an international authority with teeth that will enforce order in a disarmed world. This tendency prevents the United Nations from serious discussion on limited bargains of achievable and workable agreements of arms control. Stripped of its activities in arms control, the United Nations has become engaged in an unprecedented process of creating institutions and organs that deliberate, "negotiate," and study disarmament. But apparently bureaucratic reforms and institutional arrangements cannot compensate for the lack of political conditions for a meaningful debate on disarmament.

In July 1982, when the Second Special Session on Disarmament (SSD II) of the General Assembly fizzled out, many diplomats were reported to regard the failure of the conference as damaging to future activities of the United Nations in disarmament. According to some observers the Final Document of the SSD II was nothing but a "vague blueprint for inaction, papering over the failure of consensus. . . [and] dramatizing the collapse of an international consensus on the theoretical goals of arms control" enumerated by the SSOD.[11] SSD II failed even to reach agreement on the priority that should be accorded to various disarmament measures by the Committee on Disarmament in Geneva, the multilateral organ for disarmament negotiations.

In essence, the dismal outcome of SSD II should have been anticipated, and those disappointed were victims of their own misconceptions and unrealistic illusions. Already in 1978 it was clear that the consensus of SSD I was more of an appearance than reality. As long as the patterns of differences in the United Nations are those outlined in the preceding chapters, it is likely that "disarmament" will remain a theoretical topic that permits each group to carry on its political struggle by other means. Given the unworldly concepts of NIEO and CPD, which ignore the current world hierarchy and balance of power, and in the absence of serious confrontation of questions of security and international order, United Nations debates on disarmament are doomed to remain irrelevant to the real world outside.

NOTES

1. Madariaga, *Disarmament*, p. 62.
2. The upward trend continued into the mid-1980s and was reinforced by the electronic media with the screening of nuclear horror movies ("The Day After" in 1984) on national television.
3. Jonathan Schell, *The Fate of the Earth* (New York: Alfred A. Knopf, 1982), p. 187.
4. Ibid., p. 194.
5. Laszlo, Baker, Eisenberg, and Raman, *The Objectives of the NIEO*, p. xi.
6. Clark and Sohn, *World Peace Through World Law*.
7. Leonard Beaton, *The Reform of Power* (New York: Viking Press, 1972), pp. 202–6, 229.
8. Antony J. Dolman, *Resources, Regimes, World Order* (New York: Pergamon Press, 1981), pp. 96–97.
9. See also the speech by Andrei Gromyko to the Sixth Special Session, GAOR, A/PV.2210 (1974), in ibid., p. 97.

10. B. S. Fromin, "The New International Economic Order as Viewed in the CMEA Countries," in *Eastern Europe and the New International Economic Order*, ed. E. Laszlo and J. Kurtzman (New York: Pergamon Press, 1980), p. 6.

11. "UN Session Ends, Loss of Consensus on Disarmament Confirmed," *Washington Post*, July 11, 1982. For the document adopted at SSD II, see GAOR, Twelfth Special Session, Supplement No. 6 (A/S-12/6), Document A/S-12/32, July 10, 1982.

APPENDIX I

On Terminology

In the long course of United Nations activities in disarmament, some procedures and terminology have been introduced and institutionalized. It is evident that United Nations' international civil servants and the delegates involved in the disarmament business are using some terms differently than is the American community of arms controllers (the so-called armchair strategists). It seems, therefore, that it would be helpful to clarify the meaning which some of the terms have acquired, particularly because their use at the United Nations has somewhat drifted away from the common-sense use in the literature. Moreover, different notions given to the same terms by different delegates reveal the polemical distortion of terminology at the United Nations. The different attributions to the terms disarmament and arms control are in accordance with the fundamental approaches of East and West to the subject matter. In the meantime, the evolution of a third notion of "disarmament" at the United Nations underscores the changes in the settings of the deliberations. For the United Nations' new majority, the Third World countries, disarmament has became an integral part of their struggle against both superpowers, and therefore the term necessitated a new connotation.

Historically, as the language of the League's Covenant suggests, disarmament was the broad process by which gradual measures were welcomed to bring about limits, control, and regulations as elements of a broader strategy for disarmament. In more precise terms, *disarmament* has meant the reduction or elimination of armaments or armed forces. *Arms control* or *arms limitation*, on the other hand, means limitations of the number or types of armaments or armed forces, of their deployment or disposition, or of the use of particular types of armaments. *Arms control* also encompasses measures designed to reduce the danger of accidental war or to reduce concern about surprise attack.[1] The United Nations Charter explicitly recognized the existence of this distinction when it referred to "principles governing disarmament and the regulation of armaments."

Writers of the arms control school such as Thomas Schelling and Morton Halperin tend to broaden the term *arms control* to include all forms of military cooperation between potential enemies as part of a national security strategy.[2] Hedley Bull points out that there can be disarmament that is not controlled (unilateral or unconditional) and arms control that does not involve a reduction of armaments.[3] Arms control may also cost more and involve or imply a buildup in weapons arsenals if that minimizes the danger of accidents and false alarms and stabilizes strategic deterrence between the superpowers. As an American expert wrote at the height of arms control's popularity: "There is nothing in the concept of arms control to prevent the increase of certain types of armament, if it appears in the interest of national or world security to do so."[4]

In 1981, Secretary of State Alexander Haig elaborated on the nature of arms control: "Arms control agreements are aimed to enhance security.... Valuable agreements can be envisioned that do not save money and do not eliminate arms. The vital task is to limit and to reduce arms in a way that renders use of the remaining arms less likely."[5]

The new twist here is the recent attempt by the United States to redefine arms control in terms of arms reductions (START, Strategic Arms Reductions Talks, replaced SALT in the Reagan administration), while insisting on the enhancement of national security rather than the ideal of disarmament as the criterion.

Ironically, as experts in arms control have demonstrated, efforts to negotiate limits on arms may involve interrelated processes ("bargaining chips," "displacement effects," etc.), which may initiate or accelerate other weapons programs.[6] During the public debate in the United States concerning the ratification of the SALT II treaty (1979), it was taken for granted that implementation of the agreement would be coupled with increases in the U.S. defense budget and the development of new weapons systems. In this respect, arms control is part and parcel of superpowers' nuclear deterrence, the aim being to maintain and stabilize the international system on the basis of bipolarity. Arms control, according to this interpretation, is a policy of High Posture that aims at preserving, and possibly even widening, the gap between, on the one hand, the superpowers and, on the other, the smaller nuclear powers and non-nuclear states (see Chapter 6).

Another angle on the issue is provided by Hans Morgenthau, who presents the opinion of "political realism" on disarmament in its purest form. For Morgenthau, disarmament no less than the arms race is the reflection of the power relations among the nations concerned. This is why, explains Morgenthau, arms control attempts have been only moderately successful in the nuclear field in which the major nuclear powers reached that optimum of assured destruction beyond which it is irrational to go.[7] Arms control, as he explains, is not disarmament at all but merely a "regulation of the arms race" in the sense of a cartel agreement.[8]

The bipolar nature of the concept of arms control explains why Third World spokesmen reject it. The Indian representative suggested once that, in a particular United Nations document, the term *arms limitation* be used instead of the controversial term *arms control*. To him *arms control* has "certain unacceptable connotations since it implies "controls even without working for genuine disarmament." The ambassador underscored how the terminology is closely related to the notion of world order in stating that arms control "carries overtones of control exercised by one group of countries over another in the name of disarmament" and is therefore "discriminatory."[9] Similarly, the Brazilian ambassador blasted the superpowers for dropping the term *disarmament* from their political lexicon and replacing it with euphemistic expressions such as *arms control*.[10]

In the same vein it is understandable that Alva Myrdal, a former minister of Sweden for disarmament and a leader of the 21 Group of non-aligned countries in the committee on disarmament in Geneva, regrets that the term *arms control* has became popular, creating in her words a "terminological jungle." To make the term *control* synonymous with the limitation or regulation of armaments, says Myrdal, leads to nothing but confusion. For her, arms control is a shrewd cover-up of the superpowers game that involves "scant or nil disarmament.'' Arms control, suggests Myrdal, should be used only in the context of verification. She draws a distinction between *control* as the general regulation or control of the arms race through treaty obligation and *verification* as more specifically concerned with the methods used for ascertaining facts about compliance.[11]

In the United Nations it is informal practice to refer to disarmament as the broad term that includes all degrees of weapons reductions and limitations. Most countries (except the United States and its Western allies) avoid the use of *arms control*. During the preparatory discussions for the SSOD the delegation of Mexico submitted a working paper (August 1977) that indicated:

It seems advisable to point out that the term "disarmament" is used here in the same sense in which it has been used in the various forums of the United Nations: that is, as a generic term which encompasses and may designate any type of measures relating to the matter, whether they are measures for the prevention, limitation, reduction or elimination of armaments or for the reduction of military forces.[12]

Consequently, disarmament in United Nations discussions and documents includes a variety of measures on different levels, from general and complete nuclear disarmament to confidence-building measures in military-political relationships. The Final Document adopted at the SSOD is an excellent example of the United Nations' approach to the problem of terminology. This long document (129 paragraphs) contains a sort of checklist of virtually all possible measures of disarmament, from total prohibition of nuclear weapons to collateral-political measures aimed at the relaxation of international tension.

In this regard the Final Document marks a departure and deviation from the spirit and letter of the United Nations Charter's approach to disarmament. The expression *regulation of armaments*, which appears in the Charter as well as in the Covenant of the League, does not appear anywhere in the Document. Similarly there is no reference to *arms control* and instead the document uses *arms limitation*. Measures that are basically designed to preserve the stability of nuclear deterrence, such as "hot lines," are referred to as "confidence-building" measures.[13] At the behest of the Third World, the whole notion of arms regulation, so central in the days of the League and later adopted by the drafters of the Charter, had completely disappeared from the official document of the SSOD.

Alessandro Corradini, a former director and deputy to the assistant general of the United Nations Center for Disarmament, regarded the Final Document of the SSOD as representing the real philosophy of disarmament. The philosophy of disarmament, said Corradini, is not that of regulation of armaments or, what he regards as the same, of arms control. In his view, the Final Document "has contributed most significantly to bringing back the true meaning of disarmament, that is, the reduction and, ultimately the elimination of armaments." Even when the Document refers to arms limitation, explains Corradini, it implies reduction given the Document's clear goal as set out in its very first paragraphs and subsequent ones.[14] This interpretation coupled with the deliberate omission of the concept of arms regulation in the Final Document marks a departure from the philosophy of the Charter on the collective security system and its link to disarmament.

In the East–West confrontation on disarmament in the United Nations, terminology is not just a matter of semantics but involves political differences that go back to the beginning of post–World War II deliberations. From the outset, the Soviet Union and its satellites have used the single word *disarmament* to describe all kinds of initiatives and negotiations, even though many of them over the years have not called for disarmament or even a reduction of armaments, such as the non-use of nuclear weapons or non-use of force or even "hot lines" arrangements to reduce the risk of accidental nuclear war.[15] The Western powers, on the other hand, with greater caution have preferred to use the terms *limitation, regulation*, and *control of arms*, or since 1958, its shorter variant, *arms control*. The use of the term *arms control* coupled with the insistence by the West on inspection and verification measures immediately invites Soviet propaganda. The Soviets charge that the West is not interested in disarmament or a reduction of armaments but is concerned solely with control and the resulting penetration of the Soviet iron curtain, which in turn is vaguely linked to espionage.[16] Even in the late 1970s, when the superpowers were finalizing their second treaty on strategic arms limitations (SALT II), the Soviets made it plain that their rejection of the term *control* is an elementary factor in their approach to disarmament. In his statement to the SSOD, Foreign Minister Gromyko said the following:

Many of those present must have noticed that representatives of some countries generally find it difficult even to pronounce the word "disarmament"; they would rather speak of control. Control over what? Control over armaments; they say it openly, in so many words. But the volume of armaments in the world can be increased to five times the present level even if they are under control.[17]

The United States, aware of the Soviet–Third World coalition against "arms control," indicated already before the SSOD that it attached special significance to efforts in this field. In a letter to the secretary general on the SSOD, the U.S. ambassador called upon governments to consider the concepts involved and recommended: "The national reviews that precede the session itself should be based on a recognition that arms control arrangements have the potential of enhancing, not merely preserving, the security of the participants."[18] The American letter did not use the Soviet and Third World's terminology on general and complete disarmament but instead referred to "restrictions" and "limitations" of weapons or "tension-reducing measures," etc.

If one takes into consideration the views expressed by the Charter's framers on arms and the collective security system, the Western approach seems to be more in line with the Charter than is the Soviet maxim that "the way to disarm is to disarm" and its manifestations in their grandiloquent proposals for disarmament. The reference for the more restricted terms stems from the belief that under existing international circumstances of mistrust only a gradual and verifiable approach is feasible. Leaders of the West such as former Vice President Walter Mondale, West German Chancellor Helmut Schmidt, Prime Minister Pierre Trudeau of Canada, and James Callaghan of the United Kingdom, as well as others, in their addresses to the SSOD, referred to arms control agreements as something distinct from disarmament. Though in informal discussion and sometimes even in speeches Western delegates use the terms *disarmament* and *arms control* interchangeably, it is rather for practical reasons, in the recognition that the popular meaning of disarmament at the United Nations generally describes any subject matter in the field. A meticulous examination of the positions of states as reflected in the 1978 SSOD reveals that East–West divergencies over terminology remained the same. The Western working papers placed the distinction already in the subtitle: "Immediate Measures of Arms Control and Disarmament."[19] The socialist states (the Soviet bloc) did not use the term *arms control* at all. The Soviet view is that detente and "peaceful coexistence between states with different social systems" have created favorable conditions for successful negotiations on disarmament. Under this category the paper specifies a variety of bilateral and multilateral agreements that have been reached in the field, including SALT. Even measures aimed "at preventing nuclear war and reducing the risk of its accidental outbreak" are referred to as disarmament.[20]

Characteristically, the United States in all its official statements and publications refers to SALT and other agreements as "arms control." It was an established practice in the monthly *Bulletin* of the State Department to discuss SALT issues under the title of arms control. In Vice President Mondale's statement it was apparent that U.S. officials have adopted the logic and terminology of their fellow citizens from the arms control community, in which arms control embraces all ranges of possible measures. Mondale explained the thrust of United States policy: "The prudent policy of any nation must include both sufficient military preparedness and arms control efforts, if its security is to be assured. In the short run no nation can be asked to reduce its defenses to levels below the threats it faces." Referring to the record of President Carter's administration he said:

The United States has been engaged in the broadest set of arms control negotiations in our history. Together with our negotiating partners, the United States has developed an agenda more extensive than any nation has ever attempted. We are taking concrete action in 10 different areas—from nuclear-weapon accords to regional restraint and to limits on conventional and unconventional arms such as anti-satellite and radiological weapons.[21]

Since the Third World is in the position to determine the agenda of the General Assembly, its approach is more influential than both East and West on the terminology used in United Nations documents. In fact, to the extent that a common Third World position can be identified on the basis of their joint statements and documents, disarmament to the Third World is a generic term but subject to two qualifications: (1) every single measure should be instrumental to the broader framework of general and complete disarmament; and (2) disarmament is a process that is consciously subordinated to the establishment of a New International Economic Order (NIEO).

The eighty-two non-aligned countries' working paper submitted for the SSOD outlined a comprehensive program for disarmament that includes some immediate short-term measures to get the process started. However, only when these partial measures would lead to general and complete disarmament can they qualify as disarmament measures. In contrast to the superpowers' arms control agreements, this definition is less concerned with stability of nuclear deterrence and even less, of course, with the preservation of superpowers' bipolarity. According to this view, agreements that fail to slow down the arms race or encourage more spending on weapons programs do not serve disarmament purposes: "An assessment of disarmament efforts in the past three decades indicates that, despite some measures in the field of arms limitation, no real progress has been made on the crucial question of disarmament, and in particular, concerning the nuclear arms race." Instead, the non-aligned demanded the reorientation of the negotiations between the superpowers toward solutions that would make it possible to achieve decisive progress toward genuine disarmament. In sum: "All efforts and negotiations should be geared in a balanced and integrated way and lead to general and complete disarmament."[22]

The second qualification is critical to the understanding of the Third World approach to disarmament. Disarmament for the Third World became a secondary issue on their agenda completely subordinated to their quest for the establishment of the NIEO (see Chapter 4). In their working paper to the SSOD the non-aligned said: "The arms race is inconsistent with efforts aimed at achieving the new international economic order in view of the urgent need to divert the resources utilized for the acceleration of the arms race towards socio-economic development, particularly of the developing countries."[23]

With their overwhelming power in the General Assembly, the Third World inserted several statements that tie together disarmament with the NIEO in the Final Document of the SSOD. The reference to the comprehensive program of disarmament (CPD) in the Final Document reflects both aspects of their approach to disarmament: the goal of general and complete disarmament and the NIEO. The CPD, according to the Final Document, should encompass

all measures thought to be advisable in order to ensure the goal of general and complete disarmament under effective international control becomes a reality in a world in which international peace and security prevail and in which the new international economic order is strengthened and consolidated.[24]

In sum, analysis of the terminology used in the United Nations reveals the three different approaches to the concept of disarmament by the East, West, and Third World. The Soviet bloc, with its traditional sweeping and grandiloquent disarmament proposals, emphasizes exclusively disarmament measures without further elaboration on the political arrangements and principles surrounding it. The Western allies make a clear distinction between disarmament and arms control and emphasize the political context of the disarmament process and the requirements of world order. The Third World speaks about the link between disarmament and world order but in a different sense: disarmament is viewed as an instrument by which to achieve the NIEO. Disarmament, thus, does not require prior political settlements and new international security institutions, although essentially by disarming the major power the developing countries intend to transform the existing world order.

NOTES

1. Barton and Weiler, *International Arms Control*, p. 3

2. Thomas C. Schelling and Morton H. Halperin, *Strategy and Arms Control* (New York: Twentieth Century Fund, 1961), pp. 2, 141–43.

3. Bull, *The Control of the Arms Race*, p. vii.

4. Donald G. Brennan, in *Arms Control and Disarmament: American Views and Studies*, ed. Donald G. Brennan (London: Jonathan Cape, 1961), p. 31.

5. *New York Times*, July 15, 1981.

6. G. W. Rathjens, Abram Chayes, and J. P. Ruina, *Nuclear Arms Control Agreements: Process and Impact* (Washington, D.C.: Carnegie Endowment for International Peace, 1974), pp. 9–25.

7. Hans J. Morgenthau, *Politics Among Nations* (New York: Alfred A. Knopf, 1973), p. 401.

8. Hans J. Morgenthau, "Some Political Aspects of Disarmament," in *The Dynamics of the Arms Race*, ed. David Carlton and Carlo Schaerf (New York: Halsted Press, 1975), p. 57

9. GAOR, A/C.1/35/PV.37, November 20, 1980, p. 22.

10. GAOR, A/C.1/35/PV.17, October 28, 1980, p. 3.

11. Myrdal, *The Games of Disarmament*, pp. xvi, 293.

12. GAOR, Tenth Special Session 1978, Supplement No. 1 (A/S-10/1), Report of the Preparatory Committee for the Special Session of the General Assembly Devoted to Disarmament, Vol. II, A/AC.187/30/Add.1.

13. GAOR, SSOD Final Document, Tenth Special Session 1978, Supplement No. 4, A/S-10/4. In another meeting on disarmament sponsored by the United Nations Educational, Scientific and Cultural Organization (UNESCO) there was an obscure reference to control of arms. The World Congress on Disarmament Education convened by UNESCO in Paris in June 1980 simply could not completely disregard the vast amount of literature on arms control. The congress incorporated the concept in its definition of disarmament: ''For the purpose of disarmament education, disarmament may be understood as any form of act aimed at limiting, controlling or reducing arms, including unilateral disarmament.'' However, in this form the controlling of arms is ambiguous, and it can have the connotation suggested by Alva Myrdal—as related to verification and inspection. World Congress on Disarmament Education, *Disarmament Education Report and Final Document*, Document No. 55-80/Conf.40/37, Rev. (Paris: UNESCO, June 9–13, 1980), p. 8.

14. Alessandro Corradini, ''The Development of Disarmament Education as a Distinct Field of Study: an Introductory Analysis,'' *Disarmament* 3, no. 3 (November 1980): 63.

15. GAOR, Tenth Special Session 1978, Supplement No. 1 (A/S-10/1), Vol. VI, A/AC.187/81.

16. Bechhoefer, *Postwar Negotiations*, p. 7.

17. GAOR, Tenth Special Session 1978, Supplement No. 1 (A/S-10/1), Vol. VI, A/AC.187/96.

18. Ibid., Vol. II, A/AC.187/17, April 22, 1977.

19. Ibid., Vol. IV, A/AC.187/80.

20. Ibid., A/AC.187/81.

21. GAOR, A/S-10/PV.2, May 24, 1978.

22. GAOR, Tenth Special Session 1978, Supplement No. 1 (A/S-10/1), Vol. IV, A/AC.187/55/Add.1.

23. Ibid., A/AC.187/55. Later on in the document the non-aligned declare: ''A substantial portion of the savings derived from measures in the field of disarmament should be devoted to promoting economic and social development, particularly in the developing countries.''

24. GAOR, SSOD Final Document, Tenth Special Session 1978, Supplement No. 4, A/S-10/4, para. 109.

On Research Methods

As disappointing as the United Nations activities in disarmament are, from an academic vantage point they provide an abundant source for research. United Nations meetings are well documented and include verbatim transcripts, working papers, and draft resolutions. The 1978 United Nations First Special Session on Disarmament (SSOD) substantially expanded the work of the organization in the field, providing even more data for researchers.

Both the number of disarmament bodies and the volumes of documentation have tripled since 1978. Outside the United Nations very few specialists on disarmament and arms control know about these activities, which include extensive preparation of numerous studies on specific aspects of disarmament commissioned by the General Assembly (see Chapter 3). Some of these studies have certain political biases, which raise questions about the qualification of a politically motivated body to sponsor research projects on issues that have a direct bearing on strategic and national security interests. These studies can be requested by a simple majority of the General Assembly against the will and interest of many member states. By adopting the dictum that "the way to disarm is to disarm," these studies are often divorced from tendencies in the other spheres of diplomacy and security. It seems that by adopting these practices the United Nations majority tells the major powers, "If you won't disarm, we can at least force you to discuss it."

For instance, the basic manual prepared for the first SSOD was a 3,000-page record in seven volumes, covering eighteen months of the work of the Preparatory Committee, working papers, and special reports and studies. But the major advantage for the researcher lies in the method of work in preparing the Final Document of the session. The Preparatory Committee produced a monumental document on disarmament, which was designated as the bargaining text of the session. Through this exercise member states are forced to express their views on various aspects that encompass the whole field of disarmament.

The draft was interesting in its own right but was far more fascinating in its annotated form (see the following documents). It was loaded with brackets expressing reservations on paragraphs, clauses, and words on the part of some states or group of states. As submitted to the SSOD, the complex manuscript looked like "a forest of brackets"— illustrating the lack of agreement on the major issues of disarmament. The annotated version of this exercise in "bracketsmanship" reveals who is bracketing whom and on what issues. A systematic analysis of the document can illuminate the political and strategic meanings of respective positions. This document, in its annotated version, was circulated as an informal working paper to the delegates but for obvious reasons was not issued as an official document of the United Nations (the official document contained the brackets without indicating their affiliation). These documents combined with the academic literature on strategic and political trends and the review of major newspapers was supplemented with private notes gathered during various sessions and lengthy discussions with delegates and United Nations staff members and experts in the field.

In the following documents, portions from the draft final document of the SSOD are reproduced. To the official document (GAOR, Tenth Special Session, Supplement No. 1, A/S-10/1, 1978) we added the initials based on the informal annotated version of the draft final document. The initials explain who is bracketing whom, thus revealing the contesting opinions on each issue. The brackets together with the initials speak for themselves.

Legend for Documents 1, 2, and 3

Initials on text identify authorship; initials on square brackets indicate origin of brackets.

E - Eastern (the Soviet bloc)
NA - Non-Aligned   SU - Soviet Union
PAK - Pakistan   F - France
W - Western   US - USA
MEX - Mexico   S - Sweden
IND - India   R - Romania

Document 1
Non-Use of Nuclear Weapons

(p. 28 of the draft final document)

(d) *[Non-use of nuclear weapons and prevention of
the outbreak of nuclear war/*

The most efficient guarantee against the danger of nuclear war and use of nuclear weapons is nuclear disarmament and complete elimination of nuclear weapons.

^W   ^{NA}
[Since the use of nuclear weapons would cause indiscriminate suffering and destruction to mankind and, as such, is a crime contrary to the rules of international law and the laws of humanity, as long as nuclear weapons exist [threatening the security of all States,^{PAK} particularly the non-nuclear-weapon States], the following measures will be taken:

NA+E

- A convention on the non-use of nuclear weapons should be urgently concluded.

PAK

- Nuclear-weapon States should renounce [in a legally binding form] the use [or threat of use]^{PAK} of nuclear weapons [against States which have no^{NA} nuclear weapons on their territories] [against States not parties^{PAK} to the nuclear security arrangements of some nuclear Powers].

NA + PAK   MEX

- [Nuclear-weapon States should undertake], [jointly or individually], not to be the first to use nuclear weapons.]

Alternative 1   ^E[Strict implementation of the ^Wprinciple of non-use of force in international relations can be realized through full compliance with the Charter of the United Nations.]

189

Document 2

(p. 26 of the draft final document)

(a) *[Strategic Arms Limitation Talks (SALT)]*

Alternative 1   MEX

The Union of Soviet Socialist Republics and the United States of America should strive to conclude at the earliest possible date the agreement they have been pursuing for several years in the second series of the strategic arms limitation negotiations (SALT II) ᵂ[which should provide for ᴾᴬᴷ meaningful reduction in their deployment of nuclear weapons and a moratorium on the testing and refinement of new kinds of nuclear delivery systems]. The Governments of both countries should transmit in good time the text of this agreement to the General Assembly and should initiate promptly the third series of such negotiations (SALT III) intended to conclude another agreement including significant reductions ᵂ[from 10 up to 50 per ᴾᴬᴷ cent in their deployments of strategic nuclear weapons] and important qualitative limitations ᵂ[such as a five-year ᴾᴬᴷ moratorium on any qualitative improvement of their strategic nuclear-weapons delivery systems] as a step towards the complete, total destruction of the existing stockpiles of nuclear weapons and the consolidation of a world truly free of such weapons.

Alternative 2   MEX

The Union of Soviet Socialist Republics and the United States of America should adopt without delay all relevant measures for the effective implementation of the agreement they have concluded as a result of the second series of the strategic arms limitation negotiations (SALT II) the text of which has been transmitted by them to the General Assembly. The Governments of both States should also initiate promptly the third series of such negotiations (SALT III) intended to conclude another agreement including significant reductions ᵂ[from 10 up to 50 per ᴾᴬᶜ cent in their deployments of strategic nuclear weapons] and important qualitative limitations ᵂ[such as a five-year ᴾᴬᶜ moratorium on any qualitative improvement of their strategic nuclear-weapons delivery systems] as a step towards the complete, total destruction of the existing stockpiles of nuclear weapons and the consolidation of a world truly free of such weapons.

Alternative 3

ᵂ⁺ᴱ

There should be the earliest possible conclusion of an agreement in the second strategic arms limitation negotiations between the Union of Soviet Socialist Republics and the United States of America to be followed promptly by further strategic arms limitation negotiations between the two parties leading to agreed ᴱ ᵂ[significant] reductions and qualitative limitations.

Document 3

(pp. 25-26 in the draft final document)

> C. *[Immediate and short-term measures to halt
> and reverse the arms race/*

> 1. *[Nuclear weapons]*

Nuclear weapons pose the greatest danger to mankind and to the survival of civilization. It is essential to halt and reverse the nuclear-arms race in all its aspects in order to avert the danger of war involving nuclear weapons. The utlimate goal in this context is the complete elimination of nuclear weapons. To this end steps should be taken urgently to stop the build-up of nuclear arsenals, to reduce stockpiles of nuclear weapons and to halt further development of [and production^W of new types of] nuclear armaments. The nuclear-weapon States [particularly the two^{NA} leading nuclear-weapon States] bear a special responsibility for realization of these tasks.

Alternative 1   [Measures of nuclear disarmament^{NA} will require parallel progress^{W+E} the limitation and reduction of the armed forces of States and of their conventional weapons.] [In^{NA W} turn]

Alternative 2   [Real progress in the field of nuclear^{NA} disarmament could create an atmosphere which could contribute to progress in conventional disarmament.] [and^{NA W} vice versa.]

Alternative 3   [Progress in the limitation and^{PAK} reduction of the armed forces of States [nuclear-weapon^{IND} States and their allies] and of their conventional weapons could contribute to progress in nuclear disarmament.]

191

Bibliography

BOOKS

ACDA. *World Military Expenditures and Arms Transfers 1968-1977*. Washington, D.C.: GPO, 1978.

Alperovitz, Gar. *Atomic Diplomacy: Hiroshima and Potsdam*. New York: Simon and Schuster, 1965.

Aron, Raymond. *Peace and War—A Theory of International Relations*. New York: Anchor Books, 1973.

Bader, William B. *The United States and the Spread of Nuclear Weapons*. New York: Pegasus, 1968.

Barnet, Richard J. *Who Wants Disarmament*. Boston: Beacon Press, 1960.

Barton, John, and Weiler, Lawrence D., eds. *International Arms Control*. Stanford, Calif.: Stanford University Press, 1976.

Bauer, P. T. *Poverty, Poor Countries and Perverted Economics*. Cambridge: Harvard University Press, 1981.

Baylis, John; Booth, Ken; Williams, Phil; and Garnett, John. *Contemporary Strategy: Theories and Policies*. New York: Holmes & Meier Publishers, 1975.

Beaton, Leonard. *The Reform of Power*. New York: Viking Press, 1972.

Bechhoefer, Bernard G. *Postwar Negotiations for Arms Control*. Washington, D.C.: The Brookings Institution, 1961.

Bedjaoui, Mohammed. *Toward a New International Economic Order*. A UNESCO Publication. New York: Holmes & Meier Publishers, 1979.

Bennett, LeRoy A. *International Organizations: Principles and Issues*. Englewood Cliffs, N.J.: Prentice-Hall, 1980.

Benoit, Emile. *Defence and Economic Growth in Developing Countries*. Lexington, Mass.: Lexington Books, 1973.

Beres, Louis Rene. *Apocalypse—Nuclear Catastrophe in World Politics*. Chicago: University of Chicago Press, 1980.

Blumberg, Stanley A., and Owens, Gwin. *Energy and Conflict: The Life and Times of Edward Teller*. New York: G. P. Putnam's Sons, 1976.

Bowett, Derek. *Self-Defence in International Law*. New York: Praeger Publishers, 1958.
Brainard, Alfred Paul. *The United Nations and the Question of Disarmament 1950–1955*.
　　A Ph.D. dissertation, University of Washington, 1960. Ann Arbor, Mich.: Uni-
　　versity Microfilms, 1961.
Brennan, Donald G., ed. *Arms Control and Disarmament: American Views and Studies*.
　　London: Jonathan Cape, 1961.
———. *Arms Control, Disarmament and National Security*. New York: George Braziller,
　　1961.
Buchan, Alastair, and Windsor, Philip. *Arms and Stability in Europe*. New York: Praeger
　　Publishers, 1963.
Bull, Hedley. *The Control of the Arms Race*. New York: Praeger Publishers, 1965.
Cahn, Anne Hessing; Kruzel, Joseph J.; Dawkins, Peter M.; and Huntzinger, Jacques.
　　Controlling Future Arms Trade. 1980s Project Council of Foreign Relations. New
　　York: McGraw-Hill, 1977.
Carlton, David, and Schaerf, Carlo, eds. *The Dynamics of the Arms Race*. New York:
　　Halsted Press, 1975.
Clark, Grenville, and Sohn, Louis B. *World Peace Through World Law*. Cambridge:
　　Harvard University Press, 1967.
Claude, Inis L. *Swords into Plowshares*. New York: Random House, 1971.
Clemens, Diane Shaver. *Yalta*. New York: Oxford University Press, 1970.
Corwin, Norman. *Modern Man Is Obsolete*. New York: Holt and Co., 1945.
Crabb, Cecil V., Jr. *The Elephants and the Grass—A Study of Non-Alignment*. New
　　York: Praeger Publishers, 1965.
Dolman, Anthony J. *Resources, Regimes, World Order*. New York: Pergamon Press,
　　1981.
Donalson, Robert H., ed. *The Soviet Union in the Third World: Successes and Failures*.
　　Boulder, Colo.: Westview Press, 1981.
Dougherty, J. E., and Lehman, J. T. *Arms Control for the Late Sixties*. Princeton, N.J.:
　　D. Van Nostrand, 1967.
Dougherty, James E., and Pfaltzgraff, Robert L., Jr. *Contending Theories of International
　　Relations*. New York: J. B. Lippincott, 1971.
Dror, Yeheskel. *Crazy States—A Counterconventional Strategic Problem*. Lexington,
　　Mass.: Heath Lexington Books, 1971.
Dulles, Eleanor Lansing, and Crane, Robert Dickson, eds. *Detente–Cold War Strategies
　　in Transition*. New York: Praeger Publishers, 1965.
Dulles, John Foster. *War or Peace*. New York: Macmillan, 1950.
Dunn. Lewis A. *Controlling the Bomb—Nuclear Proliferation in the 1980s*. New Haven:
　　Yale University Press, 1982.
Dupuy, Trevor N., and Hammerman, Gay M., eds. *A Documentary History of Arms
　　Control and Disarmament*. New York: R. R. Bowker, 1973.
Epstein, William. *Disarmament—Twenty-Five Years of Effort*. Ontario: Canadian Institute
　　of International Affairs, 1971.
———. *The Last Chance—Nuclear Proliferation and Arms Control*. New York: Free
　　Press, 1976.
———, and Feld, Bernard T., eds. *New Directions in Disarmament*. New York: Praeger
　　Publishers, 1981.
Falk, Richard, and Mendlovitz, Saul H., eds. *The Strategy of World Order*, vol. 3, *The
　　United Nations*. New York: World Law Fund, 1969.

Fedder, Edwin H., ed. *Defense Politics of the Atlantic Alliance*. New York: Praeger Publishers, 1980.

Feliciano, M. McDougal. *Law and Minimum World Order*. New Haven: Yale University Press, 1961.

Finger, Seymour Maxwell, and Harbert, Joseph R., eds. *U.S. Policy in International Institutions, Defining Reasonable Options in an Unreasonable World*. Boulder, Colo.: Westview Press, 1978.

Fischer, George. *The Non-Proliferation of Nuclear Weapons*. New York: St. Martin's Press, 1970.

Gaddis, John Lewis. *The United States and the Origins of the Cold War 1941–1949*. New York: Columbia University Press, 1972.

Ginsburg, George, and Rubenstein, Alvin Z., eds. *Soviet Foreign Policy Toward Western Europe*. New York: Praeger Publishers, 1978.

Gompert, David C.; Mandelbaum, Michael; Garwin, Richard L.; and Barton, John H. *Nuclear Weapons and World Politics*. 1980s Project Council on Foreign Relations. New York: McGraw-Hill, 1977.

Goodrich, Leland M.; Hambro, Edward; and Simmons, Anne. *United Nations Charter: Commentary and Documents*. New York: Columbia University Press, 1969.

Green, Philip. *Deadly Logic: The Theory of Nuclear Deterrence*. Columbus: Ohio State University Press, 1966.

Greenwood, Ted; Feireson, Harold A.; Taylor, Theodore B. *Nuclear Proliferation: Motivations, Capabilities and Strategies for Control*. 1980s Project Council on Foreign Relations. New York: McGraw-Hill, 1977.

Hag, Khadija, ed. *Dialogue for a New Order*. New York: Pergamon Press, 1980.

Haldeman, H. R. *The Ends of Power*. New York: Times Books, 1978.

Harriman, Averell W. *America and Russia in a Changing World*. London: George Allen & Unwin, 1971.

Hening, Ruth B., ed. *The League of Nations*. New York: Barnes & Noble, 1973.

Henkin, Louis. *Disarmament*. The Hammarskjold Forums of the Association of the Bar of the City of New York. New York: Oceana Publications, 1964.

———, ed. *Arms Control—Issues for the Public*. Englewood Cliffs, N.J.: Prentice-Hall, 1961.

Herken, Gregg. *The Winning Weapon: The Atomic Bomb in the Cold War 1945–1950*. New York: Alfred A. Knopf, 1980.

Horowitz, Irving Louis. *Three Worlds of Development*. London: Oxford University Press, 1966.

Hull, Cordell. *The Memoirs of Cordell Hull*. Vol. 2. New York: Macmillan, 1948.

Independent Commission on Disarmament and Security Issues. *Common Security—A Blueprint for Survival*. New York: Simon and Schuster, 1982.

Independent Commission on International Development Issues (Willy Brandt, Chairman). *North–South: A Programme for Survival*. London: Pan Books, 1980.

Jack, Homer A. *Disarmament Workshop—The UN Special Session and Beyond*. New York: World Conference on Religion and Peace, 1979.

Jankowitsch, Odette, and Sauvant, Karl P., eds. *The Third World Without Superpowers: The Collected Documents of the Non-Aligned Countries*. Vols. 1–2. New York: Oceana Publications, 1978.

Jansen, G. H. *Afro-Asia and Non-Alignment*. London: Faber and Faber, 1966.

Kahn, Herman. *On Thermonuclear War*. Princeton, N.J.: Princeton University Press, 1960.

Kaplan, Morton A., ed. *Great Issues of International Politics*. Chicago: Aldine, 1974.

Kaplan, Morton A., and Katzenbach, Nicholas de B. *The Political Foundations of International Law*. New York: John Wiley & Sons, 1961.

Kapur, Ashok. *India's Nuclear Option: Atomic Diplomacy and Decision Making*. New York: Praeger Publishers, 1976.

————. *International Nuclear Proliferation*. New York: Praeger Publishers, 1979.

Kay, David A., ed. *The Changing United Nations: Options for the United States*. New York: Academy of Political Science, 1977.

————. *The New Nations in the United Nations 1960–1967*. New York: Columbia University Press, 1970.

Kelsen, Hans. *The Law of the United Nations*. London: Stevens & Sons, 1950.

Kennedy, D. E. *The Security of Southern Asia*. London: Chatto & Windus, 1965.

Kimche, David. *The Afro-Asian Movement Ideology and Foreign Policy of the Third World*. Jerusalem: Israel University Press, 1973.

Kincade, William H., and Porro, Jeffrey D., eds. *Negotiating Security—An Arms Control Reader*. Washington, D.C.: Carnegie Endowment for International Peace, 1979.

Kintner, William R., and Pfaltzgraff, Robert L., Jr., eds. *SALT—Implications for Arms Control in the 1970's*. Pittsburgh: University of Pittsburgh Press, 1973.

Kissinger, Henry A. *The Troubled Partnership: A Reappraisal of the Atlantic Alliance*. New York: McGraw-Hill, 1965.

————. *White House Years*. Boston: Little, Brown 1979.

————. *Years of Upheaval*. Boston: Little, Brown, 1982.

Knorr, Klaus, and Read, T., eds. *Limited Strategic War*. London: Pall Mall Press, 1962.

Kupperman, Robert H. *Facing Tomorrow's Terrorist Incident Today*. Washington, D.C.: Law Enforcement Assistance Administration, October 1977.

Kurland, Gerald, ed. *The Failure of Diplomacy—The Origins of the Cold War*. New York: Simon and Schuster, 1975.

Lall, Arthur S. *Negotiating Disarmament: The Eighteen Nation Disarmament Conference: The First Two Years 1962–64*. Cornell Research Papers in International Studies, No. 2. Ithaca, N.Y.: Center for International Studies, Cornell University, 1964.

Lambert, Robert W. *Soviet Disarmament Policy 1922–1931*. Research Report 64-2. Washington, D.C.: U.S. Arms Control and Disarmament Agency, 1964.

Laszlo, Ervin; Baker, Robert, Jr.; Eisenberg, Elliott; and Raman, Venkata. *The Objectives of the New International Economic Order*. A UNITAR Study. New York: Pergamon Press, 1978.

Laszlo, Ervin, and Kurtzman, J., eds. *Eastern Europe and the New International Economic Order*. New York: Pergamon Press, 1980.

Lieberman, Joseph I. *The Scorpion and the Tarantula: The Struggle to Control Atomic Weapons 1945–1949*. Boston: Houghton Mifflin, 1970.

Lilienthal, David E. *The Journals of David E. Lilienthal: The Atomic Energy Years, 1945–1950*. New York: Harper & Row, 1964.

Madariaga, Salvador De. *Disarmament*. 1929. Reprint ed. New York: Kennikat Press, 1967.

Mandelbaum, Michael. *The Nuclear Question: The United States and Nuclear Weapons, 1946–1976*. Cambridge: Cambridge University Press, 1979.

Miller, J.D.B. *The Politics of the Third World*. London: Oxford University Press, 1965.

Misra, K. P., ed. *Foreign Policy of India*. New Delhi: Thomson Press, 1977.

Morgenthau, Hans J. *Politics Among Nations*. New York: Alfred A. Knopf, 1973.

Mortimer, Robert A. *The Third World Coalition in International Politics*. New York: Praeger Publishers, 1980.

Myrdal, Alva. *The Game of Disarmament: How the United States and Russia Run the Arms Race*. New York: Pantheon Books, 1976.

Nicholas, H. G. *The United Nations as a Political Institution*. London: Oxford University Press, 1959.

Noel-Baker, Philip. *The Arms Race*. New York: Oceana Publications, 1960.

Osgood, Robert E., and Tucker, Robert W. *Force, Order, and Justice*. Baltimore: Johns Hopkins Press, 1967.

Perkinson, Roger. *Clausewitz—A Biography*. London: Wayland, 1970.

Pfaltzgraff, Robert L., Jr. *The Atlantic Community: A Complex Imbalance*. New York: Van Nostrand Reinhold, 1969.

Pierre, Andrew J. *The Global Politics of Arms Sales*. A Council on Foreign Relations Book. Princeton, N.J.: Princeton University Press, 1982.

Poulsode, T. T., ed. *Perspectives of India's Nuclear Policy*. New Delhi: Young Asia Publication, 1977.

Pringle, Peter, and Spigelman, James. *The Nuclear Barons*. New York: Holt, Rinehart and Winston, 1981.

Quester, George. *The Politics of Nuclear Proliferation*. Baltimore: Johns Hopkins Press, 1973.

Rapoport, Anatol, ed. *Clausewitz, on War*. London: Penguin Books, 1968.

Rathjens, G. W.; Chayes, Abram; and Ruina, J. P. *Nuclear Arms Control Agreements: Process and Impact*. Washington, D.C.: Carnegie Endowment for International Peace, 1974.

Roling, Bert V. A. *Disarmament and Development: The Perspective of Security*. Memo. Rotterdam: Foundation for Reshaping the International Order (RIO), 1979.

Rosecrance, Richard, ed. *The Future of the International Strategic System*. San Francisco: Chandler Publishing, 1972.

Rubinstein, Alvin Z., and Ginsburg, George, eds. *Soviet and American Policies in the United Nations*. New York: New York University Press, 1971.

Russell, Ruth B. *A History of the United Nations Charter—The Role of the United States: 1940–1945*. Washington, D.C.: The Brookings Institution, 1958.

———. *The United Nations and United States Security Policy*. Washington, D.C.: The Brookings Institution, 1968.

Schell, Jonathan. *The Fate of the Earth*. New York: Alfred A. Knopf, 1982.

Schelling, Thomas C., and Halperin, Morton H. *Strategy and Arms Control*. New York: Twentieth Century Fund, 1961.

Schlesinger, Arthur M., Jr., ed. *The Dynamic of World Power—A Documentary History of the United States Foreign Policy 1945–1973*. Vol.5, *The United Nations*, ed. Richard C. Hottelet. New York: Chelsea House, 1973.

Sharp, Jane M. O., ed. *Opportunities for Disarmament*. New York: Carnegie Endowment for International Peace, 1978.

Shotwell, James T., and Slavin, Marina. *Lessons on Security and Disarmament—from the History of the League of Nations*. New York: Carnegie Endowment for International Peace, 1949.

Sims, Nicholas A. *Approaches to Disarmament*. London: Quaker Peace & Service, 1979.

Singham, A. W., ed. *The Non-Aligned Movement in World Politics*. Westport, Conn.: Lawrence Hill, 1977.

Sivad, R. L. *World Military and Social Expenditures—1979*. Leesburg, Va.: World Priorities, 1979.

————. *World Military and Social Expenditures 1981*. Leesburg, Va.: World Priorities, 1981.

Sorensen, Theodore. *Kennedy*. New York: Harper & Row, 1965.

Spanier, John W., and Nogee, Joseph L. *The Politics of Disarmament: A Study in Soviet–American Gamesmanship*. New York: Praeger Publishers, 1962.

Stimson, Henry L., and Bundy, McGeorge. *On Active Service in Peace and War*. New York: Octagon, 1974.

Stoessinger, John G. *The United Nations and the Superpowers*. New York: Random House, 1977.

Szasz, Paul. *The Law and Practices of the International Atomic Energy Agency*. Vienna: IAEA, 1970.

Tate, Merze. *The Disarmament Illusion: The Movement for a Limitation of Armaments to 1907*. New York: Macmillan, 1942.

Todaro, Michael. *Economics for a Developing World*. New York: Longman, 1977.

Towards a New International Order. Report on the Joint Meeting of the Club of Rome and the International Ocean Institute, Algiers, October 25–28, 1976.

Townley, Ralph. *The United Nations: A View from Within*. New York: Scribners, 1968.

Tucker, Robert W. *The Inequality of Nations*. New York: Basic Books, 1977.

Ulam, Adam B. *The Rivals: America and Russia Since World War II*. New York: Penguin Books, 1977.

Urquhart, Brian. *Hammarskjold*. New York: Alfred A. Knopf, 1972.

Walters, F. P. *A History of the League of Nations*. Vols. 1–2. London: Oxford University Press, 1952.

Whynes, David K. *The Economics of Third World Military Expenditures*. London: Macmillan, 1979.

Wilcox, Francis O., and Kalijarvi, Thorsten V. *Recent America Foreign Policy—Basic Documents 1941–1951*. New York: Appleton-Century-Crofts, 1953.

Willetts, Peter. *The Non-Aligned Movement: The Origins of the Third World Alliance*. London: Frances Pinter, 1978.

Winnacker, Karl, and Wirtz, Karl. *Nuclear Energy in Germany*. La Grange Park, Ill.: American Nuclear Society, 1979.

Wohlstetter, Albert, et al. *Swords from Plowshares*. Chicago: University of Chicago Press, 1977.

Wolf-Phillips, Leslie, et al. *Why 'Third World'?* Third World Foundation, Monograph, No. 7. London: Third World Foundation, 1980.

Wolfe, Thomas W. *Soviet Power and Europe*. Baltimore: Johns Hopkins Press, 1970.

Young, Elizabeth. *A Farewell to Arms Control*. Harmondsworth: Penguin Books, 1972.

ARTICLES

Abott, George C. "The NIEO: What Went Wrong." *Co-Existence* (April 1978).

Ad Hoc Group on United States Policy Toward the United Nations. "The United States and the United Nations...A Policy for Today." Memo. New York, October 1981.

Ball, Nicole, and Leitenberg, Milton. "Disarmament and Development: Their Interrelationship." *Bulletin of Peace Proposals* 10, no. 3 (1979).

Bargman, Abraham. "The United Nations, the Superpowers and Proliferation." *Annals of the American Academy of Political and Social Science* 430 (March 1977). Nuclear Proliferation: Prospects, Problems and Proposals issue.

Barnaby, Frank. "The NPT Review Conference—Much Talk, Few Results." *Bulletin of the Atomic Scientists* (November 1980): 7–8.

————. "United Nations Center for Disarmament." *Bulletin of the Atomic Scientists* (January 1982): 6–7.

Bauer, P. T., and Yamey, B. S. "Against the New Economic Order." *Commentary* (April 1977).

————. "East–West/North–South: Peace and Prosperity?" *Commentary* (September 1980).

Beker, Avi. "The Oil–Arms Connection: Fueling the Arms Race." *Armed Forces and Society* 8, no. 3 (Spring 1982): 419–42.

————. "The Soviet Union and Disarmament in the United Nations." *Crossroads* (A Crane and Russak Journal on International Affairs) (Spring 1984).

Bloomfield, Lincoln P., and Cleveland, Harlan. "A Strategy for the United States." *International Security* 2, no. 4 (Spring 1978): 32–55.

Bull, Hedley. "Arms Control and World Order." *International Security* 1, no. 1 (Summer 1976).

————. "The Great Irresponsibles? The United States, the Soviet Union, and World Order." *International Journal* 35, no. 3 (Summer 1980).

Bundy, McGeorge; Kennan, George F.; McNamara, Robert S.; and Smith, Gerard. "Nuclear Weapons and the Atlantic Alliance." *Foreign Affairs* 60, no. 4 (Spring 1982): 753–68.

Claude, Inis L., Jr. "The Management of Power in the Changing United Nations." *International Organization* 15, no. 2 (Spring 1961): 219–35.

Collins, Arthur, Jr. "The Enhanced Radiation Warhead: A Military Perspective." *Arms Control Today* 8, no. 6 (June 1978). Includes a bibliography on the neutron bomb, pp. 1–6.

Corradini, Alessandro. "The Development of Disarmament Education as a Distinct Field of Study: An Introductory Analysis." *Disarmament: A Periodic Review by the United Nations* 3, no. 3 (November 1980).

———— (Secretary-General of the Conference). "The Second Review Conference of the Parties to the Treaty on the Non-Proliferation of Nuclear Weapons." *Disarmament: A Periodic Review by the United Nations* 3, no. 3 (November 1980).

Cox, Robert M. "Ideologies and the New International Economic Order: Reflection on Some Recent Literature." *International Organization* 33, no. 2 (Spring 1979).

Deutsch, Richard. "The African Arms Race." *Africa Report* (March–April 1979): 47–49.

Eilan, Arieh. "Conference Diplomacy." *The Washington Quarterly* (Autumn 1981).

Epstein, William. "A Ban on the Production of Fissionable Material for Weapons." *Scientific American* 243, no. 1 (July 1980).

————. "Banning the Use of Nuclear Weapons." *Bulletin of the Atomic Scientists* (April 1979): 7–9.

————. "UN Special Session on Disarmament, How Much Progress?" *Survival* (November–December 1978).

———. "Why a Special Session on Disarmament." *Transnational Perspectives* (Geneva) 4, nos. 1–2 (1978).

Frank, Andre Gunder. "Arms Economy and Warfare in the Third World." *Third World Quarterly* 2, no. 2 (April 1980): 228–50.

Gummett, Philip. "From NPT to INFCE: Developments in Thinking About Nuclear Non-Proliferation." *International Affairs* 57, no. 4 (Autumn 1981).

Hass, Richard. "Reviewing Opportunities for Disarmament." *Survival* (July–August 1979).

Hoffman, Stanley. "The Western Alliance: Drift for Harmony." *International Security* 6, no. 2 (Fall 1981).

Husain, M. A. "Third World and Disarmament: Shadow and Substance." *Third World Quarterly* 2, no. 1 (January 1980).

Hyder, Tarig Osman. "Inchoate Aspirations for World Order Change." *International Security* 2, no. 4 (Spring 1978).

Jack, Homer A. "A Special Session of the UN General Assembly Devoted to Disarmament." *Review of International Affairs* (Belgrade) (June 20, 1976).

———. "A UN General Assembly Special Session on Disarmament to Break the World Disarmament Conference Stalemate." *Bulletin of Peace Proposals* (Oslo) 8, no. 1 (1979).

Kaiser, Karl; Leber, George; Mertes, Alois; and Schulze, Franz-Josef. "Nuclear Weapons and the Preservation of Peace." *Foreign Affairs* 60, no. 5 (Summer 1982): 1157–70.

Kaldor, Mary. "International Military Order." *New Statesman* (May 25, 1979).

Kapur, Ashok. "Nuclear Proliferation in the 1980's." *International Journal* 36, no. 3 (Summer 1981).

———. " The Nuclear Spread: A Third World View." *Third World Quarterly* 2, no. 1 (January 1980).

Landgren-Backstrom, Signe. "The World Arms Trade: The Impact on Development." *Bulletin of Peace Proposals* 10, no. 3 (1979).

Leitenberg, Milton, and Ball, Nicole. "The Military Expenditures of Less Developed Nations as a Proportion of their State Budgets." *Bulletin of Peace Proposals*, no. 4 (1977): 310–15.

Lovins, A. B.; Lovins, L. Hunter; and Ross, L. "Nuclear Power and Nuclear Bombs." *Foreign Affairs* (Summer 1980).

Mackintosh, Malcolm. "The Evolution of the Warsaw Pact." *Adelphi Paper*, no. 58 (June 1969).

Manley, Michael. "Third World Under Challenge: The Politics of Affirmation." *Third World Quarterly* 2, no. 1 (January 1980)

Maynes, Charles William. "A UN Policy for the Next Administration." *Foreign Affairs* 541 (Winter 1975–76/July 1976).

Mazrui, Ali. "Africa's Nuclear Future." *Survival* (March–April 1980).

———. "The Barrel of the Gun and the Barrel of Oil in the North–South Equation." *World Order Models Project* (New York: Institute for World Order), no. 5 (1978).

McDougal, Myres S. "The Soviet–Cuban Quarantine and Self-Defense." *American Journal of International Law* 57 (1963): 601.

Moglewer, Sidney. "IAEA Safeguards and Non-Proliferation." *Bulletin of the Atomic Scientists* (October 1981).

Morris, Roger. "Eight Days in April: The Press Flattens Carter with the Neutron Bomb." *Columbia Journalism Review* (November–December 1978).

Neuhold, Hanspeter. "Permament Neutrality and Non-Alignment: Similarities and Differences." *Indian Quarterly* 35, no. 3 (July 1979): 285–308.

Quester, George. "Some Conceptual Problems in Nuclear Proliferation." *American Political Science Review* 66, no. 2 (June 1972).

Rajan, M. S. "Non-Alignment: The Dichotomy Between Theory and Practice in Perspective." *Indian Quarterly* 36, no. 1 (January–March 1980).

Rosen, Jane. "How the Third World Runs the UN." *New York Times Magazine*, December 16, 1979.

Rosenbaum, David. "Nuclear Terror." *International Security* 1, no. 2 (Winter 1977).

Salter, Arthur, Sir. "The United Nations and the Atomic Bomb." *International Conciliation*, no. 423 (September 1946).

Schilling, Warner R. "U.S. Strategic Nuclear Concepts in the 1970's: The Search for Sufficiently Equivalent Countervailing Parity." *International Security* 6, no. 2 (Fall 1980).

Schmidt, Helmut. "The 1977 Alstair Buchan Memorial Lecture." *Survival* 29, no. 1 (January–February 1978).

Shotwell, James T. "The United Nations Atomic Commission." *International Conciliation*, no. 423 (September 1946).

Sohn, Louis B. "Disarmament at the Crossroads." *International Security* 2, no. 4 (Spring 1978).

Sterling, Claire. "Qaddafi Spells Chaos." *The New Republic* (March 7, 1981).

Sullivan, Michael J., III. "Conference at the Crossroads: Future Prospect for the Conference of the Committee on Disarmament." *International Organization* 29, no. 2 (Spring 1975).

Sweet, William. "Delhi: A Third World Overture." *The Nation* (May 27, 1978).

Teller, Edward. "A Suggested Amendment to the Acheson Report." *Bulletin of the Atomic Scientists* 1, no. 12 (June 1, 1946).

Towle, Philip. "Nuclear Non-Proliferation: Deadlock at Geneva." *The World Today* (October 1980): 371–74.

———. "The UN Special Session on Disarmament—Retrospect." *World Today* 35, no. 8 (May 1979).

Waldock, H. "The Regulation of the Use of Force by Individual States in International Law." *81 Recueil des cours* 2 (1952).

Waltz, Kenneth N. "International Structure, National Force, and the Balance of World Power." *Journal of International Affairs* 21, no. 2 (1967).

Wolfgang, Mallmann. "Arms Transfers to the Third World: Trends and Changing Patterns in the 1970's." *Bulletin of Peace Proposals* 10, no. 3 (1979): 301–7.

Young, Elizabeth. "The Nonproliferation Treaty: An Acceptable Balance." *Bulletin of the Atomic Scientists* (November 1967): 37–38.

Official Documents of the U.S. Government Department of State Bulletin.

Dulles, John Foster. "United Nations Charter Review." Speech before the Subcommittee of the Senate Foreign Relations Committee on the UN Charter, January 18, 1954. Series 5, No. 3. Washington, D.C.: Department of State.

Postwar Foreign Policy Preparation. Washington, D.C.: Department of State, 1949.

U.S. Arms Control and Disarmament Agency. *Documents on Disarmament 1961.* Washington, D.C.: ACDA, 1962.

———. *Documents on Disarmament 1964.* Washington, D.C.: ACDA, 1965.

———. *Documents on Disarmament 1967.* Washington, D.C.: ACDA, 1968.

———. *World Military Expenditues and Arms Transfers 1969–1978.* Washington, D.C.: ACDA, 1980.

Vance, Cyrus R. "Meeting the Challenges of a Changing World." Speech by the Secretary of State before the American Association of Community and Junior Colleges, Illinois, May 1, 1979. *State Department,* No. 116.

STOCKHOLM INTERNATIONAL PEACE RESEARCH INSTITUTE (SIPRI) PUBLICATIONS

Agreements for Arms Control, by Jozef Goldblat. London: Taylor & Francis, 1982.

Armaments or Disarmament? London: Taylor & Francis, 1980.

Internationalization to Prevent the Spread of Nuclear Weapons. London: Taylor & Francis, 1980.

The NPT: The Main Political Barrier to Nuclear Weapons Proliferation. London: Taylor & Francis, 1980.

Nuclear Energy and Nuclear Weapon Proliferation. London: Taylor & Francis, 1978.

Postures for Non-Proliferation—Arms Limitation and Security Policies to Minimize Nuclear Proliferation. London: Taylor & Francis, 1979.

World Armament and Disarmament, SIPRI Yearbook 1978. London: Taylor & Francis, 1978.

World Armament and Disarmament, SIPRI Yearbook 1979. London: Taylor & Francis, 1979.

World Armament and Disarmament, SIPRI Yearbook 1980. London: Taylor & Francis, 1980.

World Armament and Disarmament, SIPRI Yearbook 1981. London: Taylor & Francis, 1981.

World Armament and Disarmament, SIPRI Yearbook 1982. London: Taylor & Francis, 1982.

UNITED NATIONS DOCUMENTS AND PUBLICATIONS

Documents

GAOR, Disarmament Commission.

General Assembly Official Records (GAOR).

General Assembly Resolutions.

Official Records of the Atomic Energy Commission.
Official Records of the Security Council.

Disarmament Publications

Disarmament: A Periodic Review by the United Nations.
The United Nations and Disarmament 1945–1970. New York: United Nations, 1970.
The United Nations and Disarmament 1970–1975. New York: United Nations, 1975.
The United Nations and Disarmament Yearbook, starting in 1976, Vol. 1; 1977, Vol. 2;
    1978, Vol. 3; 1979, Vol. 4; 1980, Vol. 5; 1981, Vol. 6.

Studies (issued as reports of the Secretary General)

"Comprehensive study on nuclear weapons." A/35/392. September 12, 1980.
Effects of the Possible Use of Nuclear Weapons and the Security and Economic Impli-
    cations for States of the Acquisition and Further Development of These Weapons.
    A/6858. New York: United Nations, 1968.
"Monitoring of Disarmament Agreements and Strengthening of International Security."
    A/34/374. August 27, 1979.
"Report of the Ad Hoc Group on the Relationship Between Disarmament and Devel-
    opment." A/S-10/9. April 5, 1978.
"Study of the Institutional Arrangements Relating to the Process of Disarmament." A/
    36/392. September 11, 1981.
"Study on the Relationship Between Disarmament and Development." A/36/356. October
    5, 1981.

Related Organs and Agencies

Conference of the Committee on Disarmament (CCD).
Disarmament Education: Report and Final Document. World Conference on Disarmament
    Education, UNESCO, Paris, June 9–13, 1980. Document 55-80/Conf.40/37 Rev.
Documents of the Eighteen-Nation Disarmament (ENDC).
"Final Declaration of the Review Conference of the Parties to the Treaty on the Non-
    Proliferation of Nuclear Weapons, 30 May, 1975." NPT/Conf/53/1. Geneva,
    1975. Annex: Final Declaration.
Second Review Conference on Nuclear Non-Proliferation Treaty Held in Geneva, 11
    August–7 September. Round-up of Session, United Nations Press Release, NPT/
    89, September 10, 1980. New York: Department of Public Information, United
    Nations.
UN Bulletin
UN Chronicle

NEWSPAPERS AND MAGAZINES

Christian Science Monitor
Disarmament Times, A special newspaper published by the Non-Governmental Organi-

zations (NGO) Disarmament Committee in New York at United Nations
Headquarters.
Newsweek
New York Times
Time
Wall Street Journal
Washington Post

Index

About the Author

AVI BEKER, currently Assistant Professor of Political Science at Bar-Ilan University, served as a member of the Israeli delegation to the United Nations from 1977 to 1982. He has published articles in *Armed Forces and Society* and *Crossroads*.